THE HOME CHEF

THE HOME CHEF

JUDITH ETS-HOKIN

CELESTIALARTS

Berkeley, California

Photographs copyright© 1988 by Celestial Arts.

Celestial Arts
P.O. Box 7123
Berkeley, CA 94707

Jacket and text design by David Charlsen

Interior photographs by Anne Dowie
Illustrations by Michael Pearce

Library of Congress Cataloging-in-Publication Data

Ets-Hokin, Judith.
    The home chef.

    Includes indexes.
    1. Cookery. I. Title.
TX715.E85   1988   641.5

ISBN 0-89087-750-5 (paper)

Manufactured in Canada

3 4 5 6 7 — 01 00 99 98 97

TABLE OF CONTENTS

PREFACE

I have always felt that cooking is a way of expressing love. Ever since I learned to cook years ago, I have been conveying my regard for my family, friends, and students with my food—comforting and sustaining, exciting and captivating. Wonderful meals are remembered because they make others feel good—and your cooking can be the force that makes that happen.

Once you understand the concepts behind the recipes, cooking will no longer be a mystery. Cooking is a skill, and just like any other skill—typing, tennis, or driving a car, for instance—it can be learned and mastered with practice.

This book is an expanded and detailed rendition of my comprehensive Basic Cooking Course—the most popular course offered in my San Francisco cooking school. Here you will find everything you need to know about cooking—including information on equipment and ingredients, the preparation of poultry and vegetables (*before* they are cooked), food terms, methods and techniques, and classic recipes voted easiest and best by my students—from the simplest soup stocks to the most elaborate pastries and hors d'oeuvre.

This detailed cooking guide is not only for the novice cook. It is also for the experienced cook who would like to know why those soufflés rise, or what makes each buttery, crisp bite of puff pastry an ecstasy.

My recipes and techniques are similar to those followed in the best hotel-restaurant schools—but are geared for the home cook. You will find that by using classic methods and techniques you will get the task done so quickly and easily that you will be able to create delicious meals for friends and family, not just on special occasions, but on a daily basis as well.

Sit back, relax, read, and enjoy. You are about to have an entertaining, fun, and informative experience.

HOW TO USE
THIS BOOK

The foundation of this book is the Basic Cooking Course offered at my cooking school. It is based on a series of sequential chapters, each, for the most part, built upon the previous one, and my intention was for the reader to follow the book through from beginning to end. However, this book may also be used as an ordinary recipe book—you can select recipes at random, referring back to former chapters for any missing information.

There are a few ingredients that I call for repeatedly which you may have difficulty finding, especially if you do not live in a large city. I urge you to make every effort to obtain those ingredients because I think they "make" the dish. However, if they are not available to you, here are some easily found substitutes.

Every time I specify olive oil, I mean virgin olive oil. You can substitute pure olive oil if virgin is not available.

Every time I specify Parmesan, I mean *Parmigiano Reggiano*. You can substitute an *ungrated* (*always* grate it yourself) domestic Parmesan if *Parmigiano Reggiano* is not available.

Every time I specify *crème fraîche,* and it is not available, you can substitute whipping cream.

Every time I specify *pancetta,* and it is not available, you can substitute bacon.

The temperatures in this book are given in degrees Fahrenheit. If you need to convert Fahrenheit to Centigrade, look in the section called *Equivalents and Measures* for directions on how to do this.

And finally, if there is a word, term, method, or ingredient in this book with which you are not familiar, look for it in the glossary, or under *Ingredients, Vegetable and Fruit Preparation,* or *Poultry Preparation.*

ACKNOWLEDGMENTS

The inspiration for this book came from the many questions asked by my students—and I wish to thank them all. Special thanks to Dorothy Northey, Linda Incardine, and Robin Leonard, who read the manuscript, and to Beverly Walker, who gave me the title. A big thank you to Jackie Wan, my editor, who patiently, conscientiously, and thoroughly read and corrected the manuscript at least five times, and to David Charlsen who designed the book.

THE BASIC KITCHEN

An accomplished cook in a well-equipped kitchen is like a conductor leading an orchestra, the result being a symphony of edible brilliance. Cooking then becomes a pleasurable and satisfying experience. I have always felt home cooks should have good quality, professional equipment. Cookware should be chosen for function and durability, and every piece of equipment should simplify and facilitate the perfect food creation.

As you go through this book, buy kitchen equipment as you need it. Consider what you have in your kitchen presently, how many people you normally cook for, and how often you will use a particular piece of equipment. Always buy carefully, and buy the most durable and best quality you can afford.

By the time you get to the last chapter of this book, you'll know how to cook just about anything, and will have the proper tools with which to do it. Following is an overview of the basic cookware and utensils for a well-equipped kitchen, plus a word on the various materials from which they are made.

Anodized aluminum pans (from left to right): 1½-quart saucepan, 2½-quart saucepan, 4½-quart saucepan, butter melter and lid.

POTS AND PANS

Accomplished cooks can talk about pots and pans and the materials of which they are made as well as they can about the food they cook. In other words, to a good cook, an awareness of how a pot cooks is as important as what is cooking in it.

Copper Copper is the most costly and most attractive metal for pots and pans. It is an excellent conductor of heat, and should be heavy (at least ⅛ inch thick) with a tin lining. It will need periodic retinning and polishing if you wish it to shine.

Aluminum Less expensive than copper, aluminum is moderately priced, durable, and a good conductor of heat. It does, however, interact with acidic foods (tomatoes, wine, or lemon juice, for instance), so always purchase anodized aluminum. (Anodized aluminum has a hard finish that is integral with the metal, and that prevents any chemical reaction with foods). Always purchase heavy gauge.

Stainless steel Stainless steel is easy to clean, but by itself, is a poor conductor of heat, so most stainless pans have a layer of copper or aluminum on the bottom. If you purchase stainless steel cookware, make sure it has a copper or aluminum bottom at least ⅛ inch thick. Stainless steel is the best metal for gadgets and other kitchen utensils since the finish will not rust or wear away.

Anodized aluminum pans (from left to right): *10-inch skillet, 3-quart sauté pan, 12-quart stock pot, 8-quart soup pot.*

Cast iron Very heavy, but durable and relatively inexpensive. Cast iron must be seasoned before it is used, and kept seasoned (see *Crêpes*, chapter 12) so that foods do not stick. If the seasoning is removed, cast iron will rust.

Earthenware Clay (earthenware) holds heat for a long time, and is therefore ideal for oven cooking and serving. Not all earthenware pots can be used on top of the stove—it is best to follow the manufacturer's instructions. If unglazed earthenware is soaked in water before it is placed in the oven, it will surround the food in the pot with a gentle vapor as it cooks.

Nonstick finishes There are a variety of coatings that are applied to the cooking surfaces of pots, pans, and utensils so that food won't stick. You do not need to use fat in cooking with these finishes but do need to use special utensils that do not scratch the finish.

Tinned or chromed ware A coating of tin or chrome over iron or steel is common in kitchen gadgets, cake pans, pie pans, bread pans, etc. The heavier the coating, the better the quality of the ware. Tinned or chromed utensils should not be scoured with abrasive cleaner since that will wear away the coating and expose the base metal, which will rust or corrode when exposed to moisture.

Here is a list of basic pots and pans that a well-equipped kitchen should have. As you gain experience and begin to develop your own "style" of

17-inch anodized aluminum roasting pan, 10-inch rectangular clay open roaster, 6-quart anodized aluminum casserole, 10-inch oval clay roaster, 6-quart clay casserole (marmite)*, 2½-quart clay casserole* (poelon)*.*

cooking, you will want to add to the basic collection. Remember—choose carefully, and buy the best quality you can afford.

Saucepans At a minimum, you will need a 1½-quart, a 2½-quart, a 4½-quart, and a 6-quart pan with covers. A 1-quart double boiler is also recommended, and each part can be used separately.

Steamer basket You will need a steamer basket or insert to fit one of your saucepans—the size depends upon the amount of food usually steamed.

Soup or stock pots You will need an 8-, 10-, or 12-quart pot with cover.

Skillets You will need an 8-, 10-, and 12-inch skillet. Covers do not come with skillets but can be purchased separately if you want them.

Omelet or crêpe pan These pans come in 5-, 6-, 7-, and 8-inch sizes (bottom measurement). Purchase the size that will be most useful to you—then use it exclusively for omelets and crêpes.

Sauté pans Sauté pans look like skillets except they have straight sides 2½ inches high. They can be used for frying as well as for boiling vegetables and making sauces. You will need a 10- or 12-inch sauté pan with cover.

Roasting pans You will need two oval or rectangular pans, 10 × 14 × 3 inches deep and 17 × 12 × 3 inches deep, with a roasting rack (one roasting rack will do for both).

Casseroles You will need a 2½-quart and a 6-quart casserole, oval, round, or rectangular, both with covers.

Water or tea kettle You will need a kettle with a 2- or 3-quart capacity.

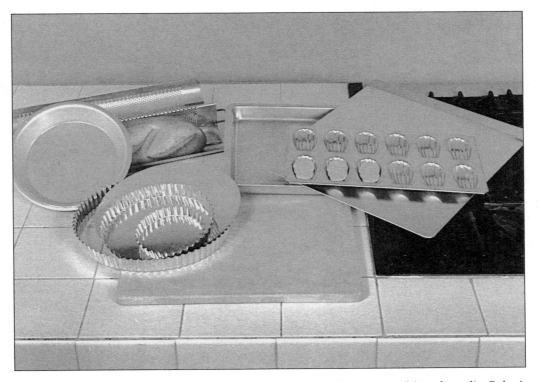

9-inch pie pan, baguette pan, 4 sizes removable-bottomed tart pans (tinned steel), Baker's stone, jelly roll pan, madeleine mold, 11 × 15-inch baking sheet.

BAKEWARE

Baking is a specialized area of cooking and requires some particular equipment. Most recipes specify standard-sized pans for breads, cakes, pies, tarts, muffins, etc. Buy baking equipment as you need it, and in that way build a collection gradually.

Baker's stone Baker's stones, sometimes referred to as "pizza stones" or "pizza bricks," are flat, stoneware discs or rectangles that you may place inside your oven. Bread may be baked directly on this stone or in bread pans while the stone is in the oven. I have found that a baker's stone, placed on the lowest rack of either a gas or electric oven and left in the oven all the time, will bake everything—cakes, cookies, stews, etc.—more evenly and quickly since the oven temperature will remain more constant.

Baking sheets You will need two 11 × 15-inch sideless pans, and an 11 × 15-inch pan with sides (a jelly roll pan).

Cake pans You will need two round pans, 8 or 9 × 1½ inches; and one square pan 9 × 9 × 2 inches.

Copper beating bowl Not absolutely essential, but better than any other type bowl, is a 10-inch unlined copper bowl for whisking egg whites—the egg whites interact with the copper, helping the egg whites expand more quickly and with greater volume.

Various size soufflé molds, stainless steel whisks.

Heavy-duty electric mixer If you intend to be mixing cakes and breads, an electric mixer—5-quart bowl capacity— is invaluable.

Flour sifter You will need a flour sifter, 4-cup size, with a hand crank and double screen.

Muffin pan Muffin pans can be used for biscuits, muffins, cupcakes, small tarts, etc. There are many sizes available; start out with a $3 \times 1\frac{1}{2}$-inch size, that bakes 12 at a time.

Parchment paper Keep parchment paper on hand to be used for lining baking sheets and pans. It comes in rolls or rounds.

Pastry or cutting board You will need an 18×24-inch area of countertop in marble, maple, or formica, for rolling and making dough. Boards of that size are available in portable units as well.

Pie and tart pans You will need a 9-inch removable-bottomed tart pan and a 9-inch pie pan.

Pastry brushes You will need two or three pastry brushes—1 to $2\frac{1}{2}$ inches wide.

Rolling pin You will need a heavy pin, 14 to 16 inches long.

Soufflé molds A straight-sided deep porcelain mold can be used for soufflés and as a versatile baking dish. One each of a 1-quart, $1\frac{1}{2}$-quart, and a 2-quart size are recommended.

(Left to right) *10-inch chopping knife, 10-inch slicing knife, serrated bread knife, all-purpose sandwich knife, boning knife, 3-inch paring knife, bird's beak paring knife.*

KNIVES

Next to pots, knives are probably the most important kitchen tools. It's a good idea to know something about the types available so that you can choose wisely. Expect to pay quite a bit for good knives. Two kinds of steel are used in knife blades, carbon steel and stainless steel. Carbon steel holds a fine edge longer, but rusts and stains easily, discoloring certain foods. Stainless steel resists stains and does not interact with any foods. When selecting your knives, be sure they are well constructed. One test of a good knife is the way the handle is attached to the blade. The shank (or tang) of the knife should extend the full length of the handle and be secured with rivets. In a cheaper knife, the tang is much shorter and is pushed into the handle, fastened with a brad or nail, and finished with a metal collar where it meets the blade. Here are some suggestions for a basic knife collection.

Chopping knife   I recommend an 8- to 12-inch long sturdy angled blade with a raised handle to allow clearance for knuckles.

Slicing knife   You will need a narrow blade 8 to 10 inches long for slicing boneless meats.

Paring knife   I recommend a paring knife with a short blade (2 to 3½ inches long), with a sharp, curved, or tapered point.

Boning knife   This is a short, sharp, thin, pointed knife from 5 to 6½ inches long, used for boning meats and poultry.

All-purpose kitchen shears, sharpening steel, knife sharpener.

Serrated bread knife   You will need a 10-inch serrated knife for cutting bread and tomatoes. You will find it invaluable for cutting cakes, especially sponge cakes.

Curved serrated knife   A small curved serrated knife, sometimes called a grapefruit knife, is used for hollowing out fruits and vegetables for stuffing, and for separating the segments of citrus fruits.

Sharpening steel   A sharpening steel should be used each time you start to use any knife, (except a serrated one) to maintain its edge. It is a good idea to have your knives professionally sharpened once a year or so.

MEASURING EQUIPMENT

Correct measuring is essential. Here are some basic tools to help you do the job.

Measuring spoons   It is a good idea to have two sets of standard ¼ teaspoon to 1 tablespoon measures.

Measuring cups   You should have three sizes in glass or plastic, each with a pouring lip—1- , 2- , and 4-cup. Metal measuring cups are used for measuring dry ingredients; you will need one graduated set.

Scale   For really accurate measurements of dry ingredients, a scale marked for both grams and ounces is recommended.

Stainless steel slotted skimmer, stainless steel mesh skimmer, meat pounder, candy-deep-fry thermometer, oven thermometer, meat thermometer.

Thermometers You will need a candy-deep-fry thermometer (they are sold under that name), for syrups and deep-frying, and an "instant read" thermometer for meats and yeast. To check the accuracy of your oven's temperature setting, you will need an oven thermometer.

MIXING EQUIPMENT

The utensils and bowls you will need to whisk, cream, stir, fold, blend, and beat are listed below.

Bowls You will need a graduated set of four or five bowls—glass, stoneware, or metal.

Spoons I recommend several 10- or 12-inch wooden spoons and spatulas, and several different sizes of metal spoons.

Rubber spatulas Rubber spatulas are good for folding as well as cleaning out bowls—several in different sizes are recommended.

Wire whisks You will need a 12-inch balloon-type whisk for whisking egg whites and an 8-inch sauce whisk.

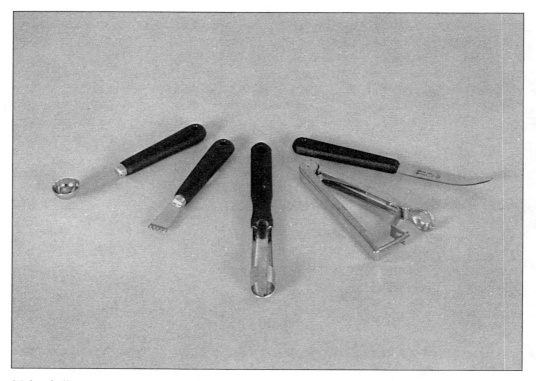

Melon baller, zester, apple corer, cherry-olive pitter, curved serrated knife.

GADGETS AND ACCESSORIES

There are hundreds of small kitchen gadgets for sale, but it is best to avoid cluttering up the kitchen with a lot of unnecessary equipment. The following items are the most commonly used, and with them, you should be able to handle almost any kitchen job.

apple corer
baster (basting bulb)
bottle or beer-can opener
can opener, hand-operated
cheesecloth
cherry and olive pitter
citrus zester
colander
corkscrew
egg slicer
garlic press
green bean julienne tool
hand grater
ladle, sauce
ladle, soup
meat pounder

melon baller
nut grinder
nutmeg grater
oyster knife
pastry cutters—for puff pastry
pepper grinder
potato masher
salad spinner
scissors, kitchen
sieves, fine and coarse
skewers
skimmer
tongs, spring-action
twine
vegetable peeler

Cooked food mill (Mouli), *with fine disc, coarse disc, medium disc.*

SPECIAL EQUIPMENT

Electric food processor   I recommend an electric food processor to help you chop, mix, slice, grate, and purée—it will save a lot of time on food preparation. If you own a heavy duty food processor, a blender is not necessary.

Pasta machine   If you intend to make your own pasta, you will find a home style pasta machine an invaluable aid.

Cooked food mill   Sometimes referred to by its French brand name *Mouli,* this tool has three different sized interchangeable mesh discs that will purée cooked foods. It is different from a blender or food processor since it will eliminate unwanted fibers, strings, or shells from any purée.

Deep-fryer   If you do a lot of deep-frying, it is best to use an electric, thermostatically-controlled deep-fryer.

Microwave ovens   Microwave cooking has one great advantage over infrared—it cooks food much faster. However, the disadvantages are many. Quick heating causes a drier or sometimes rubbery texture and foods are apt to be undercooked, overcooked, or (a common problem in microwave cooking) *unevenly* cooked. Another concern is that since the surface of the food gets no warmer than the interior, it is impossible to brown foods in a microwave. I recommend that if you decide to purchase a microwave oven you do so from a store that also gives instruction on *how to use* a microwave oven. A microwave oven is not necessary for the cooking in this book.

INGREDIENTS

One day, as I was preparing a dish in class, I overheard a lady whisper to her companion—"Well, with those ingredients, she [meaning me] can't go wrong!" I surprised her with a reply. "You are right," I said. "You understand my point precisely. With these ingredients I can't go wrong." Without being aware of it, that lady had expressed the essence of my philosophy—you must always use the best quality ingredients—they do make a difference. And, in order to select the best, you need to know something about them, and have a clear understanding of what your choices are. The following explains ingredients used in this book that may not be familiar to you.

Bread Crumbs
Bread crumbs are best made from bread that is not freshly baked, but one or two days old. If the recipe calls for fresh bread crumbs, the crumbs can be used right away. For dry, they may be spread on a baking sheet and dried in a 250° oven. (About 10 minutes will do it.) The easiest way to make crumbs is in a food processor or blender. Cut the bread into small cubes and process it in small quantities. Both fresh and dry bread crumbs store well in the freezer.

Cheese
See chapter 11.

Chocolate
Chocolate is made from fermented and dried cocoa beans that come from cocoa trees, which grow in the tropics of countries that straddle the equator. The beans are roasted, cracked, heated, and ground into a paste called chocolate mass (or liquor). From the chocolate mass, unsweetened, bittersweet, semisweet, or milk chocolate is made. Essentially, the quality of chocolate is determined by the amount and type of chocolate mass and by the amount of cocoa butter mixed back in with it during conching. (Conching is the last step in the chocolate making procedure. The chocolate, cocoa butter, sugar, etc., is poured into a container in which a very heavy roller moves back and forth continuously, grinding, mixing, and slightly heating the ingredients.) The length of time the chocolate is conched contributes to its quality—the longer it's conched the smoother its flavor becomes.
Unsweetened chocolate is pure chocolate mass.
Bittersweet chocolate contains at least 35% chocolate mass and a small amount of sugar.
Semisweet chocolate contains at least 15% chocolate mass and more sugar than bittersweet chocolate.
Milk chocolate contains at least 10% chocolate mass, milk solids, sugar, and flavorings.
White chocolate (not considered chocolate according to the U.S. standard of identity) is a combination of sugar, cocoa butter, dry milk solids, and vanilla.
Couverture is a French term used to describe the best quality coating chocolate with a high percentage of cocoa butter—at least 32%. *Couverture* is conched two to three days.
Cocoa powder is derived from chocolate liquor that has had nearly all of the cocoa butter removed. The resulting "cake" is ground into a soft powder.

Cooking with Chocolate
Unsweetened, bittersweet, and semisweet chocolate may be used interchangeably in recipes. If you use a different type of chocolate than is called for in a recipe, you will need to adjust the proportions of sugar to your taste. Keep in mind that chocolate does not need much heat to melt—it will melt in your hand. Overheated chocolate will stiffen into an unusable mass. There are two methods for melting chocolate that I use with success.
Double boiler method Break the chocolate up into small pieces and place them in the top portion of a double boiler. (If the recipe calls for cream, milk, or butter that needs to be warmed, you may combine it with the chocolate.) Fill the lower portion of the double boiler ¼ full with hot water, place it over the heat, and bring to the boil. As soon as the water boils, remove the pot from the heat and place the upper portion of the double boiler on top. Stir occasionally while the chocolate melts. Under no circumstances, should you place the pot over heat when it contains the chocolate.
Oven method Preheat the oven to 200°. Break up the chocolate into small pieces and place them in an ovenproof bowl. (If the recipe calls for cream, milk, or butter that needs to be warmed, you may combine it with the choc-

olate.) Turn off the oven and place the bowl of chocolate in the oven until melted. The following is an all-around basic chocolate sauce.

BITTERSWEET CHOCOLATE SAUCE
Makes about 2 cups

½ lb. bittersweet chocolate
¾ cup crème fraîche (see below)
2 tablespoons powdered sugar
1 teaspoon vanilla extract

In the top portion of a double boiler, break up the chocolate and combine it with the other ingredients. Following the double boiler method (see above), melt the chocolate and stir the sauce until smooth.

Cream
Cream is the yellowish fat contained in milk. If the milk is not homogenized, the cream rises to the surface naturally and separates itself from the milk. "Half-and-half" is a mixture of milk and about 10% cream. Heavy cream, also called whipping cream, is a mixture of milk and about 35% cream.

Crème Fraîche
Crème fraîche is a French term for lightly fermented or tart cream, which means that lactic acids have been added to heavy cream, thickening it and changing its flavor. Crème fraîche has a more interesting taste than sweet cream (it is somewhere between heavy cream and sour cream). It is thicker than heavy cream and can be boiled without curdling, so it is ideal for use in sauces, soups, and other cooked dishes. Crème fraîche can be kept in the refrigerator approximately 10 days. Whipped crème fraîche does not weep or separate. If you have an "incubator" (yogurt maker) you can produce an American version of crème fraîche the same way you produce yogurt, following the yogurt measurements and procedure, but using crème fraîche and heavy cream instead of yogurt and milk. (In a pinch you can use heavy cream and buttermilk to simulate crème fraîche.) Crème fraîche is available in cheese shops and some food markets. In recipes, you may substitute heavy cream if crème fraîche is unavailable, but crème fraîche is almost always preferable.

Eggs
See chapter 10.

Fats and Oils
Fats and oils are members of the same class of chemical compounds. They differ from each other only in their melting points: oils are liquid at room temperature, fats remain solid. In deciding what kinds of fats or oils to use, you must consider the cooking method (butter is never used for deep-frying, for example), and the compatibility of flavors of the fats and the food being prepared. Vegetable oils are named by the vegetables, seeds, or nuts from which they are made. Each oil tastes different, and I suggest you become familiar with some of the more common ones by purchasing and using them when recommended in a recipe. Remember that a cold-press method (usually noted on the label) of extracting oil produces the best quality oils.
Butter The best tasting butter is made from cultured cream (like crème fraîche, lactic acids are added to the cream before it is churned into butter).

Most European butters are churned from cultured cream, but cultured butter is very difficult to find here. Always use unsalted butter; salted butter is too salty and can ruin some dishes. Butter can only be used to cook foods over a low heat—when high temperatures are required, use clarified butter (see below).

Clarified butter   When the milk solids are removed from butter and only the butterfat remains, it is considered clarified. Clarified butter may be used for frying or sautéing at a higher temperature because you raise its smoke point from about 250° to 350° when you remove the butter's protein (milk solids). Clarified butter also has a longer storage life because it is primarily the protein in the butter that causes it to spoil. Here is how you make clarified butter.

1.   Melt any amount of unsalted butter slowly over a low heat.

2.   When the butter has melted, allow it to stand 5 minutes and then, with a spoon, carefully skim off the foam floating on top.

3.   Strain the remaining pure yellow fat through a fine sieve into a container, being certain to leave all the milky residue in the bottom of the pan.

4.   This pure butterfat, or clarified butter, may be stored in the refrigerator or freezer for months.

Margarine   Margarine can be used as a substitute for butter. It is 80% fat (usually vegetable oils with a small amount of animal fats), the rest of the product being milk, water, flavoring, and added vitamins. Margarine is equal to butter in calorie and nutritional value. Its taste, though, is quite different.

Grapeseed oil   This is the preferred oil to use for meat fondue, which is cooked at the table, since it has an extremely high smoke point. Its flavor is quite bland.

Avocado oil   This oil also has a very high smoke point. It has a delicate essence of avocado taste and makes a lovely mayonnaise or salad dressing. It is also an excellent cooking oil.

Walnut, hazelnut, and almond oils   All these oils have an extremely strong flavor of the nuts from which they are extracted. They can be used interchangeably with any other oil. They are especially wonderful for dressing vegetables and marinating delicate flesh such as chicken or fish.

Olive oil   There are three categories of olive oil: extra virgin, virgin, and pure—the best quality being the extra virgin. An extra virgin olive oil is as unadulterated as possible in every step of the production process. It is a first cold pressing of the olive and has less than 1% acidity. Virgin is the first cold pressing with a slightly higher acidity. Pure olive oil is the name applied to the oil obtained from subsequent pressings. It is refined and processed further, and the olives are sometimes heated for more thorough extraction. It is generally considered a lower quality product. There are also different pressing times, according to the style of the country producing the oil. An early press, December or early January, will result in a greener oil. When the olive is allowed to ripen more and is pressed later, a more yellow oil results. Early and late pressed oils have different tastes. The same quality oils will taste different depending upon where the olives from which they were made were grown.

Trade name oils   These oils are usually hydrogenated to increase shelf life. Hydrogenation converts the unsaturated oil molecules into saturated ones. These oils often contain other chemical additives and lack flavor.

Flour

There are essentially four kinds of white wheat flour: the hard wheat flour labeled "best for bread"; a combination hard wheat and soft wheat flour labeled "all-purpose" flour; flour labeled "pastry" flour; and "cake" flour. Unless otherwise specified in a recipe, use all-purpose flour. Flour proportions are important—therefore, for accuracy, flour should always be weighed on a scale, as should all other dry ingredients. (See page 240 for more information on flour.)

Herbs

Herbs are the leaves of aromatic plants. They can subtly flavor or dominate a dish, and personal taste, rather than rules, should govern their use. Dried herbs are more pungent than fresh—1 teaspoon of dried herbs is roughly equivalent to 2 tablespoons of fresh. (I always tell my students to use fresh herbs with abandon, and dried herbs with discretion. Once a woman raised her hand and, with a puzzled look on her face, asked, "What kind of food is abandon?") Dried herbs are added when a longer cooking time is required and fresh herbs are often added at the end. In buying dried herbs, always buy whole-leaf rather than ground or powdered because crushing allows the flavoring oils to evaporate.

Basil   Basil has an aromatic clove-like aroma. Its flavor increases with cooking. Use it fresh.

Bay   Bay is a leaf of a laurel tree. It is one of the few herbs that should be used only dried.

Chervil   Chervil leaves resemble fern-like parsley leaves. It has a mild flavor and brings out the flavor in other herbs. It is often used in combination with chives, parsley, or shallots.

Chinese parsley   See Cilantro.

Chives   Chives are hollow, reed-like stems of a plant of the lily family. They have a mild onion flavor. They should always be used fresh and should be snipped with a scissors rather than chopped with a knife.

Cilantro   Cilantro, also called Chinese parsley or coriander, looks like flat-leaf parsley. It has a delicate texture and a nippy taste. Cilantro leaves should only be used fresh. The seed (which is usually referred to as coriander) and the leaf of this plant have distinctly different flavors.

Dill   Dill weed is the leaf of the dill plant. It is milder in flavor than the seed and is so delicate and beautiful it is often used as a garnish.

Marjoram   Sweet marjoram is an herb from the Mediterranean basin. Its flavor is similar to oregano but milder. "Wild" marjoram is oregano.

Oregano   Oregano is best used dried. It is common in Italian, Spanish, and Mexican cooking.

Mint   There are numerous species of mint, all of which can be used fresh with fruits and vegetables and in sauces, and dried to make tea.

Parsley There are many varieties of parsley, among them Italian or "flat-leaf" parsley (which has plain, flat, glossy leaves and a rich, pungent flavor), and the common curly-leafed variety. Parsley is filled with minerals and vitamin C, so might be considered a health food as well as an herb and garnish. Always use parsley fresh, chopping it just before adding it to the dish. Parsley stems are sometimes excluded because of their coarse, fibrous texture. In flavor, however, the stems are the same as the leaves.

Rosemary Rosemary leaves look like tiny pine needles. This is an aromatic herb with a strong, distinctive flavor. It should always be used fresh and in small amounts.

Sage Sage is the leaf of an evergreen shrub that comes from the Adriatic Sea region. Its leaf is gray-green in color and may be used fresh or dry—the flowers may be used as well. Sage makes a delicious tea.

Tarragon Tarragon leaves have a unique, distinctive flavor— indispensable in Béarnaise Sauce. It makes excellent flavored vinegar and is best used fresh.

Thyme There are 60 or more varieties of thyme, all evergreen and all edible. Use the flowers as well as the leaves.

Nuts

Blanching Blanching is one way of removing the skins of nuts. I recommend that you purchase nuts already blanched, because blanching and peeling can be a time-consuming chore. However, here is a way to blanch them should you need to: Drop shelled nuts in boiling water for 30 seconds. Remove, and slip each nut out of its skin. (If this does not work easily, try 40 seconds, or more.) Don't blanch hazelnuts (filberts) or pistachios. They are more easily peeled after toasting (see below).

Toasting or roasting Toasting or roasting nuts increases their flavor. Spread the shelled nuts on a baking sheet and place in a 325° oven for 10 or 15 minutes. Watch carefully, stirring now and then, since nuts burn very easily.

Chopping and grinding To chop or grind nuts, use a chopping knife (page 7), nut grinder, or food processor. If you are using a food processor, use the "pulse" action and process just until the desired degree of fineness is reached. Overprocessing nuts causes them to release their oils and turn into butters.

Storing Store nuts, shelled or unshelled, blanched, toasted, chopped or ground, in the freezer.

Pancetta

Pancetta is Italian in origin and is the same cut of pork as bacon. It is not smoked but cured in salt and spices. Pancetta keeps approximately 3 weeks in the refrigerator. It can be frozen for 2 or 3 months. It can be eaten as is, like prosciutto (see below). Substitute bacon if pancetta is not available.

Prosciutto

Prosciutto is a dry-cured ham that can be eaten without further cooking and is used in small quantity in a great many dishes as a flavoring ingredient. It is also commonly served cold, thinly-sliced and wrapped around figs or melon slices. Its origins are Italian, and it is sometimes called Italian ham.

Seasonings

My seasonings category covers a wide range of vegetable and herb or spice blends, all of which should be used carefully to enhance, not disguise, the flavors of the dishes you are preparing. Before seasoning foods, smell or take a taste of the seasoning being used to see if it is something you like. Add a little at a time and taste again. In seasoning, practical experience is the best teacher, and taste is the real test.

Salt   Salt is used as a seasoning and preservative. Many flavors have substitutes, but there is no substitute for salt. Use more salt in foods that are to be served cold.

Seasoned salt and pepper   Finely chopped herbs, garlic, shallots, onions, etc., can be mixed with either salt or pepper, to create many all-purpose seasonings. Only your imagination is the limit.

Fine herbes   This is a French phrase meaning a mixture of herbs used for seasoning. *Fine herbes* is usually a combination of finely minced fresh or dried parsley, chervil, tarragon, and chives mixed until well blended.

Bouquet garni   Herbs, usually including parsley, thyme, and bay leaf, tied in a bunch or tied up in a small piece of cheesecloth so that they may be easily removed from the soups, stews, and sauces they may be flavoring.

Chili powder   Chili powder is a blend of spices, herbs, and chili pepper and is an American invention. It is usually a combination of cumin, coriander, chile peppers, garlic, cloves, paprika, salt, oregano, black pepper, and turmeric. It is hot, spicy, and slightly sweet, and sometimes very peppery.

Curry powder   Many spices make up curry powder. The individual blends vary considerably, but all curries will usually contain the following spices and herbs: cumin, coriander, turmeric, ginger, pepper, dill, mace, cardamom, and cloves. Together, they give the characteristic sweet-hot curry flavor and aroma.

Mustard   Mustard seeds come from a plant that grows wild in most of the world. The seeds are dried, ground, and sifted to produce dry or powdered mustard. Most packaged mustards are blends of seeds of different varieties, and will be "mild" or "hot," depending on the seeds used. Prepared mustards are made by grinding mustard seed to a paste and adding vinegar and other seasonings. In its numerous varieties, mustard is used to season just about any savory dish.

Capers   Capers are the bud of the flower of the caper bush which is found in the Mediterranean. Dried and then pickled, capers are widely used in Italian, French, German, and Spanish cooking in sauces, relishes, etc.

Sesame seeds   Sesame seeds are the flat, oval dried seed of a tropical annual. It is cultivated extensively in China. The tiny, smooth, creamy-white hulled seeds are available whole. You can also buy sesame oil. When the seeds are ground into a paste, it is called tahini. Sesame seeds must be heated to release their rich, nut-like flavor.

Onions   The flavor substance in onions is a volatile oil. Boiling onions in water minimizes the flavor. Sautéing them slowly in butter or oil converts all of the harsh raw flavor to mellow sweetness. Always use fresh onions.

Shallots   Shallots are more delicate in flavor than onions. They have the distinctive sweet taste of a mild onion with a hint of garlic. Like onions, only fresh shallots should be used.

Garlic   The aroma from its volatile oils gives garlic its pungency. When you cook with garlic, be careful not to over brown it, for it burns easily and develops a bitter taste.

Vanilla   The vanilla bean is the pod-like fruit of an orchid plant. The plant is native to Mexico, but the major production of beans today is in Madagascar. The green bean is harvested, cured, and dried before it turns a dark color and develops its characteristic fragrance and flavor. The flavor is extracted in alcohol to make vanilla extract. Vanilla makes sugar seem sweeter. A whole vanilla bean placed in a container of sugar will make "vanilla sugar."

Spices

Most spices come from a tropical region and consist of the seeds, buds, fruit or flower parts, bark, or roots of some aromatic plants. Where applicable, spices should be purchased in as whole a state as possible. Spices that are grated or ground just before use will yield the most flavor. Avoid buying preground spices.

Allspice   Allspice is the berry of an evergreen tree. The name comes from its flavor which is similar to a combination of nutmeg, cinnamon, and cloves.

Cardamom   Cardamom is native to India. It is richly perfumed and has a sweet refreshing flavor. It is used in curries and many Middle Eastern dishes.

Dried small hot chilies   Hot chilies are a member of the pepper family. They are usually removed from foods after cooking.

Cinnamon   Cinnamon is an aromatic, sweetly pungent spice made from the bark of any of several trees of Southeast Asia, Brazil, and the West Indies. The bark is stripped and dried and sold as sticks or ground into a powder.

Cloves   Cloves are the flower bud of a tree, native of China.

Coriander seed   The dried fruit of the coriander plant is ground and used in curries, sausages, and pastries. It is sometimes referred to as cilantro, although the word cilantro usually denotes the fresh leaves of the plant.

Ginger   Ginger is the rhizome of a plant and has a spicy-sweet, hot flavor. It is best used fresh.

Juniper berries   Juniper berries are the ripened fruit of an evergreen shrub. It takes three years for the berries to ripen and turn blue. They have a spicy pine aroma and sweet resinous flavor.

Mace   Mace is the lacy covering of the nutmeg. It is orange in color, and has a sweet, warm, spicy flavor.

Nutmeg   Nutmeg is the seed of a fruit of an East Indian evergreen tree. It has a warm, sweet, spicy flavor. Always purchase the whole nutmeg and grate it as needed.

Paprika   Paprika is a red powder made from a certain variety of red pepper. It ranges in taste from mild to hot. The best quality paprika comes from Hungary.

Peppercorns, black, white, and green   All peppercorns are the berries of the pepper tree, native to the East Indies. The differences between black, white, and green, are related to the harvesting time and processing methods. Black peppercorns are picked slightly immature and dried whole. White peppercorns are allowed to mature before picking, are soaked to remove the outer skin and then dried skinless. (White pepper is used in light-colored dishes.) Green peppercorns are picked unripened, and are preserved by freeze-drying them or placing them in brine. Their flavor is more delicate and aromatic than black or white peppercorns and they are used in specific dishes like Steak with Green Peppercorns, Breast of Duck with Green Peppercorns, etc. Always freshly grind peppercorns; never use preground pepper.

Saffron Saffron is the thread-like stigma of the crocus flower. It takes 225,000 hand-picked stigmas to yield 1 pound of saffron, making it the most expensive spice in the world. Its flavor is pungent and distinctive and it is used in extremely small amounts.

Turmeric Turmeric is the rhizome of a plant in the ginger family. It gives curry powder and prepared mustard their yellow color.

Sugar

Granulated white sugar is an all-purpose sugar. Superfine white sugar (a more finely granulated sugar, which is available in supermarkets or may be made by placing granulated sugar in the bowl of a food processor, and processing until the sugar is more finely ground, see page 227), will dissolve more quickly and is convenient to use in drinks and certain desserts. Powdered or confectioners' sugar is finely crushed sugar with a small amount of cornstarch added. Brown sugar contains a by-product of the sugar refining process—molasses—which gives it its distinctive flavor and color. Sugar should be stored in airtight containers.

Sugar syrups Sugar syrups are used in a variety of ways—for poaching fruit, as a base for sherbets and other frozen desserts, and to sprinkle on or soak certain cakes. If white wine is substituted for all or part of the water in the recipe, the syrup is called "White Wine Syrup." Should you substitute rum, you will produce a "Rum Syrup," etc. Here are some basic syrup recipes.

LIGHT SUGAR SYRUP

3½ oz. sugar (½ cup)
1 cup water

1. Place the sugar and water in a saucepan. Over medium heat, stir the mixture until all the sugar dissolves.
2. Bring the syrup to a boil and boil for 1 minute.
3. The syrup may be used immediately or stored in a jar in the refrigerator.

Variations:

Medium Sugar Syrup

Increase the sugar to 6 oz. (¾ cup).

Heavy Sugar Syrup

Increase the sugar to 7 oz. (1 cup).

Extra Heavy Sugar Syrup

Use 7 oz. (1 cup) sugar and decrease water to ½ cup.

Wine Syrup

Replace half the water with wine in any of the above.

Vinegar

Vinegar is a clear acidic liquid obtained by fermenting cider, wine, malt beer, or other alcoholic liquids. It is used as a condiment to season food, to make salad dressings and sauces, as a preservative, and as a marinade. Wine vinegars are very flavorful and I prefer to use them most of the time. As with oils, there is a vast array of vinegars too numerous to mention here. Don't be afraid to experiment—let your own tastes be the guide. When purchasing wine vinegar, look for pure vinegar—not one that has been watered down to a lower acidity.

Wine

Wine is the fermented juice of grapes. Although wine can be made from other plant juices—for instance cranberry wine, mulberry wine, or dandelion wine—its most common form is as fermented grapes. The subject of wine can (and does) fill whole volumes, so I will simply discuss it in the most general terms here and suggest you consult a good book on wines if you want to learn more about them.

Appetizer and dessert wines   These wines generally have a higher alcoholic content and a more pronounced flavor than other wines. Sometimes appetizer and dessert wines are the same wine in a different form, like sherry. You would select the "dry" version of sherry for an apéritif, and the "sweet" version for dessert. Some of the more popular wines in this category are vermouth, sherry, port, Marsala, French sautérnes, and Tokay.

Table wines   Wines in this category are compatible with food in general, are good "harmonizers," and are not as assertive as dessert wines. They are also dry. Table wines—red, rosé, and white—average about 12% alcohol. Very generally, with a few exceptions, you may follow the advice of red wine with red meat and white wine with white meat.

Some of the more popular red table wines are Pinot Noir, Cabernet Sauvignon, red Burgundy, red Bordeaux, Beaujolais, Zinfandel, and Chianti.

Some of the well known white table wines are Pinot Chardonnay, Chablis, Sauvignon Blanc, Chenin Blanc, white Burgundy, white Bordeaux, Vouvray, white Graves, and Gewürztraminer.

When a recipe calls for a "dry red" or "dry white" wine, any of the above table wines may be used.

Sparkling wines Champagne and sparkling Burgundy are two of the most popular sparkling wines. Champagne is quite versatile and can be served before dinner, during dinner, or with dessert. Sparkling Burgundy is sweeter and is better served as a dessert wine. In cooking with wine, remember that you are adding it for flavor, and if it is not a drinkable wine, you will not produce an edible result.

VEGETABLE AND FRUIT PREPARATION

The ability to select perfect fruits and vegetables—the perfect tomato, at the peak of its flavor and juiciness, the just-ripe melon, etc.—is a matter of experience. The best way to begin is to start shopping in a busy produce market—one that has a rapid turnover—and one that does not prepackage its fruits and vegetables, but allows you to select your own. Then make friends with the produce person so that you'll feel comfortable asking for help when you are unsure about what is "the best."

Generally, small, young vegetables are the most tender and best tasting; the biggest ones (like the giant vegetables pictured in seed catalogues) often lack taste. Look for clean, crisp, bright-colored, unblemished, smooth, shiny, and well-formed fruits and vegetables in season. Vegetables start to lose flavor and nutrients the moment they are harvested, so buy them in small quantities and cook them as soon as possible.

Most fresh produce should be stored in the vegetable drawer of the refrigerator, but shallots, garlic, onions, and potatoes do best stored in string bags or baskets in cool dark areas, not the refrigerator.

In this section, we are concerned primarily with the selection and preparation of vegetables and fruits *before* they are cooked. You will find instructions and recipes for boiling, steaming, braising, sautéing, and baking them in the chapters that follow. It is worth emphasizing these general rules now, though: In order to preserve flavors and nutrients, *do not overcook* vegetables, and *never* substitute frozen or canned vegetables for fresh with the hope of achieving the same taste or texture as fresh vegetables.

The following is a medley of methods and techniques for handling specific vegetables.

Artichokes

An artichoke is an edible thistle that may be cooked and served whole, and eaten leaf by leaf. It can also be trimmed of all its leaves, leaving a small bowl-shaped bottom (also called the heart) that can be cooked and filled with another vegetable like creamed spinach or peas. Rub all cut surfaces of the artichoke with a lemon and use a stainless steel knife when cutting the raw artichoke to minimize the discoloration that occurs.

To prepare a whole artichoke Swish the artichoke in a bowl of lukewarm water to clean. Cut off the stem end so that the artichoke will stand nicely on a plate.

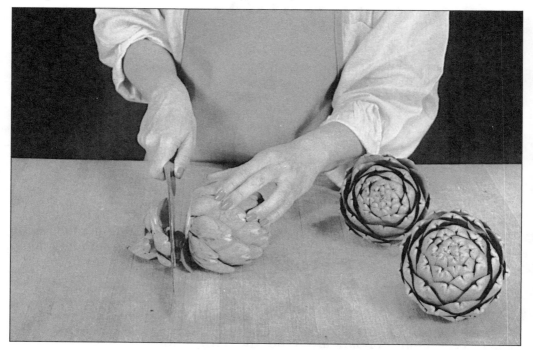

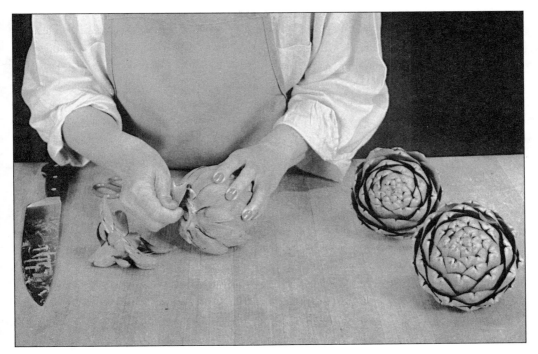

With your fingers, pull off all the tiny leaves near the bottom.

Cut off about an inch from the top of the artichoke.

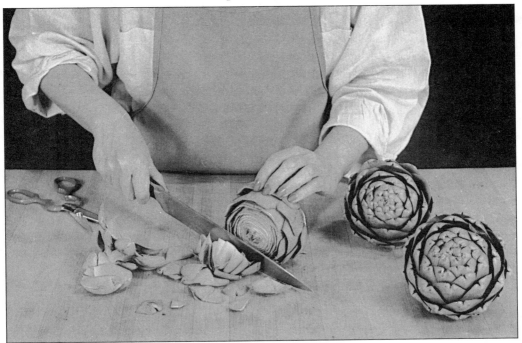

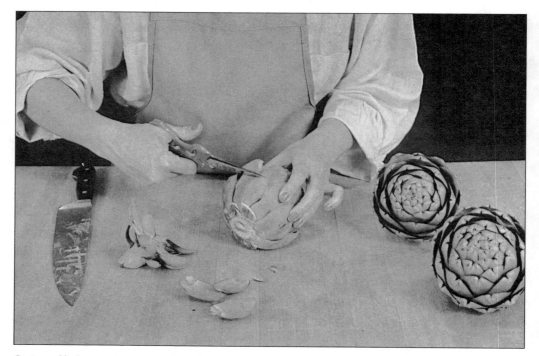

Snip off the spiny tip of each leaf with a pair of scissors.

After cooking, the choke (the feathery, inedible center portion that conceals the bottom) is easily removed before serving.

To prepare an artichoke bottom   Cut or break off the stem and all the leaves at the base of the artichoke. Cut off all the leaves just above the bottom and trim off all the visible green. Drop into boiling salted water that has lemon juice added. Lower the heat and simmer until tender. Let the bottoms cool in the cooking liquid. Remove the choke with a spoon and store in some of the cooking liquid until ready to use.

Asparagus and Celery

Both asparagus and celery should always be peeled before cooking or serving. The tough outer membrane of asparagus is stringy and fibrous and not edible even when it is overcooked. Once it is removed, the entire asparagus spear is edible. Removing the strings on celery makes it easier to chop, julienne, or slice. Lay the celery or asparagus down on a flat surface and peel with a vegetable peeler.

Beets

When selecting beets, choose small ones—no bigger than about 2 inches in diameter. Larger ones can be fibrous. Beets are available year round and are best boiled, steamed, braised, or baked. To avoid losing color and juices, do not trim or peel beets before they are cooked.

Bell Peppers

Many bell pepper recipes call for broiling (or charring or roasting) the peppers first. This makes the skin peel off easily and enhances the sweetness of the flesh. Place the pepper over a direct flame or under the broiler and char evenly, turning frequently. Allow to cool. Peel away the charred outer skin with a paring knife. This is a messy job and best done at the sink. To remove the seeds, cut the pepper lengthwise and open it out flat. Cut out the stem and core with seeds attached. Remove any remaining seeds.

Belgian Endive

Belgian endive is outstanding cooked or uncooked. However you serve it, the core should always be removed as it is bitter. Cut off the root end and, with the tip of your knife, remove the core by cutting it out with a circular motion.

Broccoli

Broccoli buds should be tightly closed; the color should be green or purple, but never yellow—which means the broccoli is old. To prepare, cut off the broccoli flowers at the ends of their stems. Cut in half or quarters any "florets" that are too large. Slice away all the fibrous outer skin of the main stalk. The "heart" of the stalk is delicious and can be prepared along with the florets or prepared on its own—sliced and sautéed, diced in a cream sauce, or in soups or salads.

Celery

See Asparagus.

Corn on the Cob

When selecting corn, the cobs should be about 6 inches long and the husks green. The corn silk should be a pale cream color and the kernels firm. See page 97 for cooking method.

Zesting an orange.

Citrus Fruits

Zesting The zest of a citrus fruit is the thin outer skin, the pigmented layer, that contains a strong citrus flavor. The zest is used a great deal in cooking when an intense citrus taste is needed. The fibrous membrane or white spongy pith beneath the zest should never be included. It will give a bitter taste to the dish. Use a zesting tool or a small paring knife to remove only the colored portion of the rind. The zest may be chopped fine and used immediately, or dried for later use.

Peeling and sectioning Using a stainless steel paring knife, cut a slice from each end of the fruit. Cut away the entire skin, being certain that all the bitter white of the rind is removed. To separate sections, cut next to the membrane. Squeeze the juice from the sectioned membrane before discarding.

Cucumbers

Since commercially grown cucumbers are coated with chemicals or "waxed" to retard spoilage, they should be peeled before use. The seeds have an unpleasant texture and hold excessive water around them, so they should be discarded, too. Using a vegetable peeler, remove the dark outer skin of the cucumber. Cut off ¼ inch from each end and cut the cucumber in half lengthwise. Use a teaspoon to scrape out the seeds. The cucumber halves may then be left as is for stuffing, sliced for salad, or cut into a julienne, depending on your needs.

Eggplant

The following technique should always be employed before cooking eggplant in any form, as it helps eliminate excess moisture and bitterness. Peel and slice or cube the eggplant according to the directions in your recipe. Arrange the eggplant pieces (cubes, slices, etc.) on paper towels and sprinkle with salt. Let drain 30 minutes, pat dry with more paper towels, and proceed with your recipe.

Garlic and Shallots

Garlic and shallots are dried after harvesting so that the papery outer dry skin will protect the inner flesh during storage. With rare exceptions, you will always need to remove the skin before using these vegetables. When selecting these vegetables, choose firm ones that have not sprouted. Store them in baskets or net bags, in a cool, dry, dark place.

To peel garlic, separate the cloves, cut off the tip ends, and hit each clove sharply with the flat side of a knife. This loosens the skin and causes it to pop off.

To peel shallots, cut off the tops and bottoms of the shallot. With a small paring knife, peel away the first layer of flesh that is attached to the thin, dry, paper-like outer skin.

Leeks

Leeks have sand deep down in the bulb and must be cleaned carefully. Generally the dark green tops of the leeks are discarded as they are very bitter in flavor. Cut off the root and the upper dark green tops of the leek just above where the white part joins the green. Split the leaves lengthwise above the bulb once, and a second time at right angles to the first cut. Under running water, carefully clean the sand out of each section, checking each portion before going on to the next. The leeks are now ready to be cooked whole, chopped, or sliced.

Mushrooms

Because of the high water content of mushrooms they should never be soaked in order to clean them. Cultivated mushrooms purchased in the supermarket can be cleaned without water by gently brushing with a mushroom brush. Wild mushrooms from the forest often have soil and sand imbedded in their "gills" and must be brushed gently under cool running water. Mushroom gills are not exposed in fresh domesticated mushrooms.

Onions

When selecting onions, choose firm ones that have not sprouted. Onions, like garlic and shallots, have a papery outer skin that must be removed and discarded. Should you wish to boil tiny onions or bake and stuff larger ones, remember not to cut off the root end. Slice off the top and peel the outer skin away. Trim the root end, but leave it intact. If the root end is cut away, the onion will fall apart as it cooks.

Store onions in a cool, dry, dark place.

Salad Greens

It is very important that you take the time to properly clean, dry, and crisp lettuce or other greens used for salad. Sandy or soggy greens will spoil the most carefully made salad sauces. Remove all the inedible parts of the lettuce—the core or any bruised, wilted, or torn outer leaves. Wash the leaves carefully in cold water and dry gently on paper towels or in a lettuce spinner. Crisp the greens in the refrigerator, wrapped in linen or paper towels and placed in plastic bags, for several hours before serving.

Note: Before washing the entire lettuce, check for dirt or sand. Many varieties of lettuce are only sandy in the outer leaves—the inner ones do not need washing.

Spinach

Spinach tends to be very sandy. With a large knife, cut off approximately 2 inches of the coarse spinach stems. Fill a large bowl with warm water (warm water is more effective in removing sand) and immerse the spinach leaves in the water. Remove the spinach and rinse out the bowl. Refill the bowl with cold water and swish the leaves in the cold water. Dry the spinach on paper towels or in a salad spinner, if it's to be used for salad. Spinach cooks beautifully using only the water that clings to the leaves after washing.

Snow Peas

Select the smallest, thinnest snow peas and be careful to remove the strings from each side of the pod. Slice or break off the stem end of the snow pea, pulling the attached string off with the stem end. Slice or pull off the opposite end, pulling the attached string along with it.

Tomatoes

Peeling   Removing the skin eliminates the possibility of the tomato skin coming off during cooking, and curling up and floating in the soup or sauce. To peel, dip the tomato in boiling water for 10 seconds. Remove the stem and slip off the skin. Tomatoes may be "dipped" and refrigerated until needed. Slip the skins off just before using.

Seeding   Seeding a tomato before it is used eliminates much of the juice as well as the seeds. To seed the tomato, cut it into quarters and remove the seeds and juice by hand. Please note that peeling and seeding tomatoes is not always called for.

CUTTING VEGETABLES

Most vegetables can be cooked whole, but they are often sliced, diced, shredded (grated), chopped, carved, or julienned, to reduce their cooking time, to expose more surface area (in order to speed up extraction of flavors), or to make them more attractive. Texture affects taste, and vegetables can be made to taste differently by cutting them into strips, carving them into ovals, etc. No matter how they are cut, all the pieces in one dish should be uniform in size and shape so they please the eye and cook evenly.

Many of the following procedures may be accomplished in a food processor.

Dicing

For most vegetables, cut a thin slice from one side and place that side down on the cutting surface to keep the vegetable from rolling around while you are cutting it.

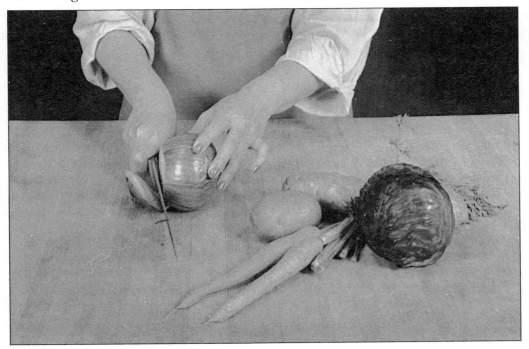

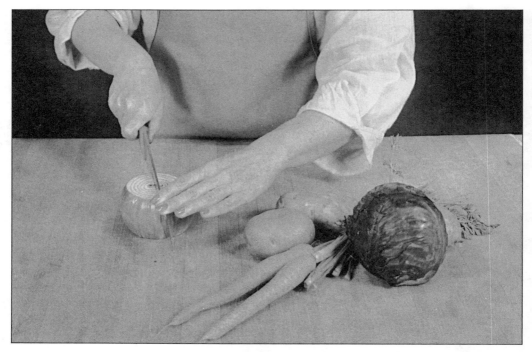

Peel and slice the vegetable to the thickness you want the finished dice to be.

Next, stack up the slices, and cut the stack into strips the same width as the first slices.

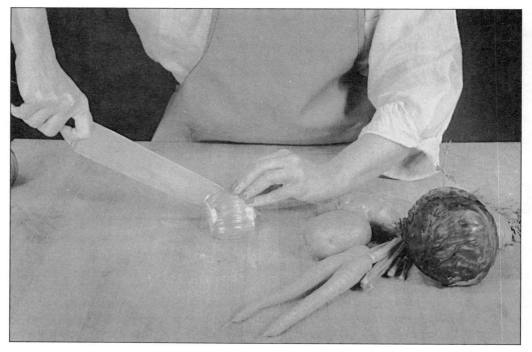

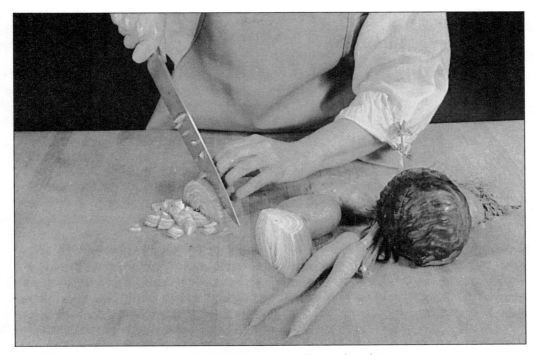

Finally, cut across the stack of strips to produce the dice.

Shredding or grating

For most vegetables, a hand grater (or the shredding disc on a food processor) will do the job quickly and easily. For leafy vegetables, you will need a knife.

For tight heads of leaves, like cabbage, halve the vegetable so that you can put the flat side down on the cutting surface, then slice it vertically with a chopping knife. The closer together you make the slices, the finer the shreds will be.

For loose leaves, like spinach or chard, stack the individual leaves, roll them into a cylinder, and cut them crosswise. Again, the closer you make the slices, the finer the shreds will be.

Julienne

To cut into julienne means to cut into strips. The strips are usually thin—about ⅛ inch in diameter—but can also be as thick as ¼ inch. If a recipe calls for "matchstick" julienne, cut the vegetable to the size of a wooden matchstick. The following are commonly julienned vegetables.

Green beans Line up 10 or 12 beans at a time, and with a large chopping knife, nip off the ends. Slice the beans into narrow strips. (There are various mechanical devices to julienne green beans.)

Carrots Scrape or peel the carrot and cut off the ends. Cut the carrot into lengthwise slices depending upon how thick you want the julienne to be. Stack 3 or 4 of the slices on top of one another and cut them again. After a long julienne has been made, the carrots may be cut crosswise to the desired length.

Diced onion, julienned carrot, chopped potato, and shredded red cabbage.

Leeks   First clean the leek (page 31,) then cut it in half. Lay the leek cut side down on the cutting board and cut into strips.

Celery   Separate the stalks, and remove the first layer of strings with a vegetable peeler. Cut the stalks into lengthwise slices, stack 3 or 4 of the slices on top of one another, and cut them again. After a long julienne has been made, the celery may be cut crosswise to the desired length.

Zucchini   Cut off the ends and cut the zucchini into lengthwise slices depending upon how thick you want the julienne to be. Stack 3 or 4 of the slices on top of one another and cut them again. After a long julienne has been made, the zucchini may be cut crosswise to the desired length.

Chopping

There are all degrees of chopping—from large chunks (as in making stock) to finely chopped parsley. Following are techniques for chopping onions, and herbs.

Parsley and other leafy herbs   Gather the herbs together tightly into a ball. Slice across the herbs several times with your chopping knife. To finish finely chopping the herbs, lightly rest the palm of one hand near the tip of the knife and continue chopping using a rocking motion until the leaves are finely chopped.

Onions   (This technique also works well for shallots or garlic.) Peel the onion and cut it in half through the root. Place the half cut side down on a chopping board. Holding the onion with one hand, slice it horizontally, being careful not to cut through the end. Hold the knife vertically and cut from top to bottom, again not cutting through the end.

Hold the onion with one hand and make thin slices across the onion. This will give you a coarsely chopped onion. Continue chopping until the onion is chopped to the desired degree of fineness.

Carving vegetables

I do not believe the elaborate vegetable carvings one sees on hotel banquet tables are appropriate for the home table. A single vegetable "rose" tastefully displayed may be an exception. Whenever you use a combination of vegetables for a garnish or accompaniment to a main dish, a rule to remember is that they must all be uniform in size.

Ovals and cylinders   It is common to carve carrots, potatoes, turnips, and other root vegetables into cylinders or ovals before cooking them. First peel the vegetables, and put any you are not working on in water. Cut the vegetable in half, slice off rounded ends, and cut into the size pieces desired. With a paring knife, carve away any sharp edges, turning the vegetable after every cut to form an oval or cylinder shape.

Tomato roses   Remove the entire tomato skin in one strip, slicing off the bottom of the tomato and leaving it still attached to the peel. The peel should not be too thick or too thin. Starting at the end, roll the peel up until the rolled peel rests on the bottom of the tomato. Apples, lemons, oranges, grapefruits, and limes can also be used to create "roses."

EXTRACTING WATER FROM VEGETABLES

Salting vegetables softens the flesh and draws out moisture. This is advisable when you don't want the juices from the vegetables to dilute a sauce or dressing. Generally the vegetables should be peeled and sliced fairly thin to expose as much surface area as possible. Spread the sliced vegetables out on paper towels, sprinkle lightly with fine salt, and allow to stand 30 minutes. Now gently blot the sliced vegetables with dry paper towels to get rid of the salty liquid.

ICING VEGETABLES

Icing vegetables has the reverse effect as salting vegetables—it refreshes and crisps the vegetables by replacing the water they have lost since harvesting. Firm vegetables such as carrots, celery, cucumbers, and radishes respond well to icing. Vegetables need to be sliced to expose sufficient surface area, then placed in a bowl with ice and refrigerated at least an hour.

PREPARING VEGETABLES FOR FILLING

There are many dishes based on a filling that is stuffed into vegetables. Sometimes a single stuffing is made and a variety of vegetables like potatoes, mushrooms, and squash are stuffed, baked, and served together.

Bell peppers   Slice off the pepper tops, leaving the stems intact, and reserve them. Scoop out the seeds and ribs and blanch the peppers and tops in boiling water for 1 minute before stuffing.

Mushrooms   Select large mushrooms and carefully break out the stems. Blanch for 1 minute in boiling water if the mushrooms are not going to be cooked after they are stuffed.

Patty pan squash   Place the squash on the work surface with the stem side down. Slice off the opposite end with a knife and with a small tool called a melon baller, scoop out the seeds and flesh.

Onions   Trim, but do not cut off the root end of the onion. Peel the onion, and cut off the top. With a curved serrated knife, cut around the inner layers of the onion. With a spoon, scoop out the flesh, leaving two or three layers to form a solid shell.

Potatoes   Scrub but do not peel the potatoes. Bake until tender. Allow to cool and cut in half either lengthwise or crosswise. Scoop out the flesh, leaving a layer ¼ inch thick next to the skin so that the potato will hold its shape when further baked.

Tomatoes   Tomatoes can be stuffed with vegetables such as spinach or peas, and then baked, or they can be filled with fish or vegetable salad and served uncooked. If a "cap" is desired, cut off the bottom of the tomato and reserve it as a lid. Hollow the tomato out with a curved serrated knife, standing the tomato on its stem end to serve. Sprinkle the inside of the tomato with salt and turn it upside down to drain for 30 minutes before using.

Zucchini   Slice lengthwise. Using a curved serrated knife, scoop out the seeds and flesh, being careful to leave a substantial "wall," so the zucchini will not break when baked. You can also cut zucchini into large chunks and remove the center of each piece with an apple corer.

Note: For more information on preparing vegetables especially for hors d'oeuvres, see page 275.

POULTRY
PREPARATION

Almost without exception, birds (from quail to turkeys or geese) need some kind of preparation *before* they are cooked.

The proper methods and techniques to accomplish those tasks are all presented in this section. I have used chickens and turkeys as examples, but the same procedures may be used for all poultry.

DISJOINTING

By cutting up your own poultry you will be able to produce precise, neat, portions exactly to your specifications. Poultry pieces are generally more expensive than a whole bird, so you will save money as well. In addition, you'll have bones and scraps to put into a soup stock. All you need is a sharp, heavy chopping knife and a cutting board.

Halving poultry

1. Place the bird on its back with the legs pointing toward you. Insert the knife into the body cavity, and cut down along one side of the backbone. (See fig. 1) Open the bird and cut along the other side of the backbone. (See fig. 2) Reserve the backbone for soup stock.

2. Place the bird breast side down and cut through the white membrane along both sides of the breastbone. Hold the poultry on each side of the breastbone and bend it backward until the breastbone snaps. Pull out and reserve the bone and cartilage for soup stock and completely cut the bird in half.

3. Cut off each wing tip at the joint and reserve for soup stock. With each half skin side down, make a small cut at the leg joint and the shoulder joint. This will keep the wing and leg flat while the bird cooks. (See fig. 3)

Cutting into 4 pieces

Follow instructions 1, 2, and 3 above, and then cut the bird where the thigh joins the breast.

Cutting into 8 pieces

Follow instructions 1, 2, 3, above and then cut the bird where the thigh joins the breast and where it joins the drumstick. Cut off the wing where it joins the body, taking a little breast meat along with the wing.

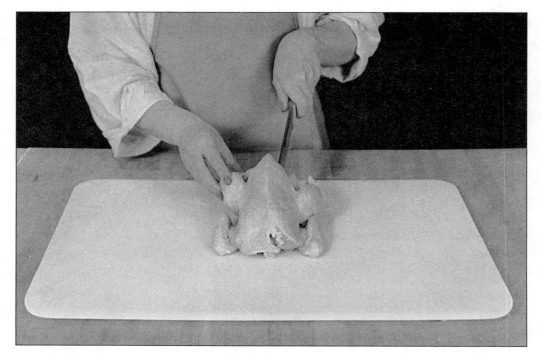

Insert knife and cut along one side of backbone.

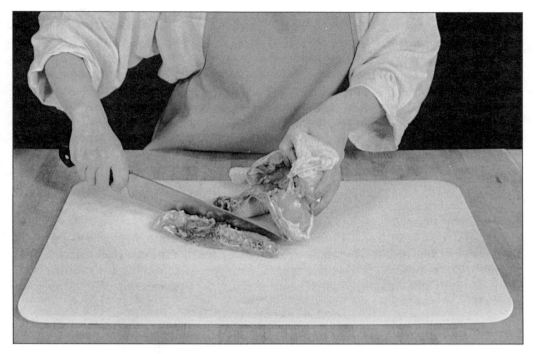

Cut along other side of backbone.

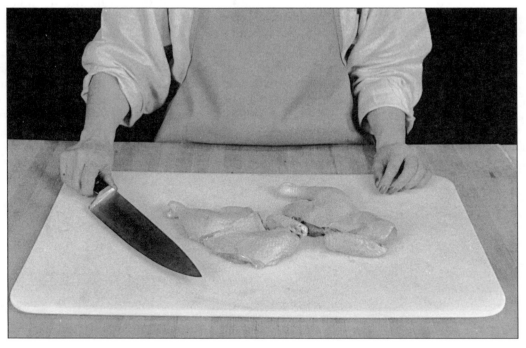

Halved poultry, breastbone and wing tips removed.

BONING AND FILLETING
CHICKEN BREASTS

Boned chicken breast recipes are featured in many cuisines. The technique of boning a chicken breast is very simple and very good to know in case you are unable to buy the breasts already boned. Filleting or cutting the deboned breast into 3 pieces is a technique that you will probably use many times, whenever boned chicken breasts are called for. Filleting the breast, and then sautéing and serving the fillets to innocent guests may evoke the same response as I have had. "Oh," they say eating the tender morsels, "this is the best veal I have ever had—where do you buy your veal?!!!"

Boning the breast

1. Start out with a whole breast and use a boning knife (see page 7). Place the whole breast skin side down on a board, and cut down the length of the breastbone to separate the breast into two half breasts. Loosen the skin from the half breast with your fingers—using the knife to cut the skin wherever it is connected.

2. Turn the half breast over, skinned side down, and insert the tip of the boning knife under the breastbone and gently separate the bone from the flesh, working the knife under the ribs, and cutting them away at the edge of the breast.

3. Insert the knife under the thin piece of cartilage attached to the narrow end of the chicken breast and cut it away.

4. Use the knife tip to cut through the flesh over the wishbone; pull it out with your fingers and cut it free. Trim off any fat or membrane to make a neat-looking fillet. (Reserve all bones for soup stock.)

Filleting the breast meat

1. On the underside of the breast, the part that was next to the bone, there is a smaller muscle that may easily be separated from the rest of the breast meat with your fingers. Finish cutting the piece off with the knife, creating one fillet.

2. Lay the remaining larger piece of breast meat on the cutting board, and, holding it flat with one hand, slice into it, holding the knife parallel to the cutting board to create two thin fillets. Now you have three fillets from one half breast.

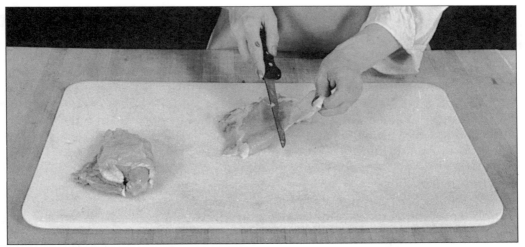

Remove skin from half breasts.

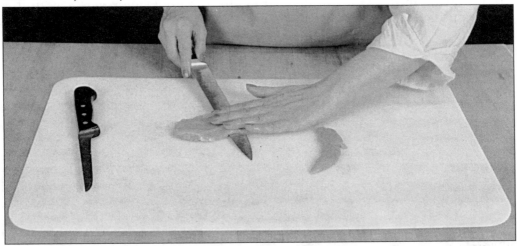

Place one hand on larger piece of boned breast meat and carefully slice into two thin fillets.

Three fillets from one half breast.

STUFFING, TRUSSING, AND
CARVING A BIRD

Stuffing a bird adds flavor, helps keep the bird juicy, and provides a side dish, all at the same time. (See pages xx for recipes.) It is not always necessary to stuff a bird, but trussing should always be done when cooking (roasting, braising, or poaching) a whole bird. Not only does it give the bird an attractive shape with wings and legs held close to the body, it also helps keep the bird moist and juicy.

Stuffing a bird
1. Fill the bird through its tail opening, being careful to pack the stuffing loosely and only about ¾ full. (Stuffing expands as it cooks.) Thread a trussing needle with twine and sew up the opening.
2. Fill the neck cavity loosely, separating the skin from the breast with your fingers, and placing a thin layer of stuffing under the skin. Sew up the neck skin flap.

Trussing a bird
Cut a piece of string 3 times the length of the bird. Cut off the wing tips at the joints. Fold the flap of neck skin over the back to close the neck opening (if the bird has not been stuffed and sewed up). Place the bird on its back.

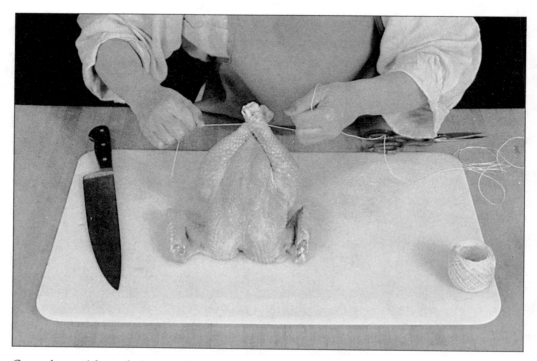

Cross drumsticks and tie securely, leaving a 2-inch piece of string at one end.

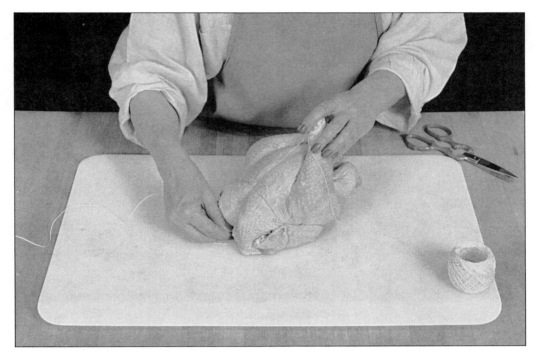

Bring longer string over breast and around the bird, securing wings.

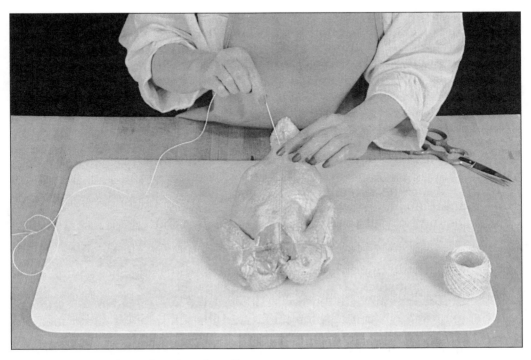

Bring string over the neck and to the tail.

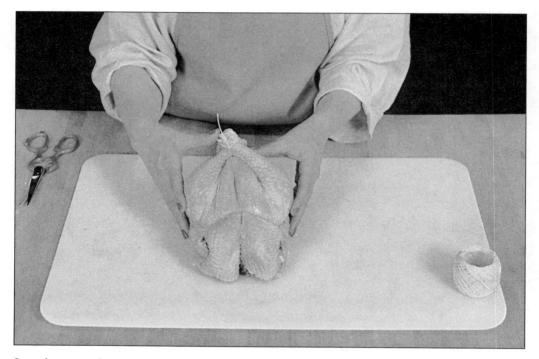

Loop longer string around drumsticks and tie securely to shorter string.

Carving a bird

Always allow the bird to rest at least ½ hour before carving. This allows the juices to be reabsorbed into the meat.

Use a pointed knife with a flexible blade and a two-tined fork to hold the bird while you carve. The same procedure used on a turkey may be used on a smaller chicken, without slicing the meat from the thigh or breast. On very small birds like squab or quail, all you do is split them in two by cutting straight down along the center of the breastbone and backbone. The following procedure is for a large turkey.

1. Place the bird on a large cutting board with a well, to catch any juices. Cut and remove the trussing string. If there is any stuffing, remove it from both the tail and neck cavities of the bird (leaving the stuffing under the breast skin, if any, intact), and transfer to serving bowls.

2. Cut the skin all around the upper thigh. Gently separate the thigh (and drumstick) at the joint from the breast, using your fork to hold the bird steady.

3. Separate the thigh from the drumstick at the joint. Slice the meat off the thigh and drumstick, and arrange it on a platter.

4. Slice down through the breast toward the wing. Move the wing to find the joint and cut through the joint. Add the wing to the sliced meat on the platter.

5. Cut the breast into slices and add to the sliced meat on the platter. Repeat the same procedure for the other side of the bird.

STOCK, BROTH, AND CONSOMMÉ

What to present as a first chapter was a difficult decision for me to make. And it was equally difficult some years ago when I first introduced this basic cooking series into my school. The first lesson is the first impression, and I wanted then, as now, to make a good impression.

So, once again I checked off all the possibilities for a first chapter. Thinking of the wonderful soups, main dishes, and sauces that I could start with, I confronted the same problem I encountered years ago—all of those great dishes depend upon a well-made stock. An obvious solution would be to use a substitute. How about a cube, or a powdered soup base, or a can of stock that has been doctored with fresh vegetables or herbs? I tried them all anew and concluded that there is still no substitute for a good homemade stock. If your stock is good, there is no doubt that your friends and relatives will be astonished at your cooking skills when they taste your French Onion Soup, Madeira Cream Sauce, or Veal Ragoût.

With that awareness, I decided to begin this book with a lesson on making stocks. It also makes a good beginning because it is so easy to make a good stock: only the most basic equipment and ingredients are used, exact measurement of ingredients is unnecessary, and once the stock is simmering, it requires very little attention.

The Difference Between Stock and Broth
Both stocks and broths are savory extractions of flavors and nutrients from bones, meats, vegetables, and herbs. Stocks are more gelatinous than broth, they are less flavorful, and are made from a combination of bones (rather than meats), vegetables, and herbs. Even though stocks are considered the foundation of cooking, a stock is never meant to be served as is. Its prime use is as a base only: you will never serve stock as a course on a menu. Broths are made from a combination of meats (rather than bones), vegetables, and herbs. A broth can be seasoned and served as is, or it can be clarified, in a process that will be explained later, to make a consommé. Sometimes, a broth and a main course can be made at the same time. Meat or chicken can be poached just long enough to flavor the broth and then be served after the soup as the main course. (See Chicken in the Pot, page 91, and Mixed Boiled Meats, page 92.)

Basic Method for Stock or Broth
The basic method for making stock or broth is the same, whether it is made with chicken, fish, vegetables, or meat. The extraction process is begun by covering the chicken, fish, or meat, with cold water and bringing the liquid slowly to a boil. (Should you wish to serve the boiled chicken or meats as a separate course, you will not start with cold water, but bring the water to a boil first, drop in the chicken or meat, and simmer until tender. That is done so that some flavor will be preserved in the poultry or meat.) The heat is then lowered and the ingredients are simmered until the desired flavor is extracted. As they are heated, the albuminous particles of protein present in the meat and bones are released. These impurities, called scum, will float to the surface and should be skimmed off. Add the vegetables after removing the scum, as it is easier to skim without interference.

Fish stock and pure vegetable stocks are usually finished in half an hour. Meat and chicken require longer cooking times, perhaps 4 or 5 hours. At the end of cooking, strain and chill the stock or broth. Chilling causes the fat to congeal on the top of the liquid so that it can be easily removed. Finally, the stock or broth can be stored, used as is, or boiled down (reduced) to $\frac{1}{3}$ or even less of its original volume. In this reduced form it is known as a stock concentrate or extraction. In either form it can be stored in the freezer for 6 months or more, or in the refrigerator for 3 to 4 days. A broth or stock may be freshened by boiling for 5 minutes if it has "soured" in the refrigerator.

Ingredients
Good stock or broth is based on raw bones or meat, with vegetables such as onions, carrots, and celery (referred to as aromatics) added for flavor. To perfume and further flavor the liquid, herbs are used, fresh or dry, loose or tied in a muslin or cheesecloth bag and called a bouquet garni (see page 19). A vegetable broth includes the usual aromatic vegetables—carrots, onions,

and celery—plus leafy vegetables such as cabbage and lettuce. White wine is added to fish stocks, and they are generally less clear and less gelatinous than meat or chicken broths. Peppercorns are used instead of ground pepper, since ground pepper sometimes becomes bitter with prolonged cooking. Salt is never used because, as the stock is reduced, the salt becomes very concentrated. The ingredients used give the broth or stock its name, i.e., lamb bones produce lamb stock and fish bones produce fish stock.

After awhile, stock making will be so easy for you that you will be able to make stock using any bones, meat, or vegetables you have on hand without having to follow any specific recipe step-by-step. The recipes that follow are meant only to be guides until you understand the concepts of stock making.

MEAT BROTH

1 onion stuck with 6 cloves
2 carrots
1 stalk celery
¼ bunch parsley
2 lbs. beef chuck
2 lbs. veal shanks or neck bones
2 lbs. chicken necks and/or backs
1 bouquet garni
a soup or stock pot—at least 8 qts.

1. Peel the onion and stick the cloves firmly in place. Clean the carrots, celery, and parsley and chop coarsely.
2. Tie up the beef chuck (always tie up any large piece of meat to keep it from falling apart). Place the chuck, veal, and chicken in the stock pot and add enough cold water to cover.
3. Bring very slowly to the boil. Once it begins to boil, use a skimming spoon to remove the surface foam (scum).
4. Add the vegetables and bouquet garni—skimming, if necessary, as the liquid returns to the boil.
5. Turn the heat down as low as possible, cover the pot, leaving the lid askew, and simmer 3 to 4 hours, depending upon how strong you want the broth and whether you want to serve the meat.
6. Strain the finished broth through a coarse sieve, then through a fine sieve or cheesecloth, and chill at least 8 hours.
7. Remove the congealed fat formed on top of the broth and store the broth in the refrigerator for 3 or 4 days or in the freezer up to 6 months.

Use either White Stock or Chicken Stock as a base for soups, or in sauces and gravies in lighter meat, vegetable, or fish dishes, since you do not want the stock to overpower the other ingredients in these dishes.

If you want your stock to be flavored by chicken only, use all chicken bones. The addition of veal bones will produce a more gelatinous stock. White Stock and Chicken Stock are interchangeable and may be substituted for each other in any recipe.

WHITE STOCK

3 lbs. chicken bones
3 lbs. veal bones

Use the same "aromatics" (vegetables) and method as for Meat Broth.

CHICKEN STOCK

6 lbs. chicken bones

Use the same "aromatics" (vegetables) and method as for Meat Broth.

In making Brown Stock, the bones and vegetables are well browned before the actual extraction begins. Brown Stock is also used as a base for soups, and for sauces and gravies in red meat and game dishes.

BROWN STOCK

3 lbs. beef bones
3 lbs. veal bones
1 onion stuck with 6 cloves
celery tops—a handful
1 leek, cleaned (see page 31)
1 carrot
¼ bunch parsley
1 bouquet garni
**a soup or stock pot—at least
   8 qts.**

1.   Put the bones on a baking sheet and place in a 375° oven until browned before starting the stock.
2.   Put the browned bones in the stock pot, and use the same "aromatics" (vegetables) and method as for Meat Broth.

A *Court Bouillon* is made with water, herbs, vegetables, and wine or wine vinegar, and is used to poach fish. If fish bones and trimmings are added, the *Court Bouillon* becomes a fish stock or *fumet*.

COURT BOUILLON

2 qts. cold water
3 sprigs parsley
1 stalk celery with leaves
1 bay leaf
1 teaspoon peppercorns
3 fennel seeds
1 onion
½ cup wine vinegar
an 8-qt. soup or stock pot

1.   Bring all the ingredients to a boil in the stock pot. Lower the heat and simmer 20 minutes.
2.   Strain.

Fish Stock can be used as the base for sauces and many fish soups and as a poaching medium for fish. The fish used to make the stock should be compatible with the dish in which the stock is to be used.

FISH STOCK

2 lbs. white fish heads and
  bones
1 onion
1 shallot
1 carrot
a handful celery tops
1 cup dry white table wine
1 bouquet garni
an 8-qt. soup or stock pot

1.   Rinse the fish heads and bones; peel the onion and shallot; clean the carrot and cut into 3 pieces; clean the celery tops.
2.   Place the fish parts in the stock pot; add the wine and enough water to cover and bring very slowly to the boil. With a skimming spoon, remove the surface foam (scum).
3.   Add the vegetables and bouquet garni, skimming if necessary as the liquid returns to the boil.
4.   Turn the heat down as low as possible, cover the pot, leaving the lid askew, and simmer 30 minutes.
5.   Strain the finished stock through a coarse sieve then through a fine sieve or cheesecloth.

The following recipe can be your guide for making a vegetable stock. You may use any vegetables to make your stock, but be aware that certain vegetables will overpower others.

VEGETABLE STOCK

2 leeks
3 stalks celery, with leaves
5 carrots
2 onions
1 bunch chard
1 head lettuce
½ bunch parsley
1 teaspoon dry thyme
½ bay leaf
2½ qts. water
an 8-qt. soup or stock pot

1.   Clean and slice the leeks, celery, carrots, and onions. Coarsely chop the chard, lettuce, and parsley, stems and all.
2.   Place all the ingredients in the stock or soup pot, and bring very slowly to a boil. Skim, then cover with the lid askew, and allow the stock to simmer gently about 1 hour.
3.   Strain the stock, being careful not to press any of the vegetables through the strainer into the stock.

Tips for Successful Stock Making
• In making chicken broth, an older hen is preferable.
• For an extraction, always begin with cold water and heat slowly.
• Cook all broths and stocks at a simmer. Rapid boiling causes the solid ingredients to disintegrate and the fat to break down into the broth.
• Use a rack to keep the meats from sticking to the bottom of the pot.
• Small amounts of liquid fat can be removed from the top of stock or broth with paper towels.
• Always chop or slice the ingredients. The more surface area exposed, the quicker the extraction will be made.
• Always tie or "truss" large pieces of meat or poultry used in the stock to prevent their falling apart with prolonged cooking.

STOCK CONCENTRATE

A stock concentrate, also called a glaze, an essence, or an extract, is a stock that has been boiled down to about ⅓ or less of its original volume. It is unseasoned and is used in sauces, soups, and braised dishes as a "flavor booster." You should always try to have a white, a brown, and a fish concentrate on hand.

1. Make a stock or broth, strain out the bones and vegetables, and chill.
2. Remove all visible fat from the chilled stock, place in a soup or stock pot and, over a medium heat, reduce slowly to approximately ⅓ or less of its original volume.
3. Pour into containers, label, and store in the refrigerator or freezer.

The following dish is a great way to use some of the bits and pieces of meat that fall off the bones when you make stock. Serve this on toast with a cocktail or glass of wine before dinner.

COOKED MEAT PURÉE
Makes about 1½ cups

5 anchovies
3 tablespoons milk
6 sprigs parsley
¼ small red onion
6 oz. cooked meat
5 tablespoons lemon juice
¼ lb. unsalted butter
salt and pepper
an individual porcelain
soufflé mold (or
equivalent serving dish)

1. Soak the anchovies in milk for 5 minutes, drain and dry on paper towels. Using a food processor or blender, process the parsley and onion until finely chopped. Add the meat and process until it is chopped finely.
2. With the machine on, add the lemon juice, butter, and anchovies, and process until well mixed. Season with salt and pepper to taste.
3. Pack into the mold and chill. Spread on toast or crackers to serve.

CONSOMMÉS

Consommé is clarified stock or broth. It is made by simmering lean chopped meat and vegetables in the broth or stock, along with egg whites and egg shells. The process of clarification depends upon the following major ingredients: raw beef or veal; egg whites and egg shells, which contain albumin, a protein that coagulates; and vinegar, lemon juice, or tomatoes, which are acidic and also help the clarification process. The protein in the egg whites and raw meat is altered chemically by the heat so that it coagulates. The coagulation absorbs minute food particles and forms a solid mass, separating them from the remaining liquid. This coagulation or floating mass is called a raft or crust. The meat and vegetables also strengthen the flavor of the consommé. A perfect consommé is judged by its clarity as well as its taste, and is one of the symbols of an elegant menu.

CONSOMMÉ
Makes about 2 qts.; serves 8

1 carrot
1 stalk celery with leaves
½ bunch parsley
4 egg whites and shells
1 lb. chopped lean beef or veal
½ bay leaf
6 peppercorns
2½ qts. cold stock or broth, any kind
1 cup cold water
2 teaspoons vinegar
salt and pepper
an 8- or 12-qt. stainless steel stock pot preferred
cheesecloth and a fine strainer

1. Clean the carrot, celery, and parsley and chop coarsely. Whisk the egg whites until fluffy but soft. In the stock pot, mix together the meat, egg whites, egg shells, vegetables, bay leaf, peppercorns, stock or broth, water, and vinegar. Bring to a boil, stirring occasionally.

2. When the mixture comes to a boil, reduce the heat immediately, and allow the consommé to simmer slowly, undisturbed, until the coagulated mass comes to the top. Cover, leaving the lid askew, and continue a gentle simmer for 1½ hours without stirring or shaking.

3. Carefully remove the pot from the heat without stirring. Allow to cool 30 minutes. Using a ladle, strain the consommé through cheesecloth. The consommé may be refrigerated at this point and any fat easily removed.

4. Before serving, season with salt and pepper, reheat to the boiling point and serve with an appropriate garnish (see below).

Garnishes for Consommé
Julienned vegetables and meats Appropriate vegetables and meats cut into thin strips and preboiled.
Whole vegetables Precooked peas, snow peas, asparagus tips, or broccoli florets.
Eggs Poached and trimmed (see page 175).
Chiffonade Leafy vegetables such as sorrel, lettuce, or spinach, rolled up and sliced into thin strips and dropped directly into the consommé just before serving.

Tips for Making Perfect Consommé
- Egg whites must be half whipped and well mixed with meat and vegetables.
- The stock must be cold to begin with.
- The boiling point must be reached under constant supervision to avoid scorching or boiling over.
- Never shake the pot as this may cloud the clarification.
- After straining, consommé can be degreased with paper towels.

Pasta   Small filled pastas, precooked.
Savory meringues   Beaten egg whites and salt, poached by the spoonful until firm.
Celestine   Basic savory crêpes (see page 191) with chopped fresh herbs, rolled up and sliced into strips.

Jellied consommé is a refreshing first course to serve in hot weather.

JELLIED HERBED CONSOMMÉ
Serves 6

1 package gelatin (1 tablespoon)
¼ cup Madeira
1½ qts. consommé
3 tablespoons chopped parsley (leaves only)
3 tablespoons chopped watercress
3 tablespoons chopped chives

1.   Soften the gelatin in the Madeira. Bring the consommé to the boil and remove from the heat.
2.   Add the softened gelatin-Madeira mixture to the consommé and stir until dissolved. Add the chopped herbs and pour the consommé into a shallow pan to chill in the refrigerator.
3.   To serve, stir the jellied consommé with a fork and pile it into chilled bouillon cups.

ASPIC

Once a full-bodied stock is clarified and cooled, it sets to a firm and luminous jelly or aspic that can used in making an array of elegant salads. First, a gelatinous stock is made by simmering meats and aromatic vegetables in water to release their gelatin and flavors (see stock recipes). Gelatin-rich meats that may be used are calves' feet, pigs' feet, veal shanks, and chicken wing tips. The gelatinous stock is next clarified (see Consommés, pages 52-53). Clarified meat stock that is made with gelatinous cuts should set readily. However, before using it as an aspic, refrigerate a spoonful for 15 minutes. If the chilled stock is not firm, stir in softened gelatin, adding 1 tablespoon for each 4 cups of stock. (See page 176 for Eggs in Aspic.)

SOUPS

Soups are perfect for our second chapter, because they are a natural step forward from stocks—indeed, most of the soups in this section would not be possible without stock. But more importantly, it is easy to make a successful soup on the first attempt, so this will build your confidence, preparing you for some later segment which may require a little more practice to master.

Soups are eaten in every country of the world, and are probably the oldest form of cooking. They are an extremely adaptable form of sustenance since they can be made from fruits, vegetables, meats, poultry, and fish; they can be served hot or cold; they can be sweet or savory, spicy or bland; and a hearty soup can be served as an entire meal, a light soup as a first course. The variety is endless, and, for the most part, preparation is simple. Measurements of ingredients do not have to be exact, and substitution of ingredients is often appropriate. So, in this chapter especially, make a point of understanding the concepts, principles, and methods of each basic soup group. If you are diligent, you will soon be able to apply the same concepts to whatever ingredients you have on hand and create your own delicious soups without following an exact recipe. This chapter covers a full range of soups: creamed soups, including purées; cold soups, which will include some uncooked soups; hearty soups, including one-dish-meal soups; and two fish chowders.

PURÉED AND CREAMED SOUPS

Creamy soups are most often made with puréed vegetables or with shell-fish, in which case they are called bisques. In addition to the main ingredient, these soups include some liquid—usually a stock—as well as an enrichment of egg yolks, butter, or cream. If the main ingredient is potatoes, beans, or rice, then no thickener is needed. If the main ingredient is a vegetable, you will need a starch such as flour to thicken the soup. A blender or food processor is invaluable in producing a purée. Should you want to eliminate fibers or seeds, a sieve or food mill is essential. All creamed soups start with *cooked* main ingredients, (which are puréed if the soup is to be a purée), and then the appropriate liquids, thickeners, and enrichments are added.

Ingredients

The ingredients of puréed, creamed soups can be economical. Almost any vegetable or shellfish may be the base for a creamed soup—and it is not necessary to use the "prime" portion of the vegetable or shellfish. For example, asparagus has a short season and can be expensive. The asparagus tips may be cooked and served in numerous ways, but the stalks are often thrown away because they are so fibrous. They actually have as much flavor as the tips and may be cooked until very soft, puréed (eliminating the inedible fiber), and transformed into a delicious, creamed soup. Dungeness crabs also have a season and are somewhat expensive. They are usually sold whole and the firm chunks of meat that come from the legs and claws make a fine dish as is. The body meat however, has a somewhat flaky texture and tends to fall apart. This body meat is perfect to purée and turn into a delicious Crab Bisque.

Milk or any stock may serve as the liquid; the type of stock need not match the ingredients. For example, you may choose to use a white or chicken stock as all or part of the liquid in a fish soup.

Flour, bread, rice, baking potatoes, and beans may be used as thickeners; and butter, cream (or crème fraîche), and/or egg yolks may be used for enrichment. When using egg yolks in this way, they should not be added directly to the hot soup, as they may curdle or scramble. It is always best to stir a little of the hot soup into the beaten eggs first, and then add it back into the soup. (For more egg information see pages 173-74.)

Potato and leek soup is a classic soup, and it serves as a perfect example of a creamed, puréed soup that is thickened with potatoes, and enriched with egg yolks and cream. For any potato-thickened purée, select baking, not boiling, potatoes. A food mill or sieve is used to purée this soup in order to eliminate the fibers from the leeks. When this soup is served cold it is called Vichyssoise.

CREAM OF POTATO LEEK SOUP
Serves 8

1½ lbs. baking potatoes
4 medium leeks
4 tablespoons unsalted
 butter
1 cup White Stock
2 cups milk
1 teaspoon Dijon mustard
salt and white pepper
2 egg yolks
½ cup crème fraîche
an 8-qt. soup or stock pot

1. Peel and slice the potatoes. Carefully clean the leeks. Slice the whites of the leeks and set aside. Cut 3 leek greens into a fine julienne. Place the leek julienne in a strainer, and place the strainer in the sink. Pour 4 cups of boiling water over the julienned leek greens and set aside to be used as garnish. This blanching will turn the leek greens a dark, deep, beautiful green.
2. Melt the butter in the soup pot. Add the potatoes and leeks to the foaming butter along with the stock, milk, mustard, and 1 teaspoon salt. Cover and simmer gently until vegetables are soft and mushy.
3. Let cool slightly, pass through a food mill, and return the soup to the pot.
4. Whisk the egg yolks with the crème fraîche. Off the heat, stir the cream mixture into the soup.
5. Taste for seasonings, and add salt and pepper as needed. Reheat very gently to serve*. Garnish each serving with some of the julienned leek greens.

(*Be cautious when you heat any soup that has an enrichment of egg yolks because eggs cook at a very low temperature. Heat slowly, stirring constantly.)

When flour is used as a thickener, it must be well cooked to get rid of its raw taste. If the main soup ingredient is a vegetable that does not require long cooking (fresh mushrooms, for instance), the solution is to use a "velouté" base (see page 72). The velouté is cooked 20 minutes so that the flour loses its raw taste before it is combined with the mushrooms—in that way, the mushrooms do not lose their delicate flavor from overcooking. Veloutés are always enriched with cream or crème fraîche.

CREAM OF MUSHROOM SOUP
Serves 8

8 mushrooms for garnish
6 cups White Stock
1 lb. mushrooms
2 shallots
4 tablespoons unsalted butter
6 tablespoons flour
2 egg yolks
1 cup crème fraîche
salt and white pepper
an 8-qt. soup or stock pot

1.   Clean and slice the 8 mushrooms and simmer in ½ cup of the stock for 1 minute; set the mushroom slices aside for garnish.

2.   Clean and chop the 1 lb. of mushrooms and the shallots. Melt the butter in the pot, and sauté the shallots until softened. Add the flour. Cook, stirring constantly, for about 3 minutes. Add the stock (including the stock used to simmer the sliced mushrooms), bring to the boil, and stir until smooth. Reduce the heat and simmer partially covered for 20 minutes. Add the chopped mushrooms and simmer uncovered for about 15 minutes.

3.   Allow the soup to cool and purée in a food processor or blender. Return to a cleaned pot.

4.   Whisk the egg yolks lightly and combine with the crème fraîche. Add the cream mixture to the soup.

5.   Heat slowly, season to taste with salt and pepper, and serve garnished with the reserved mushroom slices.

Variation:

Cream of Watercress and Mushroom Soup

Remove the large stems from a bunch of watercress and add the leaves to the soup at the same time you add the mushrooms.

Be sure to try the next soup so that you can compare the intense flavor of the dried wild mushrooms to the more delicate flavor of the fresh mushrooms in the previous soup.

WILD MUSHROOM SOUP
Serves 8

1 oz. dried wild mushrooms
  (morel, porcini,
  chanterelle, cepe)
¾ cup sherry
2 medium onions
1 lb. fresh mushrooms
¼ lb. unsalted butter
3 tablespoons flour
6 cups Chicken Stock or
  White Stock
2 teaspoons salt
½ teaspoon pepper
1 cup crème fraîche
an 8-qt. stock or soup pot

1. Rinse the dried mushrooms well under running water, then soak them in the sherry for 1 hour. Drain the mushrooms and reserve; strain and reserve the sherry.
2. Chop the onions finely; clean and slice the fresh mushrooms.
3. Melt the butter in the pot, add the flour and cook and stir 2 minutes. Add the chopped onions, fresh mushrooms, and dried mushrooms. Add the stock and reserved sherry. Bring the soup to a boil, stirring occasionally. Lower the heat, cover partially, and simmer 1 hour, or until the dried mushrooms are very tender.
4. Add the salt and pepper. Stir in the crème fraîche; taste and correct seasoning.

In the Creamy Carrot-Orange Soup following, there is no thickener added since carrots have a high starch and cellulose content. (Peas and beans do, too.) It is enriched with cream, and the addition of orange juice adds a fresh, light dimension. You may serve the soup warm or chilled. This recipe uses a technique called "sweating." In this instance, the carrots and onions are first cooked covered over a low heat, without any added liquid. This extracts juices and flavors from the carrots and onions and is a technique used in making soups and sauces in order to intensify the flavor of the liquid. This method is used with vegetables that have a high water content.

CREAMY CARROT-ORANGE SOUP
Serves 8

½ bunch parsley
2 lbs. carrots
2 medium onions
4 tablespoons unsalted
  butter
1½ qts. White Stock
1 cup fresh orange juice
1 cup crème fraîche
salt and pepper
an 8-qt. soup or stock pot

1. Discard the parsley stems, chop the leaves, and set aside for garnish. Scrub and slice the carrots; slice the onions.
2. Melt the butter and stir in the carrots and onions.
3. Lower the heat, cover, and allow to "sweat" (see above) over low heat for 15 minutes.
4. Add the stock, bring to a boil, reduce heat to low, and simmer until carrots are soft. Cool slightly.
5. Purée in a blender or food processor; add the orange juice and crème fraîche and stir to combine. Return to a clean pot, season to taste with salt and pepper, and reheat gently to serve.

The following puréed (technically not a creamed) soup has no starchy thickening added. The soup is thickened by long slow cooking, the ground nuts, and the puréed onions. It is a very unusual and delicious soup, with its origins in Italy.

BROWN ONION SOUP
Serves 8

6 oz. blanched almonds
6 medium onions
2 oz. Parmesan
4 qts. Brown Stock or Meat
  Broth
salt and pepper
2 to 3 large croûtons per
  person (see page 67)
an 8-qt. soup or stock pot

1.   Preheat the oven to 350°. Spread the almonds on a baking sheet and toast for 15 minutes—or until lightly browned. Then grind them in a nut grinder or food processor until they are like corn meal—not a powder. Coarsely chop the onions; grate the Parmesan cheese.

2.   Bring the stock to a boil and drop in the almonds and onions. Lower the heat, partially cover the pot, and simmer gently 1 hour. Season to taste with salt and pepper.

3.   Purée the soup in a blender or food processor. When ready to serve, reheat gently. Place 1 or 2 croûtons in each bowl, and spoon the soup over the croûtons. Pass the grated cheese and more croûtons at the table.

The following soup is a classic American creamed and puréed soup. The technique of first using a blender or food processor to purée the soup and then the medium blade of a food mill to eliminate the tomato seeds, fibers, and skins, is a quick way to accomplish the job.

CREAM OF TOMATO SOUP
Serves 8

3 lbs. tomatoes
1 medium onion
1 small carrot
1 small clove garlic
2 tablespoons unsalted
  butter
3 tablespoons flour
1 qt. Chicken Stock
salt and pepper
about 1 tablespoon sugar
1 cup light cream
an 8-qt. soup or stock pot

1.   Coarsely chop the tomatoes, onion, carrot, and garlic. Melt the butter in the soup pot, add the onion, carrot, and garlic, and cook slowly until lightly browned.

2.   Add the flour and mix well. Add the stock and tomatoes; cover, leaving the lid askew, and cook over low heat for 1 hour.

3.   Purée in a blender or food processor and then pass through the medium blade of a food mill. Return to the pot.

4.   Season to taste with salt, pepper, and sugar. Add the light cream and reheat slowly to serve.

HEARTY ONE-DISH-MEAL SOUPS

Soups that are a full meal were originally meant to be economical dishes, prepared with a minimum of fuel and utensils. The concept still holds true today, even though saving money may not be our primary motive. These soups include a varied selection of meats or fish that will give the broth great flavor, and beans, rice, or pasta for thickening the soup and satisfying the appetite.

SAUSAGE, PROSCIUTTO, AND BEAN SOUP
Serves 8 to 10

6 oz. dry red beans
6 oz. dry small white beans
4 oz. pancetta
2 lbs. tomatoes
1 large onion
1 lb. assorted sausages
1 prosciutto end (6 to 8 oz.)
3 qts. stock (Vegetable, White, or Brown Stock)
2 teaspoons ground cumin
2 teaspoons dry oregano
4 cloves garlic
½ lb. leafy greens
salt and pepper
cayenne pepper
crème fraîche for garnish
2 to 3 large croûtons per person (see page 67)
a 10- or 12-qt. soup or stock pot

1. Soak the red and white beans together overnight in enough water to cover.
2. Dice the pancetta, coarsely chop the tomatoes and onion, and slice the sausage into ½-inch pieces. Sauté the pancetta and sausage in the pot until lightly browned.
3. Remove the meats, drain on paper towels, and set aside. Clean the pot.
4. Bring the beans to a boil in the water in which they soaked, turn off the heat, cover, and allow to stand 15 minutes.
5. Drain and rinse the beans, place them in the soup pot along with the prosciutto end, tomatoes, soup stock, cumin, oregano, onion, and garlic. Simmer, partially covered, until the beans are completely tender, about 2 hours, adding more stock (or water) if necessary.
6. Remove the prosciutto end, shred it finely, and return to the soup; shred the greens and add them to the soup along with the reserved sausage and pancetta.
7. Season to taste with salt, pepper, and cayenne pepper. Serve the soup hot with a garnish of crème fraîche and croûtons.

Here is a hearty vegetable soup that could be a full meal—it is a perfect example of a meatless vegetable soup. Be careful not to overcook the vegetables.

MIXED VEGETABLE SOUP WITH BASIL SAUCE
Serves 8

4 oz. small white beans
2 medium leeks (whites only)
1 medium onion
3 medium carrots
½ lb. green beans
½ lb. zucchini
¾ lb. boiling potatoes
½ lb. leafy greens
2½ qts. stock (Vegetable, Chicken, or Brown Stock)
1 bouquet garni
¼ lb. tiny filled pasta (raviollini, agnolotti, tortellini, etc.)
salt and pepper
sugar
an 8- or 10-qt. stock or soup pot

1. Soak the beans overnight, drain, and cook them in water to cover until soft. Reserve, along with any remaining liquid.
2. Clean or otherwise prepare the leeks, onion, carrots, green beans, zucchini, potatoes, and leafy greens. Slice all the vegetables uniformly—shred the greens.
3. In a large soup pot, bring the stock to a boil, add the bouquet garni, leeks, onion, carrots, potatoes, the cooked white beans, and any remaining cooking liquid and simmer covered for 30 minutes.
4. Add the pasta and simmer 15 minutes. Season to taste with salt, pepper, and sugar.
5. Add the green beans, zucchini, and shredded greens and simmer another 5 minutes. Garnish each serving with Basil Sauce.

Basil Sauce

2 oz. Parmesan
1 bunch basil
1 large tomato
4 cloves garlic
salt and pepper
1¼ cups olive oil

1. Grate the cheese; cut off and discard the basil stems; peel and seed the tomato.
2. In a food processor, blender, or mortar and pestle, grind the garlic, basil, ½ teaspoon salt, and 4 turns of the pepper mill to a paste.
3. Work in half the cheese, tomato, and olive oil, *in that order*, repeating the process, until all the ingredients are incorporated into a sauce. You will not have a perfect emulsion—the sauce will have to be mixed each time it is served.

FISH SOUPS

Chowders are thick soups or stews—usually made with shellfish. The word chowder comes from the French *la chaudière*, the enormous copper pot that was used in early French fishing villages. Returning fishermen used to toss parts of their catch into *la chaudière* and the community would make a soup to celebrate the safe return of the fishermen.

The flavors of the fish and shellfish can be combined with the vegetables and cooking liquids without overcooking any ingredients if the fish or shellfish are cooked separately from the other longer-cooking ingredients, and combined with them for a brief reheating just before serving. Another method would be to begin with the longer-cooking ingredients and add the ingredients that take a shorter cooking time towards the end.

In the next two soups, be sure to use the specified type of potato. A baking potato will break down a little as it cooks to slightly thicken a soup—a boiling potato will not. Remember not to overcook the clams either in the steaming (steam just until open), or in the serving step, where they should be just gently reheated.

NEW ENGLAND CLAM CHOWDER
Serves 6

2 dozen clams
1 medium onion
2 tablespoons unsalted
  butter
¼ lb. pancetta
1 lb. baking potatoes
about 3 cups Chicken Stock
3 tablespoons unsalted
  butter
2 cups light cream
salt and white pepper
an 8-qt. soup or stock pot

1. Scrub the clams thoroughly with a stiff brush under cold running water to remove any sand. Discard any opened clams. Slice the onion; dice the pancetta; peel and dice the potatoes.
2. Steam the clams in 1 cup of the chicken stock just until they open, about 6 or 7 minutes. Strain the liquor (clam juice) through a fine sieve and reserve.
3. Remove the clams from the shells; chop them and reserve.
4. Melt 2 tablespoons unsalted butter in a heavy soup pot, lightly brown the diced pancetta; add the onion and cook until softened. Add the clam liquor and diced potatoes and enough Chicken Stock to cover.
5. Bring to a boil, reduce the heat, and simmer partially covered until potatoes are soft, about 20 minutes. Stir in the remaining 3 tablespoons of butter and light cream, add salt, freshly ground white pepper, and the reserved chopped clams. Heat gently to serve.

MANHATTAN CLAM CHOWDER
Serves 8

2 lbs. tomatoes
1 large onion
1 leek
1 lb. boiling potatoes
1 green pepper
1 stalk celery
½ bunch parsley
2 dozen clams
½ cup Chicken Stock
2 tablespoons unsalted butter
¼ lb. slice pancetta
½ bay leaf
¼ teaspoon dry thyme
1½ qts. Chicken Stock
salt and white pepper
2 teaspoons sugar
an 8-qt. stock or soup pot

1. Peel, seed, and chop the tomatoes; chop the onion; clean and chop the leek (discarding the dark green leek tops); cube the potatoes; chop the green pepper and celery. Discard the parsley stems, and chop the leaves.

2. Scrub the clams and steam them in the ½ cup Chicken Stock until they open, about 6 or 7 minutes. Strain and reserve the liquor. Remove the clams from their shells; chop the clams and reserve.

3. Melt the butter in a heavy soup pot and brown the pancetta. Add the chopped onion and leek, and cook until the vegetables are softened. Add the potatoes, the tomatoes, the celery, green pepper, bay leaf, thyme, 1½ qts. Chicken Stock, and the reserved clam liquor.

4. Partially cover the pot, bring to a boil, reduce the heat, and simmer 30 minutes.

5. Discard the pancetta. Add the clams and sugar, and season to taste with salt and pepper. Remove from heat until ready to serve.

6. To serve, warm the chowder gently—don't over-cook the clams—and serve garnished with chopped fresh parsley.

COLD SOUPS

When the weather is very warm, cold soups are particularly appealing. Most creamed soups may be served cold, provided they are made with a minimum amount of butter and are enriched with cream instead of butter. The most famous cold soup, Vichyssoise, is actually the potato and leek soup described at the beginning of this chapter, well chilled and thinned, if necessary, with a little milk or cream. Uncooked soups are also included in this section. Please remember that if the soup is not cooked, the vegetables used to make it must be at the peak of their flavor and texture.

COLD CUCUMBER-YOGURT SOUP
Serves 8

2 lbs. cucumbers
salt
¼ bunch parsley
2 cloves garlic
¼ cup olive oil
5 cups yogurt
1 cup half-and-half
white pepper
8 sprigs fresh mint

1. Peel, seed, and chop the cucumbers coarsely. Sprinkle with salt, place on paper towels, and drain for 1 hour. Pat dry and set aside.
2. Remove and discard the parsley stems and chop the leaves. Crush the garlic cloves with 1 teaspoon of salt.
3. Place the garlic salt in a large glass bowl and beat in the olive oil. Stir in the yogurt and half-and-half and mix well. Add the cucumbers and chopped parsley. Taste for seasoning and add salt and freshly ground white pepper if needed. Chill well before serving.
4. Garnish each serving with a sprig of mint.

The avocados in this soup must be extremely ripe. A novel way to serve it is in the avocado shells. Should you wish to do this, do not scoop out all the flesh from the shells as you need enough left to make a firm serving vessel.

CREAM OF AVOCADO SOUP
Serves 6

3 large ripe avocados
2 cups White Stock or
   Chicken Stock
1 cup crème fraîche
salt and white pepper
chives or dill for garnish

1. Peel and pit the avocados. In a blender or food processor purée the avocados. Add the stock and crème fraîche. Season to taste with salt and white pepper. Chill.
2. Serve garnished with snipped chives or sprigs of dill.

There are many versions of Gazpacho. In the following one, half the ingredients are puréed with bread (for thickening) and the other half are chopped, put into individual bowls, and served as a garnish to the puréed soup. The vegetables for garnish must all be uniformly chopped—a rule that holds true whenever there are different vegetables going into the same dish. This soup must be served very well chilled, and all the vegetables must be absolutely fresh.

GAZPACHO
Serves 8

3½ lbs. tomatoes (about 7)
3 medium cucumbers
2 medium bell peppers
2 medium onions
4 hard-cooked eggs
7 thick slices French bread
½ cup olive oil
1 clove garlic
1 cup any stock
¼ cup red wine vinegar
salt and pepper
1 tablespoon sugar
8 ice cubes

1. Peel, seed, and chop the tomatoes, and set 2 chopped tomatoes aside for garnish. Peel, seed, and chop the cucumbers, and set 1 chopped cucumber aside for garnish. Peel, seed, and chop the peppers, and set half aside for garnish. Chop the onions, and set half aside for garnish. Chop the hard cooked-eggs and set aside for garnish. Cut 4 of the bread slices into cubes and sauté slowly in ¼ cup olive oil and set aside for garnish.

2. In the container of a blender or food processor, place the remaining 5 tomatoes, 2 cucumbers, onion, bell pepper, and garlic clove. Process until all vegetables are a fine purée. Add the 3 slices of bread, the stock, the remaining ¼ cup olive oil, and vinegar, and process once again until the texture is uniform. (You may have to do this in two batches.) Season to taste with salt, pepper, and 1 tablespoon sugar. Chill.

3. To serve, put an ice cube in each serving bowl. Ladle the puréed soup over the ice cube. Arrange the chopped vegetables, egg, and bread cubes in small bowls and pass at the table.

Croûtons are toasted or sautéed cubes or slices of bread and are a standard garnish for soups. Depending on the soup they are to accompany, you may wish to use all butter or all olive oil to prepare them rather than a combination. Raw garlic is sometimes rubbed over the bread before it is sautéed. If a recipe does not specify, you will need to decide whether you want cubes or slices. Croûtons work best when day-old bread is used.

CROÛTONS
Serves 4

4 slices French or Italian bread, ½ inch thick
¼ lb. unsalted butter, melted
¼ cup olive oil

Method One
Preheat the oven to 375°. The bread may be left in slices or cut into cubes. Place the bread on a baking sheet and brush with the combined melted butter and oil. Toast in the oven until pale brown.

Method Two
The bread may be left in slices or cut into cubes. Heat the butter and oil in a large skillet. Add the bread and sauté over medium heat until pale brown.

SAUCES

Imagine a perfectly prepared meal—an expertly trimmed and cooked artichoke, an impeccably roasted chicken, salad greens crisped and fresh. Sounds good, doesn't it? But wait, something is missing. Let's add a dilled mayonnaise for the artichoke, a savory pan gravy made with the juices of the chicken, and a tangy mustard dressing for the salad. Now it really is perfect.

Knowing how to complement and vary foods with sauces, and how to prepare the sauces properly, are two of the factors that will distinguish you as an expert cook. I have planned this chapter with precisely those goals in mind. You will master the concepts with ease since there are not very many, and once you understand and know the sauces, it will be a simple matter for you to place the sauces with the foods they suit.

As you are probably aware, there are many sauces, and in deciding what to include here, I drew upon my experience with students, selecting the sauces they liked and used the most. I have categorized the basic sauces into four groups—the flour-based sauces; the tomato-based sauces; the butter sauces; and the emulsified sauces. Within each sauce group, I have included some variations. You will note that many sauces in this chapter are based on stock—another way in which you will use the stocks you have stored in your refrigerator or freezer.

Equipment

For sauce making, you will need a heavy 1-quart or 2-quart saucepan with *rounded* corners, a stainless steel sauce whisk, and a wooden spoon. Preferred materials for the saucepans are anodized aluminum, tin-lined copper, or heavy copper-bottomed stainless steel. Aluminum that is not anodized may interact with certain ingredients like wine, lemon, tomatoes, or eggs, and discolor the sauce. The pan must be heavy so that the butter-and-flour base used to thicken some sauces will not burn or brown before it is cooked. Use a stainless steel wire whisk to stir most sauces, a wooden spoon for mixing thicker ones. You will also need a deglazing spoon (see above), a food mill, and a sieve. A blender or food processor may also be utilized in sauce making.

FLOUR-BASED SAUCES

The flour-thickened sauces are based on a paste of melted butter and flour, called a roux, that is cooked until foaming when making white sauces, or until brown, for making brown sauces. The first cooking of the flour and butter is slow to help get rid of a raw flour taste. The next step is to add the liquid and cook slowly so that the sauce may reduce, intensifying the flavor, thickening the sauce, and eliminating the possibility of a raw flour taste. The shortest cooking times are given to the white sauces, usually 15 to 30 minutes, and the longest to the brown sauces, sometimes an hour or more. After cooking, the sauces are strained and seasoned.

In the flour-based-sauce category, there is the White Sauce (called *Sauce Béchamel* in French), made of butter, flour, and milk; and the Velouté, made of butter, flour, and any basic stock. There is also the Brown Sauce, made from a browned roux, and Pan Gravy, based on the drippings from the skillet or roasting pan.

White Sauce is bland and is generally not served as is but used as a "binder" (for example, a binder would hold the chicken together in Creamed Chicken), or as a base for creamed dishes, soufflés, and other sauces. Basic White Sauce stores well in the freezer.

BASIC WHITE SAUCE   *(Sauce Béchamel)*
Makes about 1½ cups

2 tablespoons unsalted
  butter
2 tablespoons flour
2 cups milk
salt and white pepper
freshly grated nutmeg
  (optional)

1.   Melt the butter in a heavy saucepan. Stir in the flour and cook over low heat for 3 minutes.
2.   Add the milk, whisking constantly, and continue whisking until the sauce comes to a boil. Reduce the heat and simmer 15 to 20 minutes, stirring occasionally.
3.   When the sauce is of the desired consistency, strain it and add seasonings to taste. Use immediately or store in the refrigerator or freezer.
Note: For a thicker sauce, increase the flour and butter by 1 or 2 tablespoons, but do not change the amount of milk.

Cream Sauce is a richer version of Basic White Sauce and may be used as is to make creamed vegetables, meats, poultry, and fish, or as a base for other sauces.

CREAM SAUCE
Makes about 2½ cups

1½ cups Basic White Sauce
1 cup crème fraîche
salt and white pepper

Put the Basic White Sauce in a small saucepan and whisk the crème fraîche into it. Season to taste with salt and pepper. Heat if necessary, or use as is in your recipe.

PIQUANT WHITE SAUCE
Makes about 2 cups

¾ cup Basic White Sauce
2 egg yolks
2 tablespoons tarragon
  vinegar
¾ cup olive oil
salt and white pepper

1.   Put the Basic White Sauce in a bowl. Whisk in the egg yolks and tarragon vinegar.
2.   Whisk in the olive oil slowly, as in making Mayonnaise (see page 86).
3.   Correct the seasoning with salt and pepper and perhaps a little more vinegar. Serve at room temperature with cold meats or vegetables.

Cheese Sauce may be served over toast, or with fish or cooked vegetables, or be used to make a gratin (see page 128). Make sure the Parmesan is finely grated so that it melts nicely into the sauce. (For more on cheeses, refer to chapter 11.)

CHEESE SAUCE
Makes about 2½ cups

2 oz. Parmesan
2 oz. Gruyère
¼ cup crème fraîche
2 cups Basic White Sauce
1 tablespoon Dijon mustard
salt and white pepper

1. Grate the Parmesan and the Gruyère finely.
2. In a saucepan over low heat, stir the crème fraîche into the Basic White Sauce. Add the grated cheeses and the Dijon mustard. Stir over low heat until the cheeses melt and the sauce is smooth. Taste and add salt and pepper as needed.

ONION CREAM SAUCE
Makes about 2 cups

1 medium onion
1 tablespoon unsalted
  butter
1 cup Basic White Sauce
½ cup crème fraîche
salt and white pepper

1. Slice the onion and cook covered in the butter until soft but not brown. Cool and purée in a food processor or blender.
2. In a saucepan over low heat, combine the onion purée and the Basic White Sauce. When well blended, stir in the crème fraîche and season to taste with salt and pepper. This sauce is delicious with roasted lamb or veal.

Any basic meat, poultry, or fish stock thickened with a roux becomes a light, smooth sauce called a velouté. It is made in the same way as Basic White Sauce. A roux of butter and flour is cooked for a few minutes before the liquid, in this case a stock, is whisked in. The mixture is then simmered gently to thicken the sauce, intensify the flavor, and eliminate any raw flour taste. Velouté is a base for many variations and is generally not seasoned.

VELOUTÉ SAUCE
Makes about 2 cups

4 tablespoons unsalted
  butter
4 tablespoons flour
4 cups White Stock,
  Chicken Stock, or Fish
  Stock
½ cup crème fraîche

1. Melt the butter in a heavy saucepan. Stir in the flour (creating a roux) and cook 3 minutes without browning.
2. Add the stock to the roux, whisking constantly, and continue whisking until the sauce comes to a boil. Reduce the heat and simmer about 45 minutes to reduce the sauce to approximately ⅓ its original volume.
3. Stir in the crème fraîche and strain the sauce. Use immediately or store in the refrigerator or freezer.

Tips for Successful Sauce Making

- A good sauce should enhance the flavor and texture of the food and should not overpower or be overpowered.
- Always use a drinkable wine in your sauce—the wine planned for the meal is often appropriate. A "cooking wine" is an undrinkable wine and would create an inedible sauce.
- In cooking with wine, always get rid of—cook away or "flame" away—the alcohol. An alcoholic flavor in a sauce is not desirable.
- Canned stock, bouillon cubes, or chemical flavoring agents will create a sauce reflecting those flavors.
- The flavors of velouté and brown sauces are especially dependent on your stock—be sure the stock is reduced and full flavored.
- A properly thickened sauce should just barely cling to the food.
- Get rid of a raw flour taste by cooking flour and butter well.
- If the sauce is to be reduced, do not season with salt and pepper until after the reduction.
- Basic white and brown sauces are bases for other sauces, and are usually not used as finished sauces in themselves.
- Fresh herbs are generally added just before serving.
- Always use freshly grated nutmeg, never the preground type sold in tins.
- There are two kinds of whisks, a balloon type, designed for beating egg whites, and a narrower one, called a sauce whisk, designed to get into the corners of saucepans. Be sure you select the right kind.
- A sauce spoon is a wooden spoon with a hole in it, designed to make the stirring of thick heavy sauces easier.
- A deglazing spoon is a kind of paddle with a straight bottom edge designed to scrape up the bits of coagulated juices stuck to the bottom of a pan, so that they may be incorporated into your sauce.
- Press plastic wrap or waxed paper right on top of the sauce when storing it. When you remove the plastic wrap or waxed paper, the "skin" that forms on the sauce will be removed with it.
- Most sauces will store several days in the refrigerator or 2 weeks in the freezer.
- Always taste sauces before they are served so that you may make adjustments in the seasoning.

The next three sauces are made with a base of the basic Velouté Sauce.

TOMATO-FLAVORED VELOUTÉ
Makes about 2 cups

1½ cups Velouté Sauce, made with Chicken Stock, White Stock or Fish Stock
⅓ cup (canned) tomato purée
½ cup crème fraîche
salt and white pepper

1. In a heavy saucepan, combine the Velouté Sauce and tomato purée and stir over a low heat for 1 minute.
2. Whisk in the crème fraîche and season to taste with salt and pepper.
3. Use immediately or store in the refrigerator or freezer. Serve with cooked vegetables, chicken, or fish.

This unusual variation of velouté contains julienned vegetables and is served with warm poached fish. It makes an extremely attractive presentation.

AROMATIC FISH VELOUTÉ
Makes about 2 cups

1 medium leek
1 stalk celery
1 medium green onion
4 medium mushrooms
3 tablespoons unsalted butter
2 cups Velouté Sauce made with Fish Stock
salt and white pepper

1. Trim and clean the leek; discard the green tops and make a fine julienne of the white part only. Wash and peel the celery and make a fine julienne. Clean the green onion; discard ⅓ of the green tops and make a fine julienne of the remaining part. Clean and cut the mushrooms in a julienne to match the other vegetables.
2. Sweat (see page 59) the vegetables in the butter until they are soft, about 5 minutes.
3. Add the Velouté Sauce to the vegetables and season to taste with salt and pepper.

This sauce may be served with poached chicken, or used for creamed poultry or as a base for a cream of chicken soup. When served with poached chicken, the chicken's poaching liquid is used to make the sauce.

CREAMY CHICKEN VELOUTÉ
Makes about 2½ cups

2 cups Velouté Sauce made with Chicken Stock
1 cup crème fraîche
salt and white pepper

In a heavy saucepan over a low heat, combine the Velouté Sauce and the crème fraîche, and reduce to approximately 2½ cups. Season to taste with salt and pepper.

The Basic Brown Sauce is a cousin to the Basic White and the Velouté Sauces. It is a flour-based sauce too, but the roux for this sauce is cooked very slowly until it takes on a rich, hazelnut brown color. (Be careful not to scorch the roux as it will give the sauce a bitter taste—that is why a heavy pot is recommended.) Other differences are that aromatic vegetables and herbs are used to enrich the flavors and a larger amount of liquid is used in making the sauce. The latter allows a longer reduction period so that the complex flavors have time to develop and concentrate. The concentrated stock called for in the recipe acts as a "flavor booster." Basic Brown Sauce is the base for dozens of sauces. Freeze it in 8-oz. styrofoam cups to have on hand whenever you need it. Always use a drinkable wine in making this sauce.

BASIC BROWN SAUCE

Makes about 2 cups

1 stalk celery
1 small onion
1 medium carrot
1 small leek
4 tablespoons unsalted butter
4 tablespoons flour
1 cup red table wine
4 cups Brown Stock
½ cup concentrated Brown Stock
¼ teaspoon dried thyme
1 bay leaf
3 cloves garlic
salt and pepper

1. Chop the celery, onion, carrot, and leek coarsely. In a heavy sauce pan, melt the butter, add the chopped aromatics (vegetables), and brown slowly.
2. Sprinkle in the flour, toss with the vegetables, and slowly brown the flour.
3. Stir in the wine, stock, and stock concentrate. Add the thyme and bay leaf, and the garlic through a press. Partially cover the pot and simmer about 1 hour.
4. Remove the cover, and simmer until sauce is thickened.
5. Pass through a food mill. Season to taste with salt and pepper. May be stored in the refrigerator or freezer.

Here are three simple variations on the Basic Brown Sauce. *Sauce Espagnole* or Spanish Brown Sauce is Brown Sauce to which some tomato has been added. Brown Sauce may be substituted in any recipe that calls for *Sauce Espagnole.*

SPANISH BROWN SAUCE   (Sauce Espagnole)

1 large tomato
2 cups Basic Brown Sauce
2 tablespoons tomato paste

Peel, seed and chop the tomato. Combine the tomato, Brown Sauce, and tomato paste. May be stored in the refrigerator or freezer.

RED-WINE-FLAVORED BROWN SAUCE (*Sauce Bordelaise*)
Makes 2 cups

2 shallots
½ bunch parsley
2 cups red table wine
2 cups Basic Brown Sauce

1. Chop the shallots finely. Remove and discard the parsley stems and chop the leaves. Place the shallots and wine in a small saucepan and reduce the wine by half. Strain out the shallots.
2. Combine the reduced wine and Brown Sauce and reduce to 2 cups.
3. Garnish with chopped parsley just before serving—excellent with grilled meats. Extra sauce stores well in the refrigerator or freezer.

MADEIRA SAUCE
Makes 2 cups

2 cups Basic Brown Sauce
½ cup Madeira
½ bunch parsley

1. Reduce the Brown Sauce to 1½ cups.
2. Add the Madeira and simmer gently 3 minutes.
3. Remove and discard the parsley stems and chop the leaves. Add 3 tablespoons or more chopped parsley to the sauce just before serving. Extra sauce can be stored in the refrigerator or freezer. Madeira Sauce is excellent with game, ham, beef, and pork.

During roasting, the basting liquid and the juices from the poultry or meat will drip into the roasting pan. The result is a wonderful sauce foundation. You can skim off the fat and use the juices as they are or enhance them with stock, herbs, wine, cream, etc. They may also be combined with a Velouté Sauce, egg yolks, or butter. A pan gravy is often made in the same pan that the meat was roasted in, and is always served over the sliced, roasted meats or poultry from which it is derived. The following pan gravy is very quick and simple to make.

PAN GRAVY
Makes about 2 cups

pan drippings
1 tablespoon unsalted
butter
2 tablespoons flour
1 cup any stock
1 cup crème fraîche

1. Remove the meat or bird from the roasting pan. Allow the juices to cool a little and skim off all but 2 tablespoons of fat from the roasting pan.
2. Add the butter to the pan, and, over low heat, scrape up the juices sticking to the bottom with a deglazing spatula. Add the flour and, stirring constantly, cook 3 minutes over a low heat.
3. Add the stock and crème fraîche and stir until smooth and thickened. The sauce may be strained.

DEGLAZED SAUCES

When you sauté meats or fish, the heat starts to pull the juices out of the food. If the pan is not overcrowded, the moisture evaporates, leaving flavorful bits of coagulated juices sticking to the bottom of the pan. Those juices can be the basis of a simple but tasty sauce. After you are finished sautéing the food, transfer it to a platter. Pour off any oil or butter remaining in the pan, and add some liquid (water, stock, wine, brandy, etc.*) to dissolve the bits clinging to the pan. Heat this combination and stir, while scraping up the pan juices with a deglazing spatula to incorporate them into the liquid. Flour, butter, or cream can be added to thicken the deglazed sauce. The sauce is then seasoned and served with the sautéed food. In chapter 7, there are many exact recipes for deglazed sauces.

(**Be careful when cooking with spirits that contain a high amount of alcohol, since the alcohol will sometimes flame before it evaporates. Simply allow it to flame until it stops.*)

TOMATO SAUCES

Tomatoes simmered slowly with stock, vegetables, and herbs produce a full-bodied, rich-tasting sauce that is wonderful with hamburgers, steak, rice, pasta, eggs, and hearty vegetables like sprouts, onions, and cabbage. The Basic Tomato Sauce may be used as is or as a base for more elaborate sauces. When tomatoes are out of season, this sauce may be made with canned tomatoes. My "Slightly Cooked" Tomato Sauce is a very quick, easy sauce which should only be made in the peak of the tomato season since it is dependent on ripe, fresh tomatoes. Its taste is a direct contrast to the longer-cooking Basic Tomato Sauce and it is best served on more delicate foods such as fish, chicken, or veal. I am also including a totally uncooked sauce that is excellent with cold meats.

This sauce goes well with pasta, rice, boiled meats, hamburgers, and meat loaf. Herbs, garlic, onions, or wine may be added when desired.

BASIC TOMATO SAUCE
Makes about 2 cups

2½ lbs. ripe tomatoes
1 stalk celery
1 carrot
2 shallots
2 tablespoons olive oil
2 tablespoons tomato paste
1 cup Brown Stock
1 teaspoon each salt,
    pepper, and sugar

1. Chop the tomatoes, celery, carrot, and shallots.
2. In a saucepan, heat the oil, and cook the celery, carrot, and shallots for 5 minutes.
3. Add the tomatoes, tomato paste, and stock, and simmer gently until thickened—about 35 to 40 minutes.
4. Season with the salt, pepper, and sugar.
5. Should you wish the sauce to be smooth, pass it through a coarse sieve or food mill. Store in the refrigerator or freezer.

This fresh, light sauce should only be made with ripe, tasty tomatoes and can be served on poached or steamed fish or chicken.

"SLIGHTLY COOKED" TOMATO SAUCE
Makes about 2 cups

2 lbs. ripe tomatoes
½ medium onion
1 clove garlic
4 tablespoons butter
1 teaspoon each salt,
    pepper, and sugar

1. Peel, seed, and chop the tomatoes coarsely. Chop the onion and garlic.
2. Heat the butter in a saucepan; add the onion and sauté 1 minute. Add the tomatoes and garlic, raise the heat, and toss the tomato and onion until heated through—about 3 or 4 minutes. Season with salt, pepper, and sugar and serve immediately.

The following sauce is like a relish and goes well with cold meats.

UNCOOKED TOMATO SAUCE
Makes about 2 cups

2 lbs. ripe tomatoes
½ jalapeño pepper
1 small onion
1 clove garlic
1 bunch fresh cilantro
½ bunch parsley
¼ cup olive oil
3 tablespoons wine vinegar
2 teaspoons sugar
salt and pepper

1. Peel, seed, and chop the tomatoes. Peel, seed, and chop the jalapeño. Chop the onion and garlic finely. Chop 4 tablespoons each of cilantro and parsley leaves.
2. In a nonmetal bowl, combine the tomatoes, onion, garlic, jalapeño pepper, oil, vinegar, and sugar. Add the chopped parsley and cilantro, and some salt and pepper. Taste and add more salt, pepper, chopped jalapeño, cilantro, or parsley if desired.

COMPOUND BUTTERS

Flavored butters are a popular accompaniment to grilled, steamed, or boiled meats, fish, and vegetables, and they can be used to add body and flavor to hot sauces. The base is unsalted butter, creamed so that it can be combined with other ingredients. Almost any ingredient can then be used to flavor the butter if it is chopped or pounded finely enough to blend smoothly. Herbs, garlic, shallots, anchovies, lemon zest, mustard, and paprika are common ingredients used for flavoring butters. Sometimes, lobster or shrimp shells are pounded or puréed then sieved and worked into the butter to create spreads that are out of the ordinary. Once the flavors are blended into the butter, the butter can be chilled, shaped into a log, wrapped in foil or waxed paper, and stored in the refrigerator or freezer. The compound butter can then be sliced and placed on top of grilled meats or tossed with hot vegetables. A food processor, blender, or mortar and pestle may be used successfully to create compound butters.

GARLIC-SHALLOT-HERB BUTTER
Makes about ¼ lb.

2 shallots
1 clove garlic
1 cup water
¼ bunch parsley
¼ lb. unsalted butter
salt and pepper

1.   Peel the shallots and garlic. In a small saucepan, bring the water to a boil, and simmer the shallots and garlic for 1 minute, drain, and dry.
2.   Cut off and discard the parsley stems. In a food processor, blender, or mortar, purée or finely chop the shallots, garlic, and parsley leaves.
3.   Cream the butter until fluffy and then combine it with the shallots, garlic, and parsley. Season to taste with salt and pepper.
4.   Chill the butter to firm it up. Form it into a log, wrap it in waxed paper or foil, and store it in the refrigerator or freezer. Serve on grilled fish or meats. To make garlic bread, spread the butter on sliced French bread and warm the bread in a 350° oven for 5 minutes.

ANCHOVY BUTTER
Makes about ¼ lb.

8 anchovy fillets
4 tablespoons milk
¼ lb. unsalted butter
salt and pepper

1.   Soak the anchovy fillets in the milk for 15 minutes to remove excessive saltiness. Cream the butter until fluffy.
2.   Drain the anchovies and purée them in a food processor, blender, or mortar. Combine with the creamed butter. Season to taste with salt and pepper.
3.   Chill the butter to firm it up. Form it into a log, wrap it in waxed paper or foil, and store it in the refrigerator or freezer. Serve on grilled or sautéed fish.

LEMON BUTTER

Makes about ¼ lb.

1 lemon
¼ **lb. unsalted butter**
salt and white pepper

1.   Zest the lemon (see page 30) and chop the zest very fine. Squeeze about a tablespoon of juice. Cream the butter until fluffy.
2.   Combine the juice and finely grated zest with the creamed butter. Season to taste with salt and white pepper.
3.   Chill the butter to firm it up. Form it into a log, wrap it in waxed paper or foil, and store it in the refrigerator or freezer. Serve on grilled or sautéed fish, or on boiled or steamed vegetables.

MUSTARD BUTTER

Makes about ¼ lb.

¼ **lb. unsalted butter**
2 tablespoons prepared
    mustard
salt and pepper

1.   Cream the butter until fluffy and beat the mustard into the butter. Season to taste with salt and pepper.
2.   Chill the butter to firm it up. Form it into a log, wrap it in waxed paper or foil, and store it in the refrigerator or freezer. Serve with grilled beef, sautéed or grilled fish, or vegetables, or use it for making sandwiches.

PAPRIKA BUTTER

Makes about ¼ lb.

¼ **lb. unsalted butter**
1½ tablespoons Hungarian
    paprika
1 tablespoon tomato paste
salt and pepper

1.   Cream the butter until fluffy and beat the paprika and tomato paste into the butter. Season to taste with salt and pepper.
2.   Chill the butter to firm it up. Form it into a log, wrap it in waxed paper or foil, and store it in the refrigerator or freezer. Serve with grilled meats, sautéed or grilled fish, or vegetables, or use it for making sandwiches.

MELTED BUTTERS

These melted butters are as close to instant and foolproof as sauces can be. Simple melted butter, also called drawn butter, is a sauce on its own, most often served on steamed or boiled lobster or other shellfish, or on vegetables such as artichokes and asparagus. Naturally, it is crucial that the butter be of the best quality. It should be unsalted, and preferably cultured (see page 15). In France and Germany, browned or blackened butter is commonly served with cauliflower, asparagus, and calves' brains. Blackened butter will appeal to people who like dark roast coffee and charcoal-broiled steaks. By adding coarse bread crumbs to melted butter, texture is added to the sauce, which makes a nice contrast when served with vegetables. Any of the melted butters may be enhanced, when appropriate, with herbs, mustard, garlic, or capers.

MELTED BUTTER SAUCE

¼ lb. unsalted butter
salt and pepper
a 1-qt. saucepan

In a small saucepan over low heat, melt the butter, stirring with a wire whisk. The sauce is finished as soon as the butter is melted. Add salt and pepper to taste. Serve with lobster, shrimp, fish, or vegetables.

BROWNED OR BLACKENED BUTTER

¼ lb. unsalted butter
salt and pepper
a 1-qt. saucepan

Cook the butter to a nut-brown or blackened color, whisking constantly for uniform browning. Add salt and pepper to taste. Serve with vegetables, scrambled eggs, or variety meats.

CRUMB BUTTER

¼ lb. unsalted butter
2 tablespoons coarse bread
  crumbs
1 hard-cooked egg
salt and pepper

1. Slowly melt the butter. Add the bread crumbs and continue cooking until the butter and crumbs are brown.
2. Chop the hard-cooked egg and add to the sauce. This sauce is especially good served on cauliflower, broccoli, and asparagus.

EMULSIFIED SAUCES

The rich, smooth, emulsified sauces seem to carry the most mystique, next only to soufflés and puff pastry. This is the first time my students hear my much repeated phrase, "Don't let the notion of Hollandaise [or mayonnaise or puff pastry or a soufflé] intimidate you—always remember—you are the boss!"

One day a student brought me a cartoon that had appeared in the *New Yorker*. The first four frames showed a chef merrily kneading bread dough—pulling it, punching it, stretching it, and slapping it on the board. In the fifth frame the dough had formed itself into a fist and punched the chef back, right in the nose!

The student meant it as a joke, of course, but in fact, is that what everybody is afraid of? The cartoon unwittingly proved my point—with inert ingredients, you really are the boss.

An emulsion is a mixture in which a fatty substance is suspended in tiny globules. Homogenized milk is an emulsion—unhomogenized milk would have all the cream at the top. In this lesson you will learn the most useful and typical examples of emulsified sauces. They are as follows: Vinaigrette—a mixture of oil and vinegar; Hollandaise—butter and egg yolks; White Wine Butter Sauce—wine and butter; Lemon Butter Sauce—lemon and butter; and Mayonnaise—oil and egg yolks.

Control of temperature is crucial in the hot emulsified sauces and continuous whisking of all emulsions, hot or cold, is necessary to evenly suspend and bind the elements together. Read each recipe carefully, follow the directions exactly, and, with a little practice, you will have no difficulty.

The key to a perfectly smooth butter sauce is to blend the butter and liquid so that the butter softens and thickens without melting and becoming oily. It is most important to use a good-tasting table wine and a high-quality compatible wine vinegar. The liquid should be warm, not hot, the heat low, and the butter cold. Add the butter in small amounts and whisk until it is totally absorbed before more butter is added. Butter sauces need to be served right away since they solidify when cool. Any leftover sauce may be cut into cubes and served like a compound butter. Remember not to have the serving plate too hot as the heat of the plate will cause the sauce to separate.

WHITE WINE BUTTER SAUCE
Makes about 1 cup

2 shallots
¼ bunch parsley
¼ cup white wine vinegar
½ cup white table wine
½ lb. cold unsalted butter
salt and pepper
a 1½-qt. saucepan

1.   Chop the shallots. Remove and discard the parsley stems and chop the leaves finely.
2.   Simmer the vinegar, wine, and shallots until reduced to approximately 3 tablespoons liquid. Cool to lukewarm.
3.   Over the lowest possible heat, add the cold butter, bit by bit, whisking constantly. When the last bit of butter is incorporated, remove from the heat immediately, stirring constantly. The sauce should be a creamy emulsion, not too thick, but with body.
4.   Add the parsley and season with salt and pepper. Serve with fillets of chicken breast or fish that have been poached, broiled, or grilled.
Note: You can substitute red wine vinegar and red table wine for the white vinegar and white table wine.

Before you make the following sauce, place the lemon in the oven at 350° for 5 minutes—it will give more juice.

LEMON BUTTER SAUCE
Makes about 1 cup

¼ bunch parsley
3 tablespoons fresh lemon juice
½ lb. unsalted cold butter
salt and pepper
a 1½-qt. saucepan

1.   Remove and discard the parsley stems and chop the leaves finely.
2.   Place 1 tablespoon of lemon juice in a small saucepan and over the lowest possible heat, add the cold butter, bit by bit, whisking constantly. When the last bit of butter is incorporated, remove from the heat immediately, stirring constantly.
3.   Taste and add more lemon juice, salt, and/or pepper if needed. Stir in the parsley. Serve with grilled or poached fish or boiled or steamed vegetables.

Because of its reputation, Hollandaise is a frightening sauce to some cooks. In reality, it is not at all difficult to make. There is little or no advance preparation like making stock, or chopping vegetables. All the equipment you need is a stove, saucepan, and whisk. The ingredient list is minimal too, and if you'll remember to keep the heat low and to whisk constantly, you will have no trouble. Until you are used to the sauce, place the saucepan in a water bath—a skillet half-filled with gently simmering water, to help keep the heat low. If the sauce gets too hot, the protein in the egg will shrink—which is called curdling. Simply remove the saucepan from the heat and whisk in an ice cube to smooth out the sauce.

HOLLANDAISE SAUCE
Makes 1½ cups

4 egg yolks
2 tablespoons lemon juice
½ lb. cold unsalted butter
salt and pepper
a 1½-qt. saucepan

1.   In a heavy saucepan over low heat (or set in a water bath), whisk the egg yolks together with a tablespoon of the lemon juice until light and fluffy.
2.   Cut the chilled butter into cubes. Whisking constantly, add the butter in four parts. Allow each batch of butter to combine completely with the eggs before adding more. Whisk until all of the butter is melted and the sauce is thickened.
3.   Season to taste with salt, pepper, and the rest of the lemon juice. Serve with steamed or boiled vegetables, or steamed or poached fish.

Variation:

Mousseline Sauce

Mousseline Sauce is a richer version of Hollandaise Sauce and is used in the same way. To make it, fold 3 tablespoons whipped crème fraîche into 1½ cups Hollandaise as soon as the butter has been incorporated.

Béarnaise Sauce is made in the same way as Hollandaise Sauce, except that the yolks are combined with a reduction of wine vinegar, tarragon, and shallots instead of lemon juice.

BÉARNAISE SAUCE
Makes 1½ cups

¼ bunch parsley
¼ bunch chives
3 shallots
1 cup tarragon vinegar
1 tablespoon dry tarragon
   leaves
½ lb. cold unsalted butter
4 egg yolks
salt and pepper
a 1½-qt. saucepan

1.   Remove and discard the parsley stems and chop the leaves; chop about 1 tablespoon chives. Chop the shallots. Place the parsley, chives, shallots, vinegar, and tarragon into a small saucepan. Reduce to about 3 tablespoons. Strain through a fine sieve into another saucepan.
2.   Cut the cold butter into small cubes. Over a low heat, combine the vinegar reduction, egg yolks, and 2 of the butter cubes, stirring with a whisk until light and fluffy.
3.   Whisking constantly, add the rest of the butter in three parts. Whisk until all the butter is melted and the sauce is thickened.
4.   Season to taste with salt and pepper. Serve with grilled meats.

Vinaigrette Sauce is probably the sauce you will use most of all, since it is the classic dressing for green salads and cold vegetables. In its simplest form it is an emulsion of oil and vinegar. Because of its simplicity, the quality of the ingredients is of the utmost importance—be sure to use the best quality oils, vinegars, and mustards. The usual proportions for a vinaigrette are 1 part vinegar to 4 parts oil. Should you wish it sharper, increase the vinegar. By using different oils and vinegars, and by adding mustard, chopped herbs, or garlic, a vinaigrette may be changed to suit the food with which it is to be served. A dash of sugar is added to offset the acidity of the vinegar or lemon juice in vinaigrette sauces. If you wish, you may make up a supply of vinaigrette, store it in the refrigerator, and bring it to room temperature before serving. Even though vinaigrette is an emulsion, it is expected to separate when it stands—whisk or shake it to serve.

VINAIGRETTE SAUCE

About ¼ cup or 2 servings

1 tablespoon vinegar **4 tablespoons oil** **salt and pepper** **sugar**	Combine the vinegar and oil and mix well with a whisk. Season to taste with salt, pepper, and a pinch of sugar. If you are not using the sauce immediately, stir again just before serving.

Variations:

Vinaigrette Sauce with Herbs

Add ½ teaspoon mixed chopped fresh parsley, tarragon, chervil, etc., to the basic vinaigrette.

Vinaigrette Sauce with Mustard

Add ½ teaspoon prepared mustard to the basic vinaigrette.

Vinaigrette Sauce with Tomato

Stir in ½ teaspoon tomato paste.

Vinaigrette Sauce with Egg and Shallots

Add 1 chopped hard-cooked egg and 1 chopped shallot for each 4 servings of vinaigrette.

Once you taste a homemade mayonnaise, it will be difficult for you to serve anything else. Commercial mayonnaise available in the supermarkets is acceptable only as a sandwich spread—but not as a sauce for cold meats and vegetables. By following the simple instructions carefully at first, and with some practice, you will be able to whip up a delicious mayonnaise sauce whenever you need it.

Mayonnaise is an emulsion of egg yolks and oil. The more oil incorporated into the eggs the thicker the mayonnaise. It is important that the ingredients for mayonnaise be at room temperature—chilled ingredients are too thick to emulsify easily. The egg yolks can only absorb the oil gradually so you must add the oil slowly, drop by drop at first, then in a thin stream. Oil added too quickly may cause the sauce to curdle. You can correct it by whisking another egg yolk in a separate bowl and then slowly whisking the curdled mayonnaise into the egg yolk. If the sauce is too thick, it may be thinned with a little lemon juice or vinegar. If it is too thin, it may be thickened by whisking in more oil—always slowly. Different ingredients may be added to mayonnaise to change its flavor and texture. I have included several variations following the basic recipe below. Store the mayonnaise in the refrigerator—it will keep for about a week.

MAYONNAISE
Makes about 1 cup

2 egg yolks
½ teaspoon each salt,
  pepper, and sugar
1 teaspoon Dijon mustard
2 teaspoons vinegar
1 cup cold-pressed peanut
  oil
a 1-qt. deep mixing bowl

1.   Have all ingredients at room temperature. Combine the egg yolks, salt, pepper, sugar, mustard, and 1 teaspoon of the vinegar in a mixing bowl, blender, or food processor.

2.   Whisking steadily, or with the blender or food processor running, add the oil, drop by drop at first. When about ¼ cup of the oil has been added, add the last teaspoon of vinegar, then finish adding the oil in a steady stream. Serve with cold sliced meats, raw or cooked vegetables, or cold poached fish.

Mayonnaise is a wonderfully adaptable sauce, and lends itself to the addition of various seasonings and herbs. Below are five variations on the basic Mayonnaise.

TARTAR SAUCE I
Makes about 1½ cups

1 hard-cooked egg
¼ small onion
3 sweet gherkins
1 tablespoon chopped
  chives
1 teaspoon capers
1½ cups Mayonnaise
salt and pepper

Chop the egg, the onion, and the gherkins. Combine all ingredients except the salt and pepper, and mix well. Season to taste with salt and pepper. Serve with hot or cold fish or shellfish.

TARTAR SAUCE II
Makes about 1½ cups

1 cup Mayonnaise
2 oz. chopped cornichons
1 tablespoon capers
1 tablespoon Dijon mustard
1 tablespoon chopped
  parsley
1 teaspoon dry tarragon
2 teaspoons chopped chives
2 tablespoons chopped
  black olives

Combine all ingredients. Serve with hot or cold fish or shellfish.

RÉMOULADE SAUCE
Makes 1 cup

2 small gherkins
¼ bunch parsley
1 tablespoon capers
1 tablespoon prepared
  mustard
½ teaspoon dry tarragon
1 cup Mayonnaise
salt and pepper

Chop the gherkins. Remove and discard the parsley stems and chop the leaves finely. Combine all ingredients. Serve with Crab Cakes (see page 168) or Skewered Shrimp, Scallops, and Avocado (see page 171).

GREEN MAYONNAISE
Makes about 1½ cups

4 spinach leaves
4 sprigs each parsley,
chervil, and watercress
1½ cups Mayonnaise
salt and pepper

1.   Blanch the spinach, parsley, chervil, and watercress in boiling water for 30 seconds. Drain and dry on towels.
2.   In a food processor or blender, purée finely. Combine the puréed spinach and herbs with the mayonnaise. Season to taste with salt and pepper. Serve with cold poached fish—especially good with salmon.

MINTED MAYONNAISE

¼ cup white wine vinegar
6 fresh mint leaves
a 1-qt. stainless steel
saucepan*

In a small saucepan, combine the vinegar and mint leaves. Bring to a boil, remove from the heat, cover, and allow to stand 8 hours. Strain and substitute the mint-flavored vinegar for the plain vinegar to make mayonnaise following the basic recipe above. A few chopped fresh mint leaves may be added to the mayonnaise. Serve with cold poached fish.

(*Vinegar interacts with certain metals and may give an off taste to your Mayonnaise if you use other than stainless steel.)

BOILING, POACHING, AND STEAMING

Chapter 4

In my cooking school, I am always happy to start lesson 4. At last, we are really going to start cooking. Up to this point, we have been doing scales and arpeggios—just practicing. Now, everybody is glad they practiced, because it's time to play some real music—we are going to make some perfect, finished dishes.

In this and the next four chapters, we will cover all the most common cooking methods, including stewing and braising, sautéing and frying, broiling, grilling, roasting and baking, boiling, poaching, and steaming. In these sections we will go through the basic cooking methods as they apply to meats, poultry, and vegetables. Fish and shellfish will be dealt with in a separate chapter.

Unlike other cookbooks, where dozens (sometimes hundreds) of recipes are given for you to learn, my approach is to first explain the concept and procedure of a cooking method as well as the foods best suited to that method. For example, if you understand the concepts of roasting, including the cuts of meat suited to that method, you will know that those same techniques will apply to lamb as well as beef, goose as well as turkey. Then, if your butcher does not have the rib roast you had planned for dinner, it is easy for you to change to another cut of meat suitable for roasting—and the same holds true for stewing, sautéing, and other cooking methods.

The recipes following each concept are typical examples of that particular cooking method and are designed to perfectly illustrate the principles just learned. If you practice on these dishes, the recipes will become guides instead of strict formulas, and soon you will be adding, changing, and substituting with complete confidence and freedom, creating dishes reflective of your personality.

BOILING

The notion of boiling food may make you think of the tasteless bits of meat or chicken that fall from the bones when you make stock. In fact, the opposite is true. The primary difference is that stock is always started with cold water, and brought slowly to the boil—in order to begin the extraction of flavors from the meats. Boiled beef or boiled chicken is treated in an exact opposite manner—dropped into the boiling liquid, brought back to the boil, and then the heat is lowered to a gentle simmer until the cooking is finished. By dropping the meats into boiling liquid, the flavors and juices are sealed in, and not completely extracted into the broth as in stock making. I think you will be amazed at how tasty boiled meats can be when properly cooked.

Few foods are cooked completely at a rolling boil—pasta and green vegetables are probably the only exceptions because of their short cooking times. Cooking at a full boil can also set the green color of vegetables, remove the salt from excessively salty foods, keep noodles from sticking to each other while cooking, remove excessive starch from potatoes and rice, and facilitate the peeling of nuts and tomatoes. Rapid boiling of food throughout the entire cooking time, however, would tend to disintegrate the outside of the food before the center is cooked, resulting in mushy, overcooked food. Rapid boiling for short periods, on the other hand, seals in the juices and flavor of meats. Even in the dish called Mixed Boiled Meats, meats are put into boiling water, but are then simmered until cooked.

Meats and poultry should be allowed to cool slightly in the liquid they are cooked in for the same reason that meats are allowed to stand before carving—so that they will retain their juices. If they are taken out of the broth and immediately sliced or carved, the juices would run out, leaving the meat dry, rubbery, and tasteless. The recipes following are some of the best examples of "boiled" food.

In this classic "boiled chicken" dish, a stock is made of the vegetables and veal bones and then the chicken is simmered in the stock—in that way, you get a delicious soup as well as a flavorful chicken. If you are serving the soup as a first course, you may want to add some homemade noodles (see page 197) or Herbed Crêpes (see page 191).

CHICKEN IN THE POT
Serves 8

3 lbs. veal bones
8 qts. water
2 leeks
1 large onion
5 cloves
4 carrots
1 turnip
1 bouquet garni
a 4-lb. stewing chicken
salt and pepper
a 12-qt. soup or stock pot

1.   Put the veal bones and water into the pot. Bring slowly to a boil, and skim.

2.   Clean the leeks, discarding all but 3 inches of the green tops, and cut into 2-inch pieces; peel the onion and stick it with the cloves; clean the carrots and cut into 2-inch pieces; clean the turnip and cut into 2-inch pieces. Add the vegetables and bouquet garni to the pot and simmer, partially covered, for 1½ hours.

3.   Truss the chicken (see pages 44-46), turn up the heat so that the stock boils, and add the chicken to the boiling stock. When the stock comes back to the boil, lower the heat to a simmer, partially cover the pot, and continue simmering about 1½ hours more. Turn off the heat and allow the chicken to cool in the broth.

4.   Remove the chicken to a carving board. Strain the broth, chill it, and remove the fat.

5.   To serve, heat the soup and season to taste with salt and pepper. Carve the chicken and serve it as a separate course, or you may wish to remove the skin and bones of the chicken and serve choice pieces of the meat in the soup.

The following recipe is an elaborate version of Chicken in the Pot. It is worthy of company—a platter of attractively arranged sliced boiled meats, chicken, and sausage is a beautiful dish to bring to the table. A nice feature of this dish is that it may be prepared a day ahead and reheated in the broth to serve. Allow for about 3 hours' cooking time. The Green Sauce is also good with fish, poultry, vegetables, eggs, and other meat dishes as well.

MIXED BOILED MEATS WITH A GREEN SAUCE
Serves 8 to 10

a 1-lb. sausage
a 2½-lb. chicken
a 1½-lb. beef round
1 large leek
1 medium green bell pepper
3 ribs celery
3 medium carrots
1 large onion
1 bouquet garni
1 small beef tongue
1½ lbs. veal shanks
salt and pepper
Green Sauce (see recipe
below)
a 12-qt. stock or soup pot

1.   Soak the sausage in cold water for an hour. Truss the chicken (see pages 44-46), and tie up the beef round firmly. Clean and cut up the leek (discard the dark green tops), green pepper, celery, and carrots into 2-inch pieces. Peel the onion but leave it whole.
2.   Place the vegetables and bouquet garni in a large pot, add enough water to cover the meats that will be added later, and bring to a boil. Add the beef tongue, skim the scum that comes to the top, and after the water comes back to the boil, lower the heat, and simmer with the cover askew for 1 hour.
3.   In a 4-qt. saucepan, bring 2 qts. water to the boil and drop in the sausage. When the water comes back to the boil, lower the heat, cover the pot with the lid askew, and gently simmer 45 minutes. Do not remove from the liquid until you are ready to slice it.
4.   After an hour, remove the tongue, peel away the outer skin, trim away all the fat and gristle, and return it to the pot. Bring the water back to a boil, add the veal shanks and beef round, and simmer partially covered another hour.
5.   Add the trussed chicken, and when the chicken has simmered 40 minutes, all the meats will be done. Let the pot stand 1 hour. After an hour, remove the meats, strain out the vegetables, return the meats to the broth, and chill so that you may remove the congealed fat.
6.   To serve, slowly reheat the soup with all the meats but the sausage and season the broth to taste with salt and pepper. Remove the meats, slice, and arrange all of them on a large platter. Reheat the sausage in its own liquid, slice, and arrange with the other meats. Serve the meats with Green Sauce. The soup may be served as a first course with homemade noodles (see page 197) or Herbed Crêpes (see page 191).

Green Sauce

1 slice French or Italian
  bread
6 tablespoons red wine
  vinegar
½ bunch flat-leaf parsley
4 anchovy fillets
2 tablespoons capers
1 hard-cooked egg yolk
1 clove garlic
about 1 cup olive oil
salt and pepper

1.   Sprinkle the slice of bread with the vinegar and let stand 15 minutes.

2.   In the bowl of a food processor or blender, combine the parsley (stems and all), anchovies, capers, egg yolk, garlic, and soaked bread. Process until smooth.

3.   With the processor or blender running, add the olive oil, little by little, until the sauce has a creamy texture resembling Mayonnaise.

4.   Season to taste with salt and pepper.

The next two dishes go so well together, I urge you to include them both in your next summer buffet. Both need to marinate for 24 hours; both are served cold. They are my versions of classic Italian dishes that you always see on summer restaurant menus all over Italy. They are also typical examples of "boiled" meats. The veal dish will test your memory on how to make mayonnaise.

SLICED VEAL WITH A TUNA MAYONNAISE
(Vitello Tonnato)
Serves 8 to 10

a 2½-lb. leg of veal, deboned and tied
1 medium carrot
1 stalk celery
1 medium onion
1 bunch parsley
1 bay leaf
4 qts. water
1 7½-oz. can Italian tuna
14 anchovy fillets
¼ cup fresh lemon juice
¾ cup olive oil
4 tablespoons capers
½ cup Mayonnaise (see page 86)
salt and pepper
2 lemons
an 8-qt. stock or soup pot

1.   Have the butcher debone and tie the leg of veal.
2.   Clean the carrot and cut in half; clean the celery and cut in half; peel the onion and leave it whole. Cut off the parsley stems for the stock and reserve the leaves for garnish.
3.   Place the parsley stems, celery, carrot, onion, and bay leaf in the pot. Add the water and bring to a boil. Add the tied leg of veal, and when the water comes back to the boil, lower the heat to a simmer, cover partially, and simmer gently 1½ hours or until the meat is tender but not falling apart. Let the meat cool in the broth. After the meat is cooled, remove it from the broth, and refrigerate at least 3 or 4 hours—until well chilled. Strain and store the veal broth for another use.
4.   In a food processor or blender, purée the tuna and anchovy fillets with the lemon juice. Add the olive oil gradually until the mixture is like a thin mayonnaise. Fold in 2 tablespoons of capers and the Mayonnaise. Add salt and pepper to taste.
5.   Slice the veal ⅜ inch thick and arrange on a platter so that each slice touches the next—not overlapping. Spread the sauce over the slices and put on another layer of veal. Continue to layer the veal slices and sauce until all the veal is used—finishing with sauce. Chop the reserved parsley leaves and sprinkle them with the remaining capers over the veal. Slice the lemons and decorate the platter with the lemon slices. Cover with plastic wrap (holding up the plastic with toothpicks like a tent), and allow to marinate at least 24 hours before serving.

SPICY MARINATED CHICKEN   (Pollo Forte)

Serves 8 to 10

1 carrot
1 stalk celery
1 medium onion
½ bunch parsley
3 medium red bell peppers
2 cloves garlic
1 bay leaf
3 qts. water
a 4-lb. chicken
½ cup olive oil
12 anchovy fillets
1 tablespoon flour
1½ cups Chicken Stock
salt and pepper
cayenne pepper
1 tablespoon red wine
  vinegar
3 tablespoons capers
an 8-qt. stock or soup pot

1.   Clean the carrot and celery and cut in half. Peel the onion, but leave it whole. Cut off the parsley stems for the stock and reserve the leaves for garnish. Roast the peppers (see page 29), peel, take off the tops, and remove the seeds. Cut 2 of them into strips. Chop the garlic.

2.   Place the carrot, celery, onion, parsley stems, and bay leaf in the pot. Add the water and bring to a boil. Add the chicken and when the water comes back to the boil, lower the heat and simmer 1½ to 2 hours. Allow the chicken to cool in its liquid. Remove the chicken from the stock and reserve 1½ cups of stock for making the sauce. Store the remainder for another use. Remove all the skin and bones of the chicken, and cut the meat into strips about 1 inch wide and 3 or 4 inches long. Arrange on a serving platter.

3.   Heat the olive oil in a skillet over a medium heat. Add the anchovy fillets and mash with a wooden spoon until dissolved. Add the flour and mix well. When the flour begins to brown, add the 1½ cups stock, stirring constantly. Add the whole bell pepper and the garlic. Simmer for 5 minutes and then purée the sauce in a blender or food processor.

4.   Return the sauce to the skillet, add salt, pepper, and cayenne pepper to taste; add the vinegar and mix well. Bring the sauce to a boil, stirring, and while the sauce is hot, pour it over the chicken. Cover with plastic wrap, refrigerate, and allow to marinate at least 24 hours before serving at room temperature. Chop the parsley leaves. Garnish the platter with capers and chopped parsley.

BOILING VEGETABLES

Green vegetables that remain a bright green after being cooked, are a sign of the skilled cook. Faded or "yellowish" green vegetables should *never* be served.

The natural color of green vegetables comes from chlorophyll which is affected by acids and alkalies in the presence of heat. Acid in combination with heat will denature chlorophyll. Generally, green vegetables should be cooked uncovered so that the acids may escape in the steam. (After cooking, do not marinate the vegetables in anything acidic like vinegar, lemon juice, or tomatoes; within an hour or so, the vegetables will be an unattractive gray color.)

To keep green vegetables green, the water has to be kept boiling when the vegetables first make contact with the water. (You have probably noticed that a couple of quarts of boiling water will stop boiling when vegetables are dropped in. By the time the water comes back to the boil, the vegetables have already lost their color—you can easily see how green the water has become.) Use a minimum amount of boiling salted water—just to cover—and cook in as short a time as possible, in order to preserve vitamins.

There are several methods of boiling green vegetables in order to "lock in" their color—the following is my adaptation of one of them. *My method depends upon using a utensil that can be heated dry, so be certain that the cookware you have may be safely used in this manner.* (Many of my students purchase an inexpensive but sturdy pan in a second-hand store, and then reserve it for cooking green vegetables only.)

JE-H'S SPECIAL METHOD FOR BOILING GREEN VEGETABLES

1. Wash, peel, shell, or otherwise prepare the green vegetables for cooking.

2. Place an empty saucepan or sauté pan on the burner and turn the heat on high. (This is where you would use your second-hand pan.)

3. In a teakettle or separate pot, bring to a boil an adequate amount of water, enough to barely cover the vegetables.

4. When the water is boiling and the empty pan is very hot, put the prepared vegetables in the hot pan and immediately pour the boiling water over them. Add salt and sugar (for taste) if desired. *Do not cover.*

5. Start checking for doneness with a wooden skewer after 30 or 40 seconds of cooking, depending upon the delicacy of the vegetable.

6. When the vegetables are adequately cooked, drain, dry (when appropriate), and finish according to your recipe. (The green vegetables may be boiled in advance, then finished—sautéed, creamed, puréed, etc.—several hours later. Be sure to undercook initially, to allow for the finish.)

VEGETABLE AND GARLIC SALAD
Serves 12 to 14

1 bunch broccoli
1 small head cauliflower
½ lb. mushrooms
4 medium carrots
1 lb. green beans
8 cloves garlic
½ bunch parsley
½ cup hazelnut oil (walnut, almond, or olive oil may be substituted)
salt and pepper

1. Separate broccoli and cauliflower into florets. Clean the mushrooms and cut them into quarters. Peel the carrots and cut into ¼-inch rounds; cut the green beans into 3 pieces each. Peel the cloves of garlic, and leave them whole. Remove and discard the parsley stems and chop the leaves.
2. Heat ¼ cup oil in a large skillet; crush the garlic cloves slightly by hitting them sharply with the flat side of a knife blade. Sauté the garlic for 1 minute. Remove the garlic from the oil and reserve. Add the mushrooms to the oil and sauté until softened—season to taste with salt and pepper and set aside.
3. Boil the cauliflower and carrots by conventional methods, checking for doneness with a wooden skewer—a crunchy texture is best for this salad. Drain the vegetables when done, and transfer to a large serving bowl. Cook the broccoli and green beans separately by JE-H'S Special Method, draining and adding them to the other vegetables when done. Next, add the mushrooms and any remaining oil in the skillet to the bowl of vegetables.
4. In the same skillet, heat ¼ cup more oil, remove from the heat and add the reserved garlic through the press. Pour the warm oil and garlic over the vegetables. Toss gently and season with salt and pepper and toss well. Garnish with chopped parsley.

The cooking method described here produces crisp kernels with tender juicy interiors.

CORN ON THE COB
Serves 6

6 ears of corn
5 qts. water
2 tablespoons sugar
1 tablespoon salt
6 tablespoons unsalted butter
an 8- or 10-qt. stock or soup pot with lid

1. Strip off the husks and corn silk. Fill a pot with the water, bring to a boil, and add the sugar and salt.
2. With the water boiling rapidly, drop in the corn, and bring the water back to a boil.
3. Remove the pot from the heat, cover and let stand 10 minutes before serving. Serve each corn on the cob with a tablespoon of butter. (Corn cooked in this manner can stand up to an hour before serving.)

Once boiled and tender, all vegetables can be mashed or strained to make a smooth purée. Drain the vegetables well after cooking to make sure the purée will be thick and firm. Most vegetables contain enough water to ensure a smooth purée—however potatoes contain so much starch and fiber that they will be too dry without a little milk, cream, or butter. It is a good idea to save the cooking water from the vegetables in case you need some to thin the purée.

Vegetables with a low starch content, such as young green beans, mushrooms, or leeks, should be combined with a small amount of cooked rice or potato to give the purées body. To add flavor and body to a purée, butter or cream or sometimes both are worked into it as it is heating.

MIXED VEGETABLE PURÉE
Serves 8

1 lb. russet potatoes
1 large turnip
2 medium leeks, whites only
1 medium onion
3 qts. water
1 clove garlic
salt and pepper
½ lb. unsalted butter
4 tablespoons crème fraîche
an 8-qt. stock or soup pot

1. Peel the potatoes and turnip and cut into chunks. Clean and slice the leeks, discarding the green. Slice the onion.
2. Fill the pot with the water and bring to the boil. Drop in the potatoes, turnip, leeks, onion, and garlic, bring back to a boil, and simmer gently until tender. Drain and reserve the stock for another use.
3. Purée the vegetables in a blender or food processor (except for the potatoes—you will need to use a food mill or sieve for them).
4. Transfer to a saucepan and reheat slowly, adding salt and pepper to taste, and gradually stirring in the butter and crème fraîche. Serve hot.
Note: If the purée is too loose, reduce it over a very low heat until it thickens.

Cooking Rice
There are thousands of varieties of rice, but in the United States, only a few different kinds are grown for commercial use. Generally, it is best to follow the particular recipe instructions on which type of rice to use for specific dishes, although you can experiment to see which you prefer.

Long grain rice is four to five times as long as it is wide. When cooked, the grains are separate and fluffy. Long grain rice is the overall preferred rice in the U.S.

Medium and short grain rice are very similar—the grains are shorter and plumper than the long grain types. When cooked, the grains are more moist and tender and tend to cling together. They are a good choice for desserts and molds.

Brown rice and white rice are the same grain, except that white rice has been "polished" to remove the bran layer. Brown rice is slightly more nutritious than white rice because of the small amount of vitamin E found in the bran layer.

Parboiled or converted rice has been treated during the milling process to force some of the nutrients in the bran layer to penetrate the grain. It is parboiled, steamed, and dried before packaging.

Wild rice is the seed of an aquatic cereal grass that has never been domesticated. It is not related to regular rice. It grows in wet areas near the Great Lakes and is harvested by local Indian tribes. Because of the difficulty of harvesting, it is very expensive—a luxury food.

Most packaged rice comes with accurate cooking directions and proper liquid-to-rice ratios and should be followed. If directions are not available, follow my method.

PERFECT BOILED RICE
Makes about 3 cups

7 oz. long grain rice (1 cup) **2 cups liquid** **1 tablespoon unsalted** **butter** **1 teaspoon salt** **a 2½-qt. saucepan**	Combine all ingredients in the saucepan, place over the heat, and bring to a boil, stirring once or twice. Reduce heat to a simmer and partially cover the pot. Cook 25 to 30 minutes.

Variations:

Parboiled Rice

Use 2½ cups liquid and cook 15 to 20 minutes; for a drier rice use 2¼ cups liquid. Use broth or water.

Brown Rice

Use 2½ cups liquid and cook 45 minutes.

This rice is superb served with the curries on pages 117 and 118.

LIME SAFFRON RICE
Serves 6 to 8

2 cups Chicken Stock **¼ gram (or more) saffron** **1 teaspoon salt** **7 oz. long grain rice (1 cup)** **½ bunch fresh cilantro** **¼ lb. unsalted butter** **½ cup fresh lime juice** **a 2½-qt. saucepan**	1. Bring the Chicken Stock to a boil, and add the saffron, salt, and rice. Cover and cook over low heat for about 25 minutes. 2. Remove and discard the large cilantro stems, and chop the leaves finely. In a small saucepan, melt the butter, remove from the heat, and combine with the lime juice and cilantro. 3. When ready to serve, pour the melted butter mixture over the rice.

Risotto is a special rice cooked in a particular way that is unique to northern Italy. From the Po Valley comes a short grain rice called Arborio rice. It has a pearly white spot on it that remains firm even after the rice is cooked. This is the only rice suitable for risotto and it may be purchased in Italian markets and delicatessens. Risottos in Italy are primarily first courses but the more hearty risottos with meat or fish can be main courses. In making risotto, the raw rice is first sautéed in hot butter or oil until it is very hot. Then hot stock is added little by little, stirred constantly while the rice absorbs the liquid gradually and becomes cooked. The risotto must be stirred constantly so that it does not stick or burn.

RISOTTO
Serves 6

1 medium onion
2 oz. Parmesan
3 cups (or more) stock or broth
2 tablespoons olive oil
5 tablespoons unsalted butter
7 oz. Arborio rice (1 cup)
salt and pepper

1. Peel and chop the onion. Grate the cheese. Put the stock in a small saucepan and bring to a boil.

2. In a large skillet or sauté pan, heat the olive oil and 2 tablespoons of the butter. Sauté the onion 2 minutes, add the rice, and cook, stirring, another 2 minutes. Add about ½ cup of the hot stock and keep stirring until the rice has absorbed all the liquid.

3. Season with salt and pepper and continue to add the hot stock, little by little, stirring constantly until the rice is cooked. (You may not use all the broth or you may need a little more.) The rice should be tender (except for the small white dot) and creamy rather than dry. Remove the skillet from the heat and add the remaining butter and cheese. Serve immediately.

RISOTTO CON FUNGHI *(Risotto with Mushrooms)*

Serves 8 to 10

1 oz. dry porcini
  mushrooms
1 medium red onion
1 clove garlic
2 oz. Parmesan
¼ bunch parsley
about 6 cups Brown Stock
6 tablespoons unsalted
  butter
1 tablespoon olive oil
½ cup red table wine
14 oz. Arborio rice (2 cups)
salt and pepper
a 12-inch skillet or sauté
  pan

1.   Soak the mushrooms in warm water for 1 hour. Drain and cut into strips. Chop the onion and garlic; grate the cheese. Remove and discard the parsley stems and chop the leaves. Put the stock into a saucepan and bring to a boil—lower the heat to a slow simmer.
2.   Heat 4 tablespoons of the butter and the olive oil in the pan, add the garlic, onion, and half the parsley. Sauté gently for 2 minutes and add the wine. Allow to reduce slowly.
3.   When the wine has disappeared, add the rice and sauté a minute or two more, stirring constantly. Still stirring, add a large ladle of Brown Stock and salt and pepper to taste. When the stock has disappeared, add the soaked, drained mushrooms and, still stirring, add hot broth as needed until the rice is cooked—about 20 minutes. (You may not use all the liquid or you may need more.) The rice is cooked when it is tender and creamy with a "crunchy" center.
4.   Remove from the heat, add the remaining butter, parsley, and grated Parmesan cheese. Toss and serve immediately.

I am including *Risotto alla Milanese* since it is the traditional first course served before braised veal shanks (*Osso Bucco*—page 113).

RISOTTO ALLA MILANESE *(Risotto with Saffron)*

Serves 8 to 10

1 medium onion
about 6 cups any stock
¼ to ½ gram saffron
2 oz. Parmesan
¼ lb. unsalted butter (8
  tablespoons)
14 oz. Arborio rice (2 cups)
½ cup dry white table wine
salt and pepper
a 12-inch skillet or sauté
  pan

1.   Chop the onion. Heat the stock in a saucepan and dissolve the saffron in the hot stock. Grate the Parmesan.
2.   Heat 6 tablespoons of the butter in a large skillet and sauté the onion 1 minute. Add the rice and sauté and stir for 2 minutes more.
3.   Add the wine. When the wine has disappeared, add a cup of the hot stock and cook and stir gently until the stock has been absorbed. Add another cup of stock and repeat until the rice is cooked, tender and creamy but firm in the center.
4.   Remove from the heat and season to taste with salt and pepper. Add the remaining butter and stir in the cheese. Serve immediately.

Served at room temperature, Wild Rice Salad is a perfect accompaniment for grilled meats and poultry.

WILD RICE SALAD
Serves 8

6 oz. wild rice (1 cup)
2 cups Chicken Stock
1½ lbs. peas or ¾ lb. snow
   peas
4 green onions
2 stalks celery
6 tablespoons olive oil
3 tablespoons wine vinegar
salt and pepper

1.   Boil the wild rice in the Chicken Stock until tender. Shell the peas (or, if you are using snow peas, pull off the strings). Cook the vegetables briefly using the special method (see page 96).
2.   Clean the green onions and celery and slice thinly.
3.   Combine all ingredients and toss. Season to taste with salt and pepper.

POACHING

Poaching is a method of cooking in liquid at a lower temperature than boiling. Poaching is for delicate foods that would break apart if they were boiled even for a brief time. Fish, fruit, dumplings, sausages, and chicken breasts are some foods that poach well. While poaching, the top of the liquid should not actually bubble but just shimmer.

Poaching chicken breasts is an excellent method of preparing them. Following are some of my favorite recipes.

POACHED CHICKEN BREASTS WITH A FRESH HERB SAUCE
Serves 8

8 half breasts of chicken
16 fresh basil leaves
4 sprigs fresh tarragon
4 sprigs fresh chervil
¼ bunch fresh chives
¼ bunch fresh parsley
1 medium carrot
1 stalk celery
4 qts. water
½ small onion
4 tablespoons fresh lemon
   juice
1 cup walnut oil
salt and pepper
an 8-qt. stock or soup pot

1.   Debone the breasts (see page 42), but leave the skin intact, and reserve the bones for the stock. Finely chop the basil, tarragon, chervil, chives, and parsley. Clean the carrot and celery and cut each into 3-inch pieces.
2.   Put the bones from the breasts, the carrot, celery, onion, and water in the stock pot. Bring to a boil, lower the heat, and simmer for 30 minutes with the cover askew.
3.   Drop in the chicken breasts, and simmer for 3 minutes uncovered. After 3 minutes, remove the pot from the heat, cover, and let stand 20 minutes. After 20 minutes, remove the breasts to a platter and after they have cooled, remove and discard the skin.
4.   Combine the herbs, lemon juice, and walnut oil. Season to taste with salt and pepper. While the breasts are still warm, pour the oil mixture over them. Serve at room temperature.
5.   If the stock is weak, reduce it further before storing for another use.

POACHED CHICKEN BREASTS WITH A LEMON SAUCE
Serves 6

6 half breasts of chicken
1 lemon
¼ bunch parsley
1 stalk celery
1 medium carrot
4 qts. water
½ medium onion
¼ cup white table wine
6 tablespoons unsalted
  butter
salt and pepper
an 8-qt. stock or soup pot

1. Debone the breasts (see page 42), but leave the skin intact, and reserve the bones for the stock. Squeeze the juice from the lemon and chop the parsley. Clean the celery and carrot and cut each into 3-inch pieces.

2. Put the breast bones, the celery, carrot, onion, and water in the stock pot. Bring to boil, lower the heat, and simmer for 30 minutes. Drop in the breasts and simmer 3 minutes. Remove the pot from the heat, cover, and let stand 20 minutes. Remove the breasts from the liquid to a platter; remove and discard the skin.

3. In a small saucepan, combine the lemon juice and wine, and reduce by half. Remove from the heat and swirl in the butter. Add the parsley, and salt and pepper to taste. Return the breasts to the sauce to rewarm before serving.

Poaching fruit in a wine syrup is an easy way to create outstanding desserts. Apples, apricots, peaches, pears, cherries, and plums, all poach beautifully. Apricots, peaches, and plums are usually cut in half and have the pit removed. Cherries may be pitted as well, although you may choose to poach them with the pits. Apples and pears may be poached whole. If you use a red wine syrup on a light-colored fruit like a pear, the wine turns the fruit a beautiful deep red. Use sugar to taste and add cinnamon or peppercorns for a more exotic touch. Your imagination is the only limit when it comes to combining wines and fruit.

CHERRIES POACHED IN BURGUNDY
Serves 6

5 oz. sugar (¾ cup)
½ cup water
2 cups Burgundy
1 lb. cherries

1. Combine the sugar, water, and wine in a saucepan large enough to hold the cherries. Bring to a boil, reduce the heat, and simmer 10 minutes.

2. Add the cherries, bring back to the boil, lower the heat, and simmer gently 5 minutes. Allow to cool in the syrup.

STEAMING

In this method, the food is cooked *over* boiling water rather than in it. Steamed foods have the advantage of retaining more of their natural flavors since they are not immersed in water. Another advantage to steaming is that, as the food cooks and loses its natural juices, the juices can combine with the cooking liquid to form a broth. This is especially beneficial in the cooking of clams and mussels. For vegetables, steaming takes longer than boiling, and since the pan must be covered, steaming can discolor green vegetables and intensify the flavor of strong-tasting vegetables like cabbage and Brussels sprouts. Potatoes, carrots, mushrooms, fish, shellfish, and the breast meat of chicken all steam beautifully.

I especially like steamed potatoes with herbs—and if you have a clay pot that you can soak, you can "steam" right in the oven. This recipe is an all time favorite in our classes.

STEAMED-BAKED POTATOES
Serves 8

4 cloves garlic
8 large or 16 small boiling potatoes
2 tablespoons unsalted butter
salt and pepper
fresh herbs of your choice— a bunch each of parsley, oregano, basil, dill, etc.
a 2½-qt. unglazed or partially glazed covered clay casserole

1.   Crush the garlic. Scrub or peel the potatoes and soak them in water 20 minutes. Soak the clay pot and lid in water 20 minutes.
2.   Drain the pot and place the potatoes in it without drying them. Add the butter, salt, pepper, garlic, and fresh herbs.
3.   Cover the pot and place it in a cold oven. Turn the heat to 425° and bake about 1 hour. As the unglazed clay pot dries out in the oven, the potatoes are surrounded by a gentle steam which infuses the flavors of the herbs and garlic into the potatoes. Check for doneness with a wooden skewer.
4.   Discard the used herbs and add fresh ones for serving. Serve hot, with more melted butter, if desired.

BRAISING AND STEWING

Chapter 5

When I was first married, one of the dishes I wanted to learn to make was my Grandma Minnie's delicious beef stew. So I called her, and asked her what to do. She told me how (I learned later that it is a classic "braise"), and I couldn't wait to get started. I followed her instructions exactly, put the stew in the oven, and called my husband at the office to alert him not to eat too much for lunch, since he could look forward to a mouth-watering beef stew for dinner that night. The house smelled wonderful all afternoon as the stew cooked, and cooked, and cooked.

I kept testing it for doneness—remembering that my grandmother had said that when it was tender, it was done. And yet, the more it cooked, the tougher it got. After three hours, I called my grandmother to tell her it was still tough. She said, "Don't worry, it will be tender—did you do just as I said?" "Yes, yes," I assured her. "Then be patient—I'm going out now— call me tomorrow and let me know how your husband liked the stew."

By evening, the stew was tougher than ever, inedible—we went out to dinner. The next day, when I reported the sad news to my grandmother, she was mystified and said she was coming right over with some meat and good homemade stock and this time, we would make it together. We browned the meat, put it into the casserole, added onions and garlic to the pan, and then some tomatoes and stock, cooked it a little, and poured it over the meat. My grandmother said, "Did you do all this?" I said, "Exactly." Then she covered the pot and I said, "Wait a minute—you didn't tell me to cover the pot!!!" "Well," she said, "I thought you knew—who wouldn't know that?"

Much later, after I started my cooking school, the lessons I'd learned from my grandmother's beef stew proved invaluable—number one, the braising method, and number two, when it comes to teaching cooking, don't take anything for granted.

Braising or stewing is the technique of cooking food slowly, in a *covered* casserole or pot with some liquid. Braising and stewing are identical processes, except that when the meats are cubed, they are called stews. Generally, the tougher cuts of meat are stewed or braised since the liquid and steam produced in the process act as tenderizing agents.

Sometimes, though, even tender cuts of meat or vegetables are braised— often to increase flavors when they have little flavor of their own, since the sauce created from braised food is rich and full-bodied. Often, braised meats are marinated first to increase their flavors (Sauerbraten is an excellent example.) Braises and stews are best made a day or so in advance of serving so that the flavors have a chance to integrate and develop. Braised dishes are actually time-saving, for even though it may take several hours to make a pot roast or stew, most of it is unsupervised time. They are also convenient since you can cook, store, and serve out of the same casserole. Braised dishes are a boon to the home cook, and I am sure that once you become familiar with the technique, you will want to include a braised dish in your weekly menus.

In braising, the food is browned first and then cooked covered, with aromatics, in a small amount of liquid. The braising liquid can be anything from beer or wine to stock, water, or sometimes tomatoes, or some combination of these. Always begin with enough liquid to barely cover the food. The liquid should reduce to about half the original quantity in the cooking. Add extra braising liquid during the cooking should it evaporate too rapidly. Vegetables that are cooked with the meat are sometimes discarded (they have lost their flavor to the sauce), and fresh vegetables are precooked and added at the appropriate time. The braising pot should be the proper size to hold the food being braised. If a large container and a great deal of liquid is used, you will end up boiling the food. Clayware is the traditional braising pot, but any type of cookware may be used, as long as the container can be covered and is heavy enough so that it will not allow the meat to scorch during the long cooking time. Braised meat should be cooked only until tender, as overcooking may toughen the meat.

BROWNING

Browning is a procedure done before braising and oftentimes before roasting. To "brown" means just what it says—to cause the food to take on a brown color. This serves two purposes. First, it improves the appearance of the meat (meat that is browned looks more appetizing than pale, un-browned meat), and second, if the browning is properly done, it seals in the food's juices. Browning is not a complete cooking of the food and must always be done quickly over very high heat. Do not crowd the pan when browning many small pieces of meat. The heat under the browning skillet should always be high, otherwise the food will not take on any color and will be sautéed. Clarified butter, olive oil, and vegetable oil are all suitable fats for browning. (See pages 15-17 for more information on oils.)

To brown meats, add the selected oil to a skillet or sauté pan and heat until smoking. Lightly flour the meat to be browned (to dry the meat surface), and add it to the hot oil, being careful not to fill the pan beyond ¾ full. Once floured, the meat must be browned immediately. If allowed to stand floured, the juices from the meat will soon come through the flour coating and make it gooey. Brown the meat quickly, about a minute each side. Remove quickly from the pan and add the next batch, adding more oil if necessary. Continue until finished, always working as rapidly as possible. Then proceed with your recipe.

The following recipes are all typical examples of braised or stewed dishes. I have given you a variety—including my grandmother's beef stew—all sampled and tested and longtime favorites of my students. Make each one at least two times to be sure you understand all the procedures and then try braised dishes from some of your favorite recipe books.

In making stews, be careful not to cut the meat too small as it will overcook, dry out, and become tough and chewy. A 2-inch cube is ideal. As you learned in making vegetable soups, the vegetables should all be cut to a uniform size—in this case they may be carved into ovals.

BEEF STEW
Serves 6

2½ lbs. braising beef
(preferably bottom
round or chuck)
1½ lbs. tomatoes
1 clove garlic
8 medium carrots
4 large turnips
16 tiny boiling onions
4 large boiling potatoes
16 mushrooms
flour for browning
oil for browning
salt and pepper

1 tablespoon unsalted
butter
1 tablespoon flour
1 cup Brown Stock
¼ cup concentrated Brown
Stock
¾ cup red table wine
1 bouquet garni

¼ lb. unsalted butter for
vegetables
2 tablespoons sugar for
vegetables
½ bunch parsley
a 4- to 6-qt. ovenproof
casserole

1. Cut the beef into 2-inch cubes. Dredge the beef cubes in flour and brown in a skillet over high heat, 8 or 9 pieces at a time, in about 3 tablespoons of hot oil. Season the meat with salt and pepper and transfer the pieces to the casserole as they are browned.
2. Discard the browning fat from the skillet, add 1 tablespoon of butter, sprinkle with 1 tablespoon of flour, and cook the roux over a medium heat, stirring, until it is browned.
3. Gradually add the stock, stock concentrate, and wine, stirring constantly until smooth. Pour the liquid over the meat.
4. Preheat the oven to 375°. Peel, seed, and chop the tomatoes; chop the garlic. Add the garlic, tomatoes, and the bouquet garni, and cook slowly, covered, in the oven, until meat is tender—about 2 hours. Replenish the braising liquid if it evaporates too rapidly during cooking.
5. While the meat is cooking, carve the carrots into 24 small, uniform, oval pieces. Do the same with the turnips and potatoes. Clean the mushrooms and cut into quarters. Peel the onions, leaving the root ends intact.
6. Preboil the vegetables about 5 minutes each and then sauté them in ¼ lb. butter with the sugar until they are shiny and just beginning to brown. Season to taste with salt and pepper.
7. When the meat is done, arrange the vegetables on top of the meat and spoon the sauce over all. Season to taste with salt and pepper. (The entire dish can go into the refrigerator at this point for up to 2 or 3 days.)
8. Reheat slowly to serve. Chop the parsley, and garnish each serving with chopped parsley.

Sauerbraten—beef marinated in spiced vinegar and served with a sweet and sour sauce—is found in every region of Germany. This recipe came over with my husband, who is from the western part of Germany. You will need to marinate the meat for 4 days before cooking.

SAUERBRATEN
Serves 6

2 medium onions
2 cloves garlic
2 cups water
1 cup red wine vinegar
2 slices lemon, seeded
2 cloves
4 peppercorns
1 bay leaf
a 2½-lb. piece bottom round
flour for browning
4 tablespoons oil
2 tablespoons tomato paste
1 tablespoon paprika
1 tablespoon sugar
salt and pepper
1 cup crème fraîche
a 4- to 6-qt casserole

1. Chop the onions and garlic. Place the onions, garlic, water, vinegar, lemon slices, cloves, peppercorns, and bay leaf in a saucepan and bring to the boil. Simmer 5 minutes and allow to cool.

2. Place the meat in a deep, nonmetal bowl and pour the cooled marinade over the meat. Cover and refrigerate for 4 days, turning each day so the marinade reaches all parts of the meat.

3. Preheat the oven to 375°. Drain the meat, reserving the marinade. Pat the meat dry with paper towels, and dredge it in some flour. Heat 4 tablespoons oil in a skillet. Brown the meat on all sides over a high heat and transfer to the casserole.

4. Spoon the onions and garlic from the marinade over the meat. Remove the bay leaf, cloves, and peppercorns from the marinade and add the tomato paste, paprika, sugar, and 2 teaspoons of salt. Pour the marinade over the meat—just covering the meat. Cover the casserole and braise the meat in the oven until well done and tender, about 2 hours.

5. Remove the meat to a serving platter. Purée the sauce in a blender or food processor. Add enough crème fraîche to give the sauce the right consistency and add more salt, pepper, and sugar to achieve a "sweet and sour" taste. Return the meat to the casserole, pour the sauce over all, and reheat to serve.

6. To serve, cut the meat into thick slices, and pass the sauce at the table.

This is my version of the classic French dish, *Coq au Vin.* It is a good example of a braised dish that, once assembled, requires no attention. In this one, mushrooms and onions cook right along with the meat.

CHICKEN IN RED WINE
Serves 8

2 chickens, about 2½ lbs. each
¼ lb. pancetta
24 tiny boiling onions
2 cloves garlic
4 green onions
1 lb. mushrooms
2 tablespoons oil
3 tablespoons flour plus flour for browning
3 cups red table wine
1 cup Chicken Stock
salt and pepper
½ bunch parsley
a 4- to 6-qt. casserole

1. Quarter each chicken (see page 40). Dice the pancetta. Peel the boiling onions, leaving the root end intact so the onions do not fall apart. Chop the garlic, slice the green onions, and clean and quarter the mushrooms. Preheat the oven to 350°.

2. Heat the oil in a skillet and sauté the pancetta over medium heat until lightly browned. Remove from the skillet with a slotted spoon and transfer to the ovenproof casserole.

3. Lightly flour the chicken pieces and brown them in the fat remaining in the skillet. Remove the chicken pieces to the casserole. Add the boiling onions, the green onions, and the garlic to the skillet, and sauté 1 or 2 minutes. Add the mushrooms and sauté a minute longer.

4. Sprinkle the 3 tablespoons of flour over the vegetables and toss well with a wooden spoon. Add the wine and stock, stirring constantly, season to taste with salt and pepper, and bring to a boil. Pour the wine and vegetable mixture over the chicken.

5. Cover the casserole and braise the chicken in the oven for about 2 hours. The chicken should be very well cooked.

6. For each serving of the chicken, spoon on 2 tablespoons of the sauce and some onions and mushrooms. Chop the parsley and garnish each serving. Pass the remainder of the sauce at the table.

Braised vegetables have a full-bodied flavor that is developed by the long cooking time. Since vegetables contain a lot of water, you do not need as much braising liquid as you would with meat. Other vegetables that braise well are carrots, mushrooms, turnips, onions, cauliflower, and potatoes.

BRAISED LEEKS WITH DILL
Serves 6

8 medium leeks
2 medium onions
1 clove garlic
1 large tomato
4 sprigs fresh dill
3 tablespoons olive oil
½ cup White Stock or
  Brown Stock
salt and pepper
a 4-qt. clay casserole

1. Clean the leeks and halve them lengthwise—include about 2 inches of the green tops. Slice the onions, chop the garlic, and peel, seed, and chop the tomato. Chop the dill. Preheat the oven to 375°.
2. Heat the oil in a large skillet. Sauté the onions and garlic for 2 minutes, and transfer to the casserole. Add the leeks, the tomato, and the stock to the casserole. Sprinkle with salt and pepper and cover the casserole.
3. Place the casserole in the oven and braise for 30 to 45 minutes. Serve hot or cold, garnished with the chopped dill.

Make this vegetable stew as is the first time and then try substituting vegetables to create your own combination.

VEGETABLE STEW
Serves 6 to 8

1 lb. squash (any kind)
6 green onions
1 green bell pepper
1 red bell pepper
1 small head Boston lettuce
2 cloves garlic
1 medium onion
½ lb. mushrooms
1½ lbs. tomatoes
½ jalapeño pepper
¼ cup olive oil
salt and pepper
½ cup Brown Stock or
  White Stock
a 6-qt. clay casserole

1. Clean the squash and cut into ¼-inch slices. Clean the green onions and cut into 2-inch pieces. Halve and seed the bell peppers and cut into ½-inch strips. Shred the lettuce, chop the garlic and onion, clean and quarter the mushrooms. Peel, seed, and chop the tomatoes. Seed and chop the jalapeño pepper. Preheat the oven to 375°.
2. Heat the olive oil in a 12-inch skillet. Add the green onions, onions, and garlic and sauté 1 minute. Add the bell peppers and mushrooms and sauté another minute. Season with salt and pepper and transfer to the casserole.
3. Add the squash and tomatoes to the casserole, and 1 teaspoon of the chopped jalapeño pepper. Scatter the lettuce on top, add the stock, cover, and place in the oven for 45 minutes or until the vegetables are done to your taste. Season with additional salt and pepper if needed. This dish can be served hot or cold.

Cassoulet is a hearty French dish ideally served in winter. It is tradition-ally made in a tall, deep clay pot called a *marmite*. There are many versions of this dish—it may contain sausages, duck, preserved goose, pork, lamb or mutton, or bacon in some combination. All versions have one thing in com-mon—white beans. My version is made with pork, lamb, and sausage, and is best made with the quantities given. Unused portions may be frozen. This is a dish well suited for entertaining large groups, and should be made sev-eral days before serving and stored in the refrigerator. If it seems dry when you are ready to reheat it, add a cup or more of liquid (water or stock) before reheating.

CASSOULET
Serves 14

Beans
2 lbs. small white beans
1 large onion
4 cloves
12 oz. pancetta or salt pork
4 cloves garlic
1 carrot
1 stalk celery
1 tablespoon salt
1 bouquet garni
an 8-qt. soup or stock pot
an 8-qt. clay casserole

Meats
2 lbs. tomatoes
2 large onions
2 lbs. boneless lamb
2 lbs. boneless pork
1 lb. spicy sausage
4 tablespoons oil
salt and pepper
2 tablespoons tomato paste
1 tablespoon sugar
1 cup dry white table wine
1 cup fresh bread crumbs

1. Soak the beans overnight in water to cover.
2. Stick the cloves into the onion. Cut the pancetta or salt pork into small cubes. Chop the garlic cloves coarsely.
3. Drain the beans and put them into the soup pot with the remainder of the "beans" ingredients. Add enough water to cover the surface of the beans.
4. Bring the beans to a boil, skim the surface of any scum, partially cover the pot, and simmer approxi-mately 2 hours or until the beans are soft and most of the liquid absorbed. Discard the onion, celery, car-rot, and the bouquet garni. Transfer the beans to an 8-qt. ovenproof casserole.
5. Peel and chop the tomatoes coarsely. Chop the 2 onions. Cut the lamb and pork into 2-inch cubes and slice the sausage into ¼-inch thick rounds.
6. Preheat the oven to 375°. Heat the oil in a large skillet and brown the lamb and pork cubes; season the meat with salt and pepper and combine with the cooked white beans in the casserole. Add the chopped tomatoes, onions, tomato paste, sugar, wine, and sliced sausage. Mix well with a large wooden spoon. Cover the casserole and place in the oven for 1½ to 2 hours, until the meat is tender.
7. Taste for seasoning and add salt and pepper if necessary. At this stage, the Cassoulet may be refrig-erated for 2 or 3 days if you wish. To reheat before serving, cover the top of the beans with the crumbs and bake uncovered in a 400° oven until the crumbs are brown and the beans are heated through—about 1 hour. Serve from the casserole.

The section on braising would not be complete without the classic Italian dish—*Osso Buco*. It is traditionally served with *Risotto alla Milanese* (see page 101).

OSSO BUCO   *(Braised Veal Shanks)*
Serves 6

3 lbs. hind veal shanks
1 large onion
2 cloves garlic
2 carrots
1 stalk celery
1 lemon
1 1-lb. can Italian tomatoes
1 sprig fresh rosemary
4 tablespoons unsalted
**   butter**
flour for browning
3 tablespoons olive oil
1 cup dry white table wine
½ cup brandy
1½ cups Brown Stock
1 bay leaf
salt and pepper
2 teaspoons sugar
1 bunch parsley
a 6-qt casserole

1. When you purchase the veal shanks, have the butcher saw them into 2-inch thick pieces. Finely chop the onion, garlic, carrots, and celery. Zest the lemon and chop the zest finely. Coarsely chop the tomatoes. Finely chop the rosemary.

2. Melt the butter in a browning skillet and gently sauté the onion, garlic, celery, and carrot until softened—about 3 minutes. Transfer to the casserole. Sprinkle the vegetables with the lemon zest.

3. Dredge the veal shanks in flour and to the same skillet, add the olive oil. When the oil is hot, brown the shanks on all sides. Lay the shanks on top of the vegetables in the casserole.

4. Preheat the oven to 350°. Pour off any remaining fat in the skillet, and add the wine, brandy, stock, and tomatoes. Reduce by about ¼, scraping up any brown bits remaining in the pan.

5. Pour the braising liquid over the veal shanks; add the rosemary and bay leaf. Season with 2 teaspoons of salt and 1 teaspoon of pepper (or to taste), and the sugar. Cover and braise in the oven about 2 hours, or until the shanks are very tender.

6. Chop the parsley and garnish each serving with parsley.

Here is a "pot roast" of pork that is marinated for several days (like Sauerbraten) before it is braised. It is served with an unusual sauce made with raisins and pine nuts. The dish comes from Italy.

BRAISED PORK LOIN
Serves 6

½ medium onion
1 stalk celery
1 carrot
1 sprig fresh rosemary
1½ cups tarragon vinegar
1½ cups white table wine
6 tablespoons olive oil
12 juniper berries
2½ lbs. boneless pork loin
flour for browning
salt and pepper
Sauce for Pork Loin (see
   recipe below
a 4- to 6-qt. casserole

1. Chop the onion, celery, and carrot coarsely. Chop the rosemary finely. Combine the vinegar, wine, 2 tablespoons olive oil, the onion, celery, carrot, juniper berries, and rosemary.
2. Place the pork in a deep nonmetal dish and pour the marinade over all. Marinate 3 days, turning once each day.
3. Remove the meat from the marinade and wipe it dry with paper towels. Reserve the marinade. Heat 4 tablespoons olive oil in a browning skillet, dredge the meat in flour, and brown on all sides.
4. Preheat the oven to 375°. With a slotted spoon, transfer the vegetables from the marinade to the casserole. Place the browned meat on top of the vegetables, and pour in enough of the marinade to barely cover the meat and vegetables. Stir 1 teaspoon salt and 1 teaspoon of pepper (or to your taste) into the marinade in the casserole.
5. Cover the casserole and braise in the oven for 1½ to 2 hours, until tender. Serve the meat sliced with the following sauce.

Sauce for Pork Loin

2 tablespoons pine nuts
1 lemon
2 tablespoons
   Worcestershire sauce
2 tablespoons white raisins
1 teaspoon potato starch
1 cup Brown Stock
salt and pepper
a 1-qt. saucepan

1. Place the pine nuts on a baking sheet and toast for 5 minutes in a 350° oven. Zest the lemon and chop the zest finely. Squeeze the juice.
2. Place the lemon zest, lemon juice, Worcestershire sauce, and raisins in the saucepan. Dissolve the potato starch in the Brown Stock and add to the saucepan. Bring to a boil and simmer gently until slightly thickened. Add the toasted pine nuts and taste for seasoning—adding salt and pepper if necessary. To serve, spoon the sauce over the sliced pork.

Lamb Cacciatore is another classic "stew" from Italy. Notice that there are none of the usual aromatic vegetables in this braised dish and that the sauce is flavored with anchovies. Please try it—it is a favorite of my students.

LAMB CACCIATORE
Serves 8

3 lbs. boneless lamb
3 cloves garlic
3 fresh sage leaves
1 sprig fresh rosemary
flour for browning
4 tablespoons olive oil
salt and pepper
¾ cup Brown Stock
¼ cup red wine vinegar
6 anchovy fillets
a 6-qt. casserole

1. Cut the lamb into 2-inch cubes. Chop the garlic finely; chop the sage and rosemary.
2. Dredge the lamb in flour. Heat the olive oil in a skillet and brown the lamb on all sides. Sprinkle with salt and pepper and transfer to the casserole. Sprinkle the garlic, rosemary, and sage over the lamb.
3. Preheat the oven to 375°. Pour off any remaining fat in the skillet and add the stock and vinegar. Bring to a boil, scraping up any bits stuck to the bottom of the pan, and pour over the lamb in the casserole. Cover the casserole and braise in the oven until tender—about 1½ hours.
4. Mash the anchovies and combine with 4 tablespoons of the sauce. Return the anchovies to the casserole. Turn and mix the lamb well before serving.

Usually, ground meat loaves are baked. In this recipe, the loaf is braised, which makes it very juicy and produces a wonderful sauce. The rich flavor of the sauce comes in large part from the dried mushrooms. Dried mushrooms have an intense flavor, so they are only used in very small amounts, and must always be softened in liquid before they are added to a dish. Any one or a combination of the following mushrooms may be used: porcini, morel, cepe, chanterelle, or shiitake.

BRAISED MEAT LOAF WITH A WILD MUSHROOM SAUCE
Serves 6

1 oz. dried mushrooms (see above)
1 small onion
2 cloves garlic
2 slices prosciutto, $\frac{1}{16}$ inch thick
3 tablespoons milk
1 thick slice bread
2 oz. Parmesan
1 lb. ground beef
$\frac{1}{4}$ lb. ground pork
2 teaspoons salt
teaspoon pepper
1 egg yolk
fine dry bread crumbs (about 1 cup)
3 tablespoons olive oil
$\frac{3}{4}$ cup white table wine
2 tablespoons tomato paste
a 4-qt. clay casserole

1. Put the dried mushrooms in a bowl, pour 1 cup boiling water over them, and let them soak for 1 hour. Chop the onion, garlic, and prosciutto finely. Sprinkle the milk over the bread. Grate the cheese.
2. Place the beef, pork, bread, onion, prosciutto, salt, pepper, Parmesan, and garlic in a large mixing bowl. Combine all the ingredients thoroughly. Add the egg yolk and mix well.
3. Shape the meat into a compact salami-like loaf. Roll the loaf in the bread crumbs until it is evenly coated.
4. Drain the mushrooms, reserving the water in which they have been soaking, and chop them coarsely. Strain the mushroom liquid through a paper towel to eliminate any sand and set aside.
5. Preheat the oven to 375°. Heat the oil in a large skillet, and brown the loaf on all sides. Transfer to the casserole. Discard any remaining oil in the skillet, and add the wine and strained mushroom liquid. Boil briskly for 2 minutes, add the mushrooms and tomato paste, and stir. Pour this sauce over the meat loaf.
6. Cover and braise in the oven about 1 hour. Let the meat rest 30 minutes in the casserole before slicing and serving. Spoon a little sauce and some mushrooms over each serving.

In the next two dishes, the browning step is eliminated and the cooking time is brief, unlike the rest of the dishes in the lesson. Some years ago, I was lucky enough to be able to engage the wife of the Indian Consulate to teach a series of classes. Following are adaptations of two of her recipes, the most delicious curries I have ever tasted.

VEGETABLE CURRY
Serves 6 to 8

a 4-inch piece fresh ginger root
1 large onion
3 cloves garlic
1½ lbs. tomatoes
1 bunch cilantro
1 lb. peas
½ lb. green beans
1 small head cauliflower
2 large boiling potatoes
4 tablespoons clarified butter
salt and pepper
1 teaspoon ground cumin
½ teaspoon ground turmeric
½ teaspoon Hungarian paprika
¼ teaspoon cayenne pepper
2 cups White Stock
1 teaspoon curry powder

1. Peel and finely chop 3 tablespoons of ginger root. Chop the onion and garlic finely. Peel and chop the tomatoes. Rinse and chop the cilantro. Shell the peas and cut the green beans into 2-inch pieces. Separate the cauliflower into small florets, and peel and cut the potatoes into ½-inch dice.

2. In a sauté pan large enough to hold all the vegetables, heat the clarified butter. Add the onions and sauté until softened. Add 1 tablespoon of chopped ginger, 2 teaspoons salt, garlic, cumin, 1 tablespoon chopped cilantro, turmeric, paprika, cayenne pepper, and tomatoes. Simmer 2 minutes uncovered.

3. Add the potatoes and cauliflower and enough stock to cover. Add 1 teaspoon curry powder, bring to a boil, lower the heat, cover the pan, and simmer gently 5 minutes. Add the peas and green beans, and more stock if necessary. Cover and simmer until all vegetables are done—about 5 minutes more.

4. Taste the sauce and add more cilantro, ginger, curry powder, salt, or pepper as needed. Serve over Lime Saffron Rice (see page 99).

Note: Any vegetables may be substituted.

CHICKEN CURRY
Serves 6 to 8

6 half breasts of chicken
(about 3 lbs.)
1 lime
3 hard-cooked eggs
1 bunch cilantro
2 medium onions
3 cloves garlic
a 4-inch piece fresh ginger
root
¼ cup peanut oil
2 teaspoons curry powder
1 teaspoon ground cumin
1 teaspoon ground turmeric
¼ teaspoon ground fennel
1 teaspoon ground chili
peppers
salt
1 cup yogurt
½ cup Chicken Stock
1 tablespoon unsalted
butter
3 oz. whole raw cashews
(½ cup)
1 small bunch fresh mint
a 12-inch skillet or sauté
pan

1.   Have the butcher debone the chicken breasts, or do it yourself (see page 42). Either way, reserve the bones for stock. Cut the meat into ½-inch strips the length of the breast. Juice the lime. Chop the eggs. Remove and discard the lower stems of the cilantro and chop the remainder. Chop the onions and garlic. Peel and chop the ginger root—you will need at least a tablespoon of chopped ginger.

2.   Heat the oil in the skillet or sauté pan and sauté the onions for 2 minutes. Add the garlic, a tablespoon of chopped ginger, a tablespoon of chopped cilantro, curry powder, ground cumin, turmeric, fennel and chili peppers, salt, and yogurt. Add the stock and stir with a spoon until the mixture comes to a boil. Add the strips of chicken, cover the pot, and lower the heat; braise gently for 1 minute. Remove from the heat.

3.   In a small skillet, melt the butter, add the cashews and sauté 3 minutes. Add the lime juice and combine the lime cashew mixture with the chicken. Add more salt, curry powder, and cilantro to taste.

4.   Reheat to serve. Garnish each serving with mint leaves and chopped egg.

ROASTING AND BAKING

Roasting, or baking, is a method of cooking by dry heat. The two terms, roasting and baking, refer to the same process but each word is, by convention, used with certain foods. You would say, for instance, *roasted* lamb or turkey, but *baked* potatoes or meat loaf. In this chapter we discuss meats, poultry, and vegetables. Baked cakes, custards, breads, and pastries, will be dealt with in their respective chapters.

Many years ago, all roasting was done on a spit over an open fire. Today, most roasting is done in ovens. When the hot air of an oven first heats the food, the outermost layer is quickly cooked. Then, the food's own juices spread the heat inward to finish the cooking and allow the flavors of the food to develop fully. Meats and poultry to be roasted should be tender, so for this method of cooking, select young birds and tender meat cuts such as the ribs or tenderloins of beef, pork, etc.

ROASTING

Oven temperature   Roasting should be done in a hot oven, so that the outer food surfaces will brown as soon as possible and seal the juices inside. The smaller the food roasted, the hotter the oven can be—for example, a 2½-lb. chicken can be roasted from start to finish at 400°. However, if you try to cook a large turkey at a high temperature for the full cooking time, the outer surface will get too brown before the bird cooks at the center. You could roast a 25-lb. turkey at 425° for the first 30 minutes to brown it, but then you would lower the heat to 350° for the remainder of the cooking.

Trussing poultry   All birds that are roasted whole, either stuffed or un-stuffed, need to be trussed or tied up. When the bird is trussed, the legs and wings are held close to the body, which keeps the meat succulent and moist. A trussed bird is also easier to turn and more attractive to serve.

Basting   Basting means to spoon liquid over the food. By periodically moistening the food while it is roasting, an outer crust that is nicely browned and crisp will develop. Roasted meats and poultry, when not on a spit, need to be basted often with liquids, and if the meat or poultry being roasted is lean, fat needs to be added to the basting liquid. Basting may be done with a bulb baster or a large serving spoon. If the basting liquid evaporates, it should be replaced.

Testing for doneness   Properly roasted meat or poultry should be well browned on the outside and tender and juicy on the inside, whether it is to be served rare or well done. The degree of rareness depends on personal taste and on the variety of meat or poultry. Follow recipes as guides for cooking times. If you use a meat thermometer, follow the printed guide on the thermometer. Or, you may wish to learn to tell when meats are done by the way they feel. Touch the meat raw, and again after 10 minutes or so of cooking. You will notice that the softer it feels, the rarer it is. Another test for doneness is to insert a skewer into the thickest part of the meat—the juices that run out will be pink for rare and colorless for well done. If you find that the breast of a poultry is browning too fast, cover the bird loosely with foil.

Standing   Always allow time for the roasted meat or poultry to stand covered loosely with foil for at least 20 minutes (longer for birds or roasts over 10 pounds). This allows the juices to be reabsorbed by the tissues so the meat will be juicy. Otherwise, the juices run out and the slices of meat or poultry become dry and rubbery.

Pan gravies   During roasting, the basting liquid and the juices from the poultry or meat will drip into the roasting pan and the result is a wonderful sauce foundation. You can skim off the fat and use the juices as they are or enhance them with stock, herbs, wine, cream, etc. They may be combined with a velouté sauce (see page 72, 73), egg yolks, or butter. A pan gravy (see page 76), is always served over the sliced, roasted meats or poultry from which it is derived.

This same basic method may be used to roast any bird from a squab to a goose.

PERFECT ROAST CHICKEN
Serves 4

a 2½- to 3-lb. chicken
salt and pepper
paprika
1 small onion
6 tablespoons unsalted
 butter
trussing string
an open roaster (preferably
 clay) and rack

1.   Sprinkle the inside of the chicken with salt, pepper, and paprika. Peel the onion and place it in the body cavity. Put 2 tablespoons of butter inside the bird and truss the bird (see pages 44-46).

2.   Melt the remaining butter. With a brush, spread the butter over the skin of the bird. Sprinkle the bird liberally with salt, pepper, and paprika.

3.   Lay the bird on its side on the rack in the roasting pan. Pour ⅓ cup water into the pan and roast the chicken in a preheated 425° oven until done (a 2½-lb. chicken roasted at 425° in a clay roasting dish is cooked after approximately 1 hour and 5 minutes).

4.   Midway through the cooking, turn the bird onto its other side. Baste at least 2 times with liquid from the bottom of the pan. Add more liquid if necessary.

5.   Allow the chicken to stand at least 20 minutes before carving.

All birds can be roasted without a stuffing, but by adding a stuffing you not only flavor the meat but help keep it moist and juicy, too. Place some of the stuffing under the skin of the breast, and the breast of the bird will be self-basting.

HERBED STUFFED ROASTED CHICKEN
Serves 6

a 4-lb. chicken
1 chicken liver
1 medium onion
2 stalks celery
4 tablespoons unsalted
  butter
3 oz. pecans (½ cup)
1 small apple
4 sprigs fresh oregano
2 sprigs fresh thyme
4 fresh sage leaves
6 oz. croûtons, cubed (2
  cups) (see page 67)
salt and pepper
¾ cup crème fraîche
½ cup Chicken Stock
olive oil
trussing string and needle
a clay roaster and rack

1.   Remove the neck and giblets from the chicken. Chop the chicken liver; chop the onion and celery finely. Melt the butter in a skillet and sauté the liver, onion, and celery for 5 minutes. Transfer to a large bowl. Toast the pecans (see page 18) and chop them coarsely. Peel, core, and chop the apple. Remove and discard the stems from the fresh herbs and chop the leaves finely.
2.   Add the croûtons to the chicken liver mixture; add the herbs, nuts, and apple. Season to taste with salt and pepper. Add the crème fraîche and stock, and toss the stuffing with your hands until the mixture is moist and holds together. Taste again for seasoning and correct.
3.   Loosen the skin of the chicken, starting at the neck and working over the breast, thighs, and drumsticks. Sew any tears in the skin, and salt and pepper the body cavity lightly. Work the stuffing under the skin, reserving half for the body cavity. Stuff the body ¾ full, leaving enough room for the stuffing to expand. (Any remaining stuffing can be heated in a casserole.) Sew up the opening and truss the bird for roasting (see pages 44-46).
4.   Brush olive oil over the skin and sprinkle with salt and pepper. Place the bird on its side on the rack in the roasting pan. Pour ½ cup water in the pan and roast the chicken at 400° approximately 2 hours. Halfway through the cooking turn the chicken on its other side. Baste several times, replacing the basting liquid if necessary.
5.   Allow the chicken to stand at least 20 minutes before removing the stuffing and carving.
Note: Any fresh herbs in this recipe may be replaced by ¼ teaspoon dry herbs.

The following roasted chicken has an unusual stuffing that contains an Italian almond cookie (amaretti) available in supermarkets and Italian delicatessens.

ROAST CHICKEN WITH A NUT STUFFING
Serves 8

a 6-lb. chicken or capon
1 carrot
2 stalks celery
1 small onion
¼ bunch parsley
1 bay leaf

¾ lb. shelled walnuts
   (1½ cups)
6 amaretti cookies
¼ lb. Parmesan
6 juniper berries
¾ cup crème fraîche
2 oz. dry bread crumbs
   (¾ cup)
¼ lb. unsalted butter
5 egg yolks
½ teaspoon pepper
¼ teaspoon each grated
   nutmeg and ground
   cloves

olive oil
salt and pepper
paprika
Giblet Pan Gravy (see
   recipe below)
a clay roaster and rack

1.   Remove the neck, wing tips, and giblets from the chicken, reserving the liver for another use. Make a stock with the chicken parts and the carrot, celery, onion, parsley, and bay leaf. Strain the stock; chop the giblets and neck meat. Reserve the stock and chopped meats for the gravy (recipe follows).

2.   Spread the walnuts out on a baking sheet and place in a 325° oven for 10 minutes; chop finely. Crush the amaretti (in a food processor or blender, or with a rolling pin), and grate the cheese. Chop the juniper berries. In a bowl, mix together the walnuts, crème fraîche, bread crumbs, amaretti, butter, egg yolks, pepper, freshly grated nutmeg, ground cloves, juniper berries, and grated Parmesan. Mix well with your hands, taste, and correct seasoning. Loosely stuff the chicken with the mixture, about ¾ full, and put any extra stuffing in a covered ovenproof casserole. Sew or skewer the neck and body openings closed.

3.   Preheat the oven to 375°. Truss the chicken for roasting (see pages 44-46), brush with olive oil, sprinkle with salt, pepper, and paprika. Roast approximately 2½ hours, basting every 45 minutes. Halfway through the cooking turn the bird on its other side.

4.   Allow the chicken to stand at least 30 minutes before removing stuffing and carving. Serve with Giblet Pan Gravy.

Giblet Pan Gravy

4 tablespoons unsalted
   butter
1 tablespoon potato flour
2 cups stock or defatted pan
   juices
½ cup white table wine
¼ cup cognac or brandy
½ teaspoon dry thyme
reserved giblets and neck
   meat
salt and pepper

1.   Melt the butter in a heavy saucepan, add the potato flour, and stir until dissolved. Add 2 cups giblet stock and/or pan juices, wine, cognac or brandy, and thyme.

2.   Cook over a low heat until the sauce thickens. If the sauce becomes too thick, add a little more stock.

3.   Add the chopped giblets and neck meat and salt and pepper to your taste. Reheat when ready to serve.

The following recipe is excellent for lamb, pork, or veal. If you are serving the meat hot, the defatted pan juices are all that is called for in a sauce. These roasts are also wonderful served at room temperature, sliced and arranged on a platter surrounded with long sprigs of fresh rosemary for garnish. Mustard or Mayonnaise (see page 86) may be served with the cold meats.

ROAST PORK WITH ROSEMARY AND GARLIC
Serves 8

a 4-lb. center pork loin*
4 sprigs fresh rosemary
1 head of garlic
salt and pepper
trussing string
a roasting pan and rack

1.   Have the butcher bone the meat and weigh it so you can calculate roasting time. Strip the rosemary sprigs, discard the stems, set aside 8 leaves, and chop the remainder. Peel and crush 8 (or more) cloves of garlic.

2.   Lay the meat out flat and sprinkle it with ½ teaspoon salt, ½ teaspoon pepper, 1 tablespoon chopped rosemary leaves, and 4 cloves of crushed garlic. Roll the meat and tie it securely. Make 4 incisions in the top of the roast, and insert 2 whole rosemary leaves and 1 clove of garlic in each. Sprinkle with salt and pepper.

3.   Place on the rack of a roasting pan, pour enough water in the pan to barely cover the bottom, and roast in a preheated 375° oven about 30 minutes per pound or until a meat thermometer registers 160°. Baste 3 times throughout the roasting period using the juices that accumulate in the bottom of the pan, adding more water if necessary.

4.   Allow to stand 30 minutes before carving.

(**A veal sirloin or leg of lamb may be substituted. Reduce the cooking time if you prefer the meat rare.*)

The following meat loaf is unusual because the ground meat is wrapped around a stuffing of sausage, cheese, and eggs.

"STUFFED" MEAT LOAF
Serves 8 to 10

½ bunch parsley
6 fresh basil leaves
1 lb. Italian sausage
¼ lb. Parmesan
3 eggs
3 lbs. ground beef
3 oz. dry bread crumbs (1 cup)
1¼ teaspoon salt
1¼ teaspoon pepper
olive oil
4 hard-cooked eggs
4 slices Provolone, ⅛ inch thick
Basic Tomato Sauce (see page 78)
a 14-inch roasting pan

1.   Chop the parsley and basil; boil the sausage. Grate the Parmesan cheese; beat the eggs.
2.   Combine the ground beef, bread crumbs, basil, 4 tablespoons of the chopped parsley, the beaten eggs, half the Parmesan, and 1 teaspoon each of salt and pepper.
3.   Lightly oil a cutting board, place the meat mixture on it and flatten it out into a large rectangle, about ½ inch thick. Place the sausage on the meat, the hard-cooked eggs between the sausages, and the sliced cheese over all. Sprinkle the remaining Parmesan cheese, and ¼ teaspoon each salt and pepper over the Provolone, and carefully roll the meat until you have a firm tubular roll.
4.   Transfer the meat loaf to a roasting pan and bake in a preheated 400° oven for 45 minutes. Reduce heat to 350° and bake an additional 20 minutes.
5.   Allow to stand 20 minutes before slicing. Serve with Basic Tomato Sauce.

SPICY BEEF RIBS
Serves 4 to 6

1 small onion
3 cloves garlic
¼ cup fresh lemon juice
½ cup olive oil
4 tablespoons Dijon mustard
2 dry chili peppers
3 lbs. beef short ribs
salt and pepper
cayenne pepper
a roasting pan and rack

1.   Chop the onion and garlic finely. Combine the onion, garlic, lemon juice, olive oil, mustard, and chili peppers, and mix well.
2.   Pour the marinade over the short ribs and marinate overnight.
3.   Drain the ribs and place them on a rack in a roasting pan, fat side up. Sprinkle with salt, pepper, and a little cayenne.
4.   Roast in a preheated 400° oven 30 minutes. Reduce the heat to 350° and roast 1 hour more, or until meat is tender. Serve warm.

PERFECT ROAST BEEF
Serves 8 to 10

a 5-lb. beef rib or sirloin tip
  roast
coarse salt
freshly ground pepper
1 cup crème fraîche
4 tablespoons prepared
  horseradish
a roasting pan

1.   Place the roast on its bones, fat side up, in a roasting pan. Sprinkle with salt and pepper.
2.   Roast in a preheated 375° oven 17 minutes per pound for rare meat or a reading of 120° on a meat thermometer.
3.   Allow the roast to stand at least 20 minutes before carving.
4.   Combine the crème fraîche and horseradish to serve with the roasted beef.

This eggplant is marvelous served as an accompaniment to roasted leg of lamb.

BAKED STUFFED EGGPLANT
Serves 6

1 medium eggplant
salt
4 tablespoons olive oil
2 oz. pitted black olives
1 clove garlic
6 anchovy fillets
¼ teaspoon dry thyme
pepper
a baking sheet
a baking dish

1.   Cut the eggplant in half lengthwise—do not remove the stem.
2.   Using a curved, serrated knife, remove the flesh, being careful not to break the skin, leaving a shell about ¼ inch thick. Cut the flesh into cubes, sprinkle with salt, and drain on paper towels for 30 minutes. Sprinkle the shells with salt and turn upside down on paper towels to drain for 30 minutes.
3.   Preheat the oven to 400°. Oil the baking dish with a tablespoon of oil; wipe the eggplant cubes dry and place in the baking dish. Grease the baking sheet with a tablespoon of oil; wipe out the eggplant shells and place them on the baking sheet. Bake the shells 15 minutes, and the cubes 25 minutes.
4.   Chop the olives and garlic finely. Heat the remaining oil in a skillet. Add the anchovies and crush them with a fork. As soon as they have dissolved into a paste, remove them from the heat and mix in the garlic and olives.
5.   Mash the eggplant cubes and combine with the anchovies, garlic, olives, and thyme. Add freshly ground pepper to taste.
6.   Stuff the eggplant shells with the filling. Return the eggplants to a 350° oven for 10 minutes, or until heated through. Serve hot. (Up to the point of the final reheating, the eggplant can be prepared several hours in advance.)

The following recipe serves as a model for any kind of hash. Use your imagination and create your own. For example, you may use beef instead of lamb, and oregano instead of mint. Hashes are fun, since they allow you complete creative freedom. Generally, hash is made with already cooked meat—and then baked, thereby combining several cooking methods.

LAMB HASH
Serves 6 to 8

1 lb. boneless cooked lamb
1 lb. boiling potatoes
1 large onion
2 cloves garlic
1 green bell pepper
1 jalapeño pepper
6 fresh mint leaves
2 oz. Parmesan
3 tablespoons unsalted
  butter
1 tablespoon olive oil
2 tablespoons soy sauce
¼ cup Brown Stock
  concentrate
salt and pepper
Basic Tomato Sauce (see
  page 78)
a 4-qt. ovenproof casserole

1.   Chop the lamb coarsely. Peel and boil the potatoes and cut them into dice. Chop the onion, garlic, and green pepper. Cut off the stem and seed and chop the jalapeño; chop the mint leaves. Grate the Parmesan cheese.
2.   Heat the butter and oil in a skillet, and sauté the onion and garlic 1 minute—add the lamb and continue to cook until lightly browned.
3.   Preheat the oven to 375°. Remove the lamb mixture from the heat and add all the remaining ingredients—mix well and add salt and pepper to taste. Transfer to the casserole and bake until the top of hash is brown and crisp—about 20 minutes.
4.   Serve with Basic Tomato Sauce.

GRATINS

Gratin means crust, so all dishes prepared "au gratin" have a crust whether the dish has been simply sprinkled with bread crumbs or cheese and placed under the broiler, covered with a cheese custard and baked, or steeped in cream and baked as in the recipe below.

POTATO GRATIN

Serves 8

2 lbs. boiling potatoes
1 clove garlic
½ lb. unsalted butter
salt and pepper
2½ cups light cream
a 12-inch gratin dish

1.   Peel and slice the potatoes thinly—about ⅛ inch thick. Rinse and dry them. Cut the garlic clove in half, rub the inside of the dish with it, and discard. Use a little of the butter to grease the inside of the dish and layer the potatoes in overlapping rows, salting and peppering each layer as you go.
2.   Preheat the oven to 325°. Cut the remaining butter into small pieces and dot the potatoes with them. Pour the cream over all. Bake about 1½ hours, until the potatoes are tender and the cream has formed a pale brown crust over the surface. Let rest at least 10 minutes before serving.

EGGPLANT GRATIN
Serves 8

1 large eggplant
salt
1½ lbs. tomatoes
1 medium onion
1 clove garlic
12 fresh basil leaves
1 teaspoon each green,
   white, and black
   peppercorns
2 oz. Parmesan
1 cup olive oil
½ cup ricotta
1 egg
1½ cups crème fraîche
a 12-inch gratin dish

1.   Peel the eggplant and cut lengthwise into ¼-inch thick slices—sprinkle with salt and allow the eggplant to stand 30 minutes. Wipe the slices with paper towels. Peel, seed, and coarsely chop the tomatoes. Peel and chop the onion; chop the garlic and basil leaves. Grind the peppercorns; grate the Parmesan.

2.   Preheat the oven to 350°. Brush a baking sheet with olive oil; place the eggplant slices on it and brush the eggplant with oil. Bake until soft—about 30 minutes.

3.   In a skillet, heat 2 tablespoons of olive oil and sauté the onion, garlic, and tomato until most of the tomato liquid disappears. Season with some of the combined freshly ground peppercorns and a little salt to taste.

4.   Combine the ricotta, egg, crème fraîche, and half the Parmesan, to create a thick custard to pour over the eggplant.

5.   Preheat the oven to 450°. Arrange half the eggplant slices in the bottom of the gratin dish. Sprinkle with some of the combined ground peppers and half the chopped basil.

6.   Spread the tomato mixture over the eggplant— sprinkle with the remainder of the basil and peppers. Cover with the rest of the eggplant and pour on the cheese and cream mixture. Sprinkle the remainder of the Parmesan over the top.

7.   Bake for 10 minutes at 450°, then reduce the oven temperature to 350° and bake approximately 20 minutes more, until the surface is golden brown and puffed.

This gratin combines meat, pasta, and vegetables, and may serve as a complete meal in one dish. It is my adaptation of a Greek dish.

PASTA, EGGPLANT, AND LAMB GRATIN
Serves 8

2 medium onions
4 cloves garlic
2 lbs. tomatoes
½ lb. elbow macaroni
3 oz. Parmesan
1 large eggplant
salt
½ cup olive oil
¼ lb. unsalted butter
1 lb. ground lamb
½ teaspoon dry oregano
pepper
7 eggs
3 tablespoons flour
3½ cups milk
1½ cups ricotta
a 14-inch gratin dish

1.   Peel and chop the onions and garlic. Chop the tomatoes coarsely. Cook and drain the pasta; toss it with 1 tablespoon of the olive oil. Grate the Parmesan cheese.

2.   Peel and slice the eggplant into ¼-inch thick slices. Sprinkle with salt and drain on paper towels 30 minutes. After 30 minutes, wipe dry with paper towels, place on an oiled baking sheet, brush with oil, and bake in a preheated 375° oven for 30 minutes.

3.   Grease the gratin dish with 2 tablespoons of butter.

4.   Melt 3 tablespoons of butter in a large skillet and sauté the lamb, onions, and garlic for 5 minutes. Add the chopped tomatoes, the oregano, and salt and pepper to taste. Simmer 5 minutes or until most of the liquid has evaporated. Beat 3 of the eggs and combine with the grated Parmesan. Add the Parmesan-egg mixture to the meat.

5.   Combine the cooked pasta and meat mixture, and transfer to the buttered gratin dish. Place the eggplant slices over the meat mixture.

6.   Preheat the oven to 350°. In a saucepan, melt the remaining 3 tablespoons of butter. Add the flour and cook over low heat 2 minutes, stirring constantly. Add the milk and cook over low heat, stirring occasionally, until the mixture begins to thicken, about 10 minutes. Remove this white sauce from the heat. Beat the remaining 4 eggs and combine them with the ricotta. Stirring constantly, combine the white sauce and the ricotta-egg mixture. Mix well and pour over the eggplant.

7.   Sprinkle with the remaining Parmesan, and bake for 30 minutes or until the custard is puffed and brown. Let stand 30 minutes before serving.

SAUTÉING AND DEEP-FRYING

Sautéing, or pan-frying, as it is commonly called, is the absolute opposite cooking method of stewing or braising. When foods are sautéed, they are cooked quickly and without liquids, producing food with an outer firmness and an inner tenderness and succulence. Only very tender foods are suitable for sautéing—lean fish, young chicken, the tenderloin or rib chops of red meats, liver, ground meat patties, onions, mushrooms, and so on. Since sautéed food can be cooked so quickly—often in as little as two or three minutes—it is a good idea to have the rest of the meal ready to serve as soon as the sauté is finished.

Sautéed foods may be served just as they come from the pan, without a sauce, or, as often as not, with a deglazed sauce (that is, a sauce based on the pan juices—see page 77).

The fat you use for sautéing or pan-frying is a matter of personal preference. You might let the national origin of your dish determine what you use. For example, olive oil is preferred in Italy, Greece, and Spain; butter is preferred in France, Germany, and Holland. Clarified butter, olive oil, hazelnut oil, almond oil, and walnut oil are all excellent for sautéing. Sauces for sautéed foods are often finished with butter, even if another oil was used for the sautéing.

Whatever kind of food you sauté, the basic technique is the same: Begin with a hot pan and a small amount of hot butter or oil, sear the food on each side to seal the outside surfaces, then, depending on how thick the food is, lower the heat to finish the cooking. If the food is very thin, like veal scallops, the minute or so it takes to brown each side is sufficient to cook the meat as well. Generally speaking, the food to be sautéed should be at room temperature and the recipe will often call for it to be dredged in flour before it is sautéed, to allow an even browning.

Ideally, the frying pan, skillet, or sauté pan should not be deeper than 2 inches and the sides may slant out or be straight. Tin-lined copper, anodized aluminum, and cast iron work well if the metal is thick enough. Because sautéing is done over high heat, a thin pan may overcook the food or burn the outside of the food before it is done. The pan must be large enough to accommodate all the food without overlapping, since that would trap the juices and stew or steam the food instead of frying it.

The following recipe is a typical sauté with a deglazed sauce. The shortness of the cooking time is dependent on the chicken breasts being deboned and filleted or sliced very thin. Any apéritif-dessert wine may be substituted for the sherry.

CHICKEN BREAST FILLETS WITH A WINE CREAM SAUCE
Serves 6

6 half breasts of chicken
½ bunch parsley
flour
4 tablespoons unsalted
  butter
¾ cup concentrated White
  Stock
½ cup sherry
¾ cup white table wine
1 cup crème fraîche
salt and pepper
a 10-inch skillet or sauté
  pan

1. Skin, debone, and fillet each half breast (see pages 42-43), cutting each into 3 pieces. Chop enough parsley so that you will have about 4 tablespoons.

2. Heat the butter in the skillet. Lightly flour the chicken fillets and sauté them over high heat 30 seconds each side. Remove the fillets from the pan, cover, and set aside until ready to serve. (Covered so they will not dry out, the chicken will hold nicely for 2 or 3 hours.)

3. Pour off any butter remaining in the pan, add the concentrated stock and both wines, and reduce by half. Add the crème fraîche and continue to reduce further, until the sauce is thick enough to just cling to the food.

4. Taste the sauce and add salt and pepper as needed. Add the chopped parsley to the sauce. Just before serving, gently heat the fillets in the sauce. Each serving should be a half breast (3 fillets) with 2 or 3 tablespoons of sauce.

The delicious and unusual sauce served with the following sautéed chicken is a form of Hollandaise. Before making this dish you should review Hollandaise Sauce (see page 84).

CHICKEN BREAST FILLETS WITH A DIJON MUSTARD SAUCE
Serves 6

6 half breasts of chicken
½ bunch parsley
4 sprigs fresh tarragon
2 shallots
½ lb. unsalted butter
flour
¼ cup white table wine
¼ cup Chicken Stock
¼ cup brandy
2 tablespoons tomato paste
2 tablespoons Dijon mustard
4 egg yolks
salt and pepper
a double boiler
a 10-inch skillet or sauté pan

1. Skin, debone, and fillet each half breast (see pages 42-43), cutting each into 3 pieces. Discard the parsley stems, and chop enough parsley leaves so that you will have about 4 tablespoons. Remove and discard the tarragon stems and chop the leaves. Chop the shallots.
2. Heat 4 tablespoons butter in the skillet. Lightly flour the chicken fillets and sauté them over high heat, 30 seconds each side. Remove to a platter.
3. Pour off any butter remaining in the pan. Add the shallots, wine, stock, brandy, and tomato paste to the skillet and stir to combine. Over moderate heat, reduce the sauce by about half. Strain out the shallots, and add the mustard, chopped tarragon, and parsley to the sauce.
4. Cut the remaining butter into 12 pieces. In the top of a double boiler, whisk the egg yolks. Over a medium heat, whisking constantly, add the pieces of butter to the egg yolks, in three parts, alternating with the tomato sauce mixture. Whisk the sauce until it is as smooth and thick as whipped cream. Taste for seasoning, and add salt and pepper as needed. (The sauce and chicken may be held for 2 or 3 hours before serving.)
5. When ready to serve, warm the breasts in the oven and the sauce in the double boiler. Each serving should be a half breast (3 fillets) with several table-spoons of sauce spooned over all.

The following chicken breast dish begins with a sauté and is finished in the oven.

CHICKEN BREASTS WITH PARMESAN AND PROSCIUTTO
Serves 6

6 half breasts of chicken
2 oz. Parmesan
6 tablespoons unsalted
  butter
flour
salt and pepper
¾ cup dry Marsala
½ cup Chicken Stock
½ cup dry white table wine
6 thin slices prosciutto
a 10-inch skillet or sauté
  pan
a 10-inch clay roaster

1. Skin and debone the chicken breasts (see page 42). Grate the Parmesan.
2. Heat 4 tablespoons butter in the skillet. Lightly flour the chicken breasts, and sauté 4 minutes each side. Season with salt and pepper and transfer to the clay roaster in a single layer.
3. Pour off any butter still remaining in the skillet and add the Marsala, stock, and wine. Over a moderate heat, reduce the mixture by half.
4. Sprinkle the cheese over the breasts, and place a slice of prosciutto over each—if the ham is too large, fold so that it fits. Sprinkle the reduced Marsala sauce over all and dot each breast with butter. Cover the dish with foil.
5. Place the dish in a 375° oven for 10 minutes or until the cheese melts. To serve, spoon a little sauce over each portion.

When pan-frying chicken with the bone in, a longer cooking time is required than with boneless chicken fillets; however, you cannot use a high heat the entire time, since the chicken would probably burn on the outside before it is cooked on the inside. To allow for this, a combination of frying techniques is used in this recipe.

PAN-FRIED CHICKEN
Serves 4 to 6

a 3-lb. chicken
¼ lb. flour (¾ cup)
salt and pepper
about ½ cup milk
½ cup clarified butter
a 12-inch skillet or sauté
  pan

1. Cut the chicken into 8 pieces (see page 40). Combine the flour, 1 teaspoon salt, and ½ teaspoon pepper in a plastic bag. Pour the milk into a bowl.
2. Dip the chicken pieces in the milk. One by one, shake the pieces in the bag of flour so that they are well coated with flour.
3. Melt the butter in the pan, and, over high heat, brown the chicken quickly on each side. Lower the heat, and cook the chicken covered, about 15 minutes.
4. Remove the cover, raise the heat, and let the chicken crisp for about 3 minutes each side. Sprinkle with additional salt and pepper. Serve warm or at room temperature.

This has become a classic dish and serves as a perfect example of a sauté with a deglazed sauce. Green peppercorns are available freeze-dried or packed in brine. For this dish, the ones in brine are preferred.

STEAK WITH A GREEN PEPPERCORN SAUCE
Serves 6

2 shallots
4 teaspoons green
peppercorns in brine
¼ cup clarified butter
6 sirloin steaks
¼ cup cognac
½ cup Brown Stock
¼ cup Madeira
½ cup red table wine
1 teaspoon Dijon mustard
salt and pepper
½ cup crème fraîche
a 12-inch skillet or sauté
pan

1. Peel and chop the shallots. Rinse the peppercorns in water, and crush them with the back of a spoon. Heat the butter in the skillet and sauté the steaks 2 minutes each side over high heat. Transfer to a platter.
2. Pour out any butter remaining in the skillet and add the shallots, cognac, stock, Madeira, and red wine. Cook over moderate heat until reduced by half. Add the crushed peppercorns, mustard, and salt and pepper to taste. Stir in the crème fraîche and reduce by half once again.
3. When ready to serve, put the steaks into the sauce and reheat about 1 minute. Each serving should be accompanied by 3 tablespoons sauce.

The procedure for making this dish is identical to that for the preceding one, but the two dishes taste completely different. The olive oil, tomato paste, and Marsala reveal the Italian origins of this dish.

STEAK WITH A PIQUANT TOMATO SAUCE
Serves 6

2 cloves garlic
½ bunch parsley
4 tablespoons olive oil
6 sirloin steaks
salt and pepper
¾ cup Marsala
¾ cup red table wine
2 tablespoons tomato paste
¼ teaspoon cayenne pepper
a 12-inch skillet or sauté
pan

1. Chop the garlic finely. Remove and discard the parsley stems and chop the leaves. Heat the olive oil in the skillet and sauté the steaks 2 minutes each side over high heat. Season with salt and pepper and transfer to a platter.
2. Pour out any oil remaining in the pan, being careful not to lose any of the meat drippings.
3. With the heat still on high, add the Marsala and red wine, and boil while scraping up the drippings stuck to the pan. Reduce by half. Add the garlic, tomato paste, and cayenne. Reduce by half once again. Add salt and pepper to taste and more cayenne if desired.
4. When ready to serve, reheat the sauce, return the steaks to the sauce, and heat about 1 minute—until warm. Serve each steak with 2 or 3 tablespoons of sauce. Sprinkle chopped parsley over each serving.

The following recipe is basically our familiar hamburger, but the anchovies, tomatoes, and cheese give it a little different twist. Because of those additions, no sauce is required.

BEEF PATTIES WITH ANCHOVIES, CHEESE, AND TOMATOES
Serves 6

½ bunch parsley
2 large tomatoes
½ lb. mozzarella
¼ cup milk
2 slices white bread
4 tablespoons olive oil
2 lbs. ground beef
1 egg
2 teaspoons salt
1 teaspoon dry oregano
1 teaspoon pepper
2 oz. dry bread crumbs
 (¾ cup)
12 anchovies
a 10-inch skillet
a 12-inch baking dish

1. Discard the parsley stems and chop the leaves. Slice off the top and bottom of each tomato and cut those end pieces of tomato into about ¼ inch wide strips (to be used for garnish). Cut 6 slices of tomato, each ¼ inch thick. Cut the mozzarella into 6 slices, each ¼ inch thick. Sprinkle the milk over the sliced white bread and crumble it up. Grease the baking dish with 1 teaspoon of olive oil.
2. In a large mixing bowl, place the beef, egg, salt, crumbled bread, oregano, and pepper. Mix well and form into 6 patties. Coat each patty with dry bread crumbs and set aside.
3. Heat the remaining oil in the skillet and sauté the patties over high heat 2 minutes each side. Transfer to the baking dish.
4. Place a slice of tomato over each patty and a slice of cheese over the tomato. Over the cheese place a crisscross of anchovies with a strip of tomato in the center.
5. Heat in a 350° oven 10 minutes, or until the cheese melts. Serve hot.

This is a very simple version of a classic dish. We are deglazing the pan with Marsala only. If you want a richer sauce, ½ cup crème fraîche could be added.

VEAL SCALLOPS WITH A MARSALA SAUCE
Serves 6

2 lbs. veal scallops
½ bunch parsley
4 tablespoons clarified
   butter
flour
salt and pepper
¾ cup Marsala
3 tablespoons cold unsalted
   butter
a 12-inch skillet or sauté
   pan

1. If the scallops were not pounded by the butcher, you will need to place them between two pieces of waxed paper and hit them lightly with a meat pounder until thin. Then snip the outer membrane with a scissors two or three times around the edge of each scallop. This will keep them from curling up when they are sautéed. Remove the parsley stems and chop the parsley leaves.

2. Melt the clarified butter in the skillet and when it is hot, dredge the scallops in the flour and sauté 1 minute each side. Transfer the meat to a platter and season with salt and pepper.

3. Pour off any oil left in the pan and, over a high heat, add the Marsala. Reduce the sauce by half, scraping up any brown bits left clinging to the pan with your deglazing spatula. When the sauce is reduced, turn off the heat and swirl in the cold butter.

4. Return the veal scallops to the sauce, reheat 1 minute, and serve the veal with the sauce, garnished with chopped parsley.

This is another classic dish and a good example of a breaded sauté.

WIENER SCHNITZEL
Serves 6

6 veal cutlets (leg)
4 hard-cooked eggs
3 lemons
2 eggs
1½ teaspoons salt
3 oz. bread crumbs (1 cup)
5 oz. flour (1 cup)
1 teaspoon pepper
½ cup clarified butter
12 anchovies
2 tablespoons capers
a 12-inch skillet or sauté
   pan

1. The cutlets should be between ¼ and ½ inch thick. Slice the hard-cooked eggs with an egg slicer. Cut the lemons in half.

2. Break the 2 remaining eggs into a wide bowl, add ½ teaspoon salt and mix well with a fork. On a large plate, combine the bread crumbs, flour, pepper, and remaining teaspoon of salt.

3. Dip the cutlets in the raw egg and then into the crumb mixture. Let stand uncovered in the refrigerator for 1 hour so the coating dries.

4. Heat the butter in the skillet and sauté the cutlets over medium heat 5 minutes each side. Garnish each cutlet with 3 slices of hard-cooked egg, a crisscross of anchovies, and a few capers. Serve the half lemon on the side.

In this veal sauté, we are again combining methods. The pancetta and cheese eliminate the need for a sauce.

VEAL RIB CHOPS WITH PANCETTA AND FONTINA

Serves 6

2 sprigs fresh rosemary
2 eggs
1½ teaspoons salt
1½ teaspoons pepper
5 oz. flour (1 cup)
3 oz. bread crumbs (1 cup)
6 veal rib chops
½ cup clarified butter
¼ cup white table wine
¼ cup brandy
6 slices Italian Fontina
6 slices pancetta (or bacon)
a 10-inch skillet or sauté
pan
a 10-inch baking dish

1. Remove and discard the rosemary stems and chop the leaves.
2. Break the eggs into a wide bowl, add ½ teaspoon each salt and pepper, and beat lightly. On a large plate, combine the flour, bread crumbs, and 1 teaspoon each pepper and salt. Dip the rib chops in the egg and then in the seasoned crumbs. Let stand 1 hour uncovered in the refrigerator, so the coating dries.
3. Heat the butter in the skillet and sauté the cutlets over medium heat 3 minutes each side. Transfer to the baking dish.
4. Pour off any butter remaining in the pan and deglaze the pan with the wine and brandy. Reduce the liquid by half, and add the chopped rosemary. Spoon the sauce over the rib chops. Place a slice of Fontina and a slice of pancetta on each chop. (If you wish, the dish can be made ahead to this point.) When you are ready to serve, bake in a preheated 375° oven 10 minutes to melt the cheese and warm the chops.

Any vegetable, (such as cauliflower, broccoli, zucchini, etc.) may be substituted in this dish. Because the vegetables are cooked so quickly, you must constantly toss everything so that all will be evenly cooked. For a medley of vegetables, it is important to cut everything the same size, for eye appeal and so that different vegetables will cook evenly. Even then, you should begin with vegetables that take longest to cook.

SAUTÉED VEGETABLES
Serves 8

½ lb. green beans
8 mushrooms
6 tiny artichokes
3 stalks celery
6 green onions
¼ cup walnut, hazelnut, or
  almond oil
¼ bunch parsley
2 cloves garlic
salt and pepper
a 12-inch skillet or sauté
  pan

1.   Slice (or julienne) the green beans, mushrooms, artichokes, celery ribs, and green onions uniformly.
2.   Heat the oil in the pan. Add the beans first and toss them 3 or 4 minutes over medium-high heat. Add the artichokes, celery, green onions, and mushrooms. Shake and toss the vegetables for 3 or 4 minutes until all are tender but crisp.
3.   Remove and discard the parsley stems and chop the leaves; chop the garlic. Season the vegetables to taste with salt and pepper and toss with the parsley and garlic. Serve immediately.

For pan-frying, if you shred vegetables instead of slicing them, the shreds will cook quickly, as in these pancakes. For variety, grated cheese or chopped herbs can be added to the potatoes. The coarse grater on either a hand grater or food processor is the best way to prepare the potatoes for pancakes.

POTATO PANCAKES
Makes about 20 pancakes

2 lbs. baking potatoes
1 small onion
3½ oz. flour (⅔ cup)
2 eggs
2 teaspoons salt
1 teaspoon pepper
vegetable oil
a 12-inch skillet or sauté
  pan, or griddle

1.   Peel and shred the potatoes. Place the potatoes on a towel and press out excess moisture. Shred the onion. Combine the onion, flour, eggs, salt, and pepper. Stir the potatoes into the egg mixture.
2.   Heat ¼ cup oil in the skillet. When the oil is hot, drop in spoonfuls of the potato mixture and flatten them into pancakes with a spatula. When the bottoms brown (about 1 minute), turn the pancakes over. Brown the second side, then remove the pancakes and drain them on paper towels. Continue until all the batter is finished.
3.   Sprinkle the pancakes with more salt and pepper, and serve immediately.

DEEP-FRYING

Deep-frying is a quick way to cook small pieces of tender foods. The immersion in hot fat creates a kind of seal around the food, preventing the fat from penetrating, and keeping the food's juices locked in. Correctly cooked deep-fried foods should have a delicate crisp surface and a soft succulent interior—they should never be greasy or soggy.

For deep-frying, use the highest quality vegetable oils, solid or liquid. Any fat or oil used must be of a kind that will not smoke or burn when it is heated to temperatures of 380°. Peanut oil is a preferred oil, because its smoking point is 425°, it is economically priced, and it stores well. Oils may be reused two or three times. If you wish to do this, strain the oil through a fine sieve lined with cheesecloth before storing in a cool place.

The most important point to remember when deep frying is that the temperature of the oil must be correct (380° for most foods) and must remain constant. If the oil is not hot enough, the food absorbs the fat; if the oil is too hot, the food burns immediately. A thermometer is essential and must be constantly checked so that the correct temperature can be maintained.

Most deep-fried foods need a coating before they are to be fried. The simplest—milk and flour—may be used on fish, fruits, and vegetables. If a crustier finish is desired, bread crumbs and eggs may be added. For a fritter batter, beer is often added.

If you are using bread crumbs for a crusty finish, allow the breaded food to stand an hour before deep-frying so that the coating can dry. Be sure that all utensils are dry before they come in contact with the hot oil as water will cause the oil to spatter. Do not "toss" the pieces of food into the hot oil as that will cause the oil to spatter as well. Large pieces of poultry such as turkey, goose, or duck will burn on the outside before being cooked inside and are not suitable for deep-frying. Always place deep-fried foods on a plate covered with a cloth napkin and serve immediately.

Use a high-sided pan designed for deep-frying. When you fill the pan with 3 inches of oil, it should be only half full. You will also need a candy-deep-fry thermometer so that you can monitor the temperature of the oil. A removable basket is convenient for lifting foods such as french fries in and out of the pan, or a wire skimmer may be used to remove and drain foods. If you plan to do a lot of deep-frying, you might consider an automatic deep-fryer.

In this dish, the chicken is marinated first, thereby sealing a delicious flavor inside the meat. Letting the breaded chicken stand an hour allows the coating to dry; it will then be less likely to fall off when cooked.

DEEP-FRIED CHICKEN
Serves 8

2 chickens, about 2 lbs. each
½ bunch parsley
2 lemons
4 cloves garlic
10 oz. flour (2 cups)
3 eggs
salt and pepper
6 oz. bread crumbs (2 cups)
oil for deep-frying
a deep-fryer
a deep-fry thermometer

1. Remove the wing tips and cut each chicken into 8 pieces (see page 40). Remove and discard the parsley stems and chop the leaves. Squeeze the juice from the lemons. Cut the garlic cloves in half and crush them with the flat side of a knife. Combine the parsley, lemon juice, and garlic, and marinate the chicken pieces overnight.

2. Dry each piece of chicken and flour each piece separately. Beat the eggs with 2 teaspoons of salt and dip each floured piece of chicken into the beaten egg. Then coat each piece with bread crumbs. Let stand uncovered in the refrigerator for 1 hour so the coating dries.

3. Preheat 3 inches of oil in a deep-fryer to 375°. First add the legs and thighs. Five minutes later, add the breasts and 10 minutes later the wings.

4. When the pieces are nicely browned and done— about 20 minutes, drain them on paper towels. Salt and pepper them lightly and arrange on a folded napkin to serve. This chicken is also delicious served cold.

The batter for the apple fritters may be used on any small delicate food to be deep-fried. The beer causes the batter to puff when it hits the hot oil and creates a delicate crispy shell for the warm tart apple slices. Both the batter and the apples need to be prepared at least an hour in advance of cooking time.

APPLE FRITTERS
Serves 2

1 large tart apple
sugar
rum
**Fritter Batter (see recipe
  below)**
oil for deep-frying
powdered sugar
a deep-fryer
a deep fry thermometer

1. Peel and core the apple and slice the apple into rings ¼ inch thick. Sprinkle with sugar and rum (or any preferred spirit) and allow to stand at least 1 hour.
2. Make the Fritter Batter.
3. Pat the apple rings dry and drop them into the batter.
4. In the deep-fryer, heat about 3 inches of oil to 370°. Remove the apple rings one at a time from the batter, gently slip them into the hot fat, and fry until golden—keeping the temperature at 370°—about 1 minute on each side. Drain on paper towels. Sprinkle with powdered sugar; serve on a folded napkin immediately.

Fritter Batter

2½ oz. flour (½ cup)
½ teaspoon salt
1 tablespoon melted butter
1 slightly beaten egg
½ cup beer
1 egg white

1. Combine the flour and salt. Add the melted butter, whole egg, and beer.
2. Put the batter in a warm place to stand at least 1 hour, until light and foaming.
3. Just before using the batter, whisk the egg white until soft peaks form and fold it into the batter.

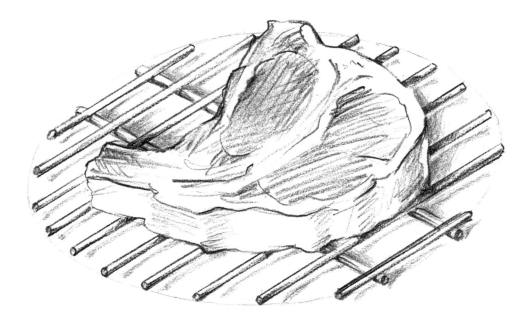

BROILING AND GRILLING

Chapter 8

My mother was the cook in our household. My father rarely went into the kitchen—but he loved to cook outside over the charcoal grill. Nestled in a corner of the garden, at the very edge of our patio, we had an elaborate brick arrangement built to my father's specifications—with a chimney, a large grill, and plenty of counter space so that platters of marinated meats could wait their turn to be cooked, and afterwards, tantalizingly displayed, wait to be consumed. The biggest and best parties we ever had were in the summer, when friends and relatives were invited to "a barbecue." My mother would have the meats marinating on platters; my father would put on his special barbecue apron, collect all his tools, including a bottle of water that had a "whiskey pourer" inserted (his own contrivance) to put out unwanted flames, and a long brush and a bowl of sauce for the meats. He would arrange all his equipment, and then he would go to work, first lighting the coals, and then checking to see if the coals were evenly covered with gray ash signaling their readiness. All of a sudden, he would announce that the coals were "perfect"—and happily, sometimes totally enveloped in smoke,

143

he would stand, turning, moving, and poking the meats, asking everyone how they liked their steaks, and then making sure everyone got exactly what they wanted.

Today, most people do not have the space for elaborate equipment, but grilled meats remain as popular as ever, with numerous restaurants specializing in "the grill." Whether it is called barbecuing, broiling, or grilling, it is the same cooking method. It is a relatively brief, dry-heat method of cooking, only suitable for tender cuts of meat. Grilling outdoors over charcoal is called barbecuing, but grilling may also be done over a gas flame or electric coil indoors. Broiling is the same method, but the heat source is from above, rather than below. All three procedures involve cooking by direct heat, first on one side, then the other.

Foods Suitable for Grilling

Meats and poultry Meats that are fat but naturally tender, and that are cut not more than 2 inches thick grill the best. Pork ribs, beef steak, and hamburgers grill well. Lean, thinly sliced veal scallops do not grill well by themselves, because of the lack of fat. If the meat has a border of fat around it, don't trim it off—slash it with a knife to keep it from curling. Chicken (and other poultry) can be grilled split, quartered, or cut into parts. Because it has a mild flavor, chicken quickly absorbs the grilled, smokey flavor. Lean meats must be brushed with fat or a sauce, or be covered with bacon, or, in the case of poultry, be cooked with the skin on. Leave the meats at room temperature for at least 2 hours before cooking. They can be marinated, trimmed, skewered, or otherwise prepared in advance—but the actual cooking should be done at the last minute.

Vegetables Vegetables grill very well, since the dry intense heat seals the outside of the vegetables, allowing the inner flesh to cook in its own juices. Always brush the outside skins or flesh with oil and start the cooking over the highest heat. The vegetables can be moved away from the hottest part of the grill to finish cooking. To check doneness, poke with a skewer.

Seafood Fish and shellfish can also be grilled with good results. It is best to marinate seafood beforehand and baste it as it grills. Be very careful not to overcook. See pages 169-71 for more on grilling seafood.

Grilling Procedure

Preheating the grill or broiler All the dishes in this section, may be cooked under the broiler, or on an outside or inside gas, electric, or charcoal grill. It is essential that the grill or broiler be preheated so that the meat can be seared rapidly. Searing is a little more difficult under a home broiler, since home broilers do not get as hot as charcoal or commercial grills. Therefore, the broiler should be preheated for 30 minutes with its rack and pan in place. If you are using a charcoal grill, light the fire about an hour in advance; the coals should be covered with gray ash before you start cooking. If the grill is not hot enough, the meat won't sear, and the juices will run into the fire.

Marinating Marinating adds flavor to the food, helps keep it from drying out, and in some instances, tenderizes as well. Marinades for grilling should contain oil, especially if the marinade is to be used for basting as well. The longer the food is left in a marinade, the more flavor it absorbs. Usually 2 or 3 hours is sufficient, but meats can be marinated for up to 24 hours.

Searing Searing is the crucial step that gives grilled foods their rich crisp crust and distinctive grilled flavor and aroma. In order to sear, food is placed on the hottest possible grill, 3 to 5 inches above the coals, or 1 inch below a preheated gas or electric broiler, for about 1 to 2 minutes each side. After the initial searing, grilling becomes a matter of learning to judge when the food is done.

Checking for doneness of meats and poultry

Timing depends on the temperature of the grill or broiler and how far away the food is from the source of heat.

- For very rare meat, the 1 or 2 minute searing process is adequate—the meat will be soft when touched and red when it is cut. Allow a total cooking time of about 4 minutes for a 1½-inch thick cut.
- For rare meat, turn the meat when the blood begins to come to the surface—the meat will still be fairly soft, and when cut will be a deep pink inside. Allow a total cooking time of about 6 minutes for a 1½-inch thick cut.
- For medium, the meat feels firmer and more resistant than rare meat before it is turned and when cut it is pink. Allow a total cooking time of about 9 minutes for a 1½-inch thick cut.
- For well done, the meat will feel firm before it is turned, and when cut there is no trace of pink inside. Allow a total cooking time of about 12 minutes for a 1½-inch thick cut.
- For poultry with the bone in, allow about 15 minutes to the pound. Chicken should be halved or quartered and started with the skin side down. Boned chicken can easily be overcooked—grill boned chicken pieces only about 5 minutes per side. Squabs or Cornish game hens should be split and cooked a total of 20 minutes, and should be turned and basted several times as they cook. To test poultry for doneness, prick the meat near the thigh bone. If the juices run clear, it is done. If the juices are pink, cook the poultry a little longer and test again.

Equipment

Long-handled tools are ideal for grilling. Spring-loaded tongs (preferred over the scissors type) can be used to turn the meat and move the coals. A basting brush with a 45-degree bend near the bristles may be used to brush on the marinade, sauce, or oils, during grilling. A bottle with a shaker top or spray attachment comes in handy to sprinkle water over unwanted flare-ups. A wire brush is recommended to scrape the grill each time it is used, since burnt-on grease gives an unpleasant flavor to the food. A fireproof mitt should be used to handle hot cooking racks, skewers, etc. Hinged grills are useful for cooking vegetables or skewered foods. And a carving board with a juice catcher is necessary to save the juices that may run out of the meat when it is carved.

Below is a marinade and a barbecue sauce especially suited to grilled meats and poultry. Meat and poultry can be marinated at room temperature for up to 3 hours, or in the refrigerator for 24 hours. Turn food several times as it marinates. The marinade can also be used to baste during grilling. For a different result, substitute white wines for red in the Barbecue Sauce or the Red Wine Marinade that follow. The Barbecue Sauce is excellent for brushing on meats toward the end of cooking. For a more piquant sauce, increase the Tabasco.

BARBECUE SAUCE
Makes about 2 cups

1 tablespoon unsalted
  butter
1 tablespoon olive oil
1 small onion
1 clove garlic
½ cup red wine vinegar
½ cup beer
¼ cup red table wine
1 large tomato, coarsely
  chopped
¼ cup tomato paste
1 tablespoon brown sugar
1 tablespoon Worcestershire
  sauce
1 tablespoon sweet mustard
4 drops Tabasco
½ teaspoon salt
½ teaspoon pepper

1. Heat the butter and oil in a saucepan. Chop the onion and garlic finely and sauté over a low heat 5 minutes.
2. Add the remaining ingredients, stir well, and simmer gently for 15 minutes. Stores well in the refrigerator.

RED WINE MARINADE
Makes about 2 cups

1 small onion
1 small carrot
1 clove garlic
1 teaspoon black
  peppercorns
1½ cups red table wine
¼ cup red wine vinegar
½ cup olive oil
1 bay leaf

Peel and slice the onion, carrot, and garlic. Crush the peppercorns. Combine all ingredients in a bowl.

Sirloin steaks are cut from the loin, and grill very well.

GRILLED SIRLOIN STEAK
Serves 4

4 1½-inch thick sirloin steaks, about ½ lb. each
Red Wine Marinade
olive oil for the grill
salt and pepper

1.   Marinate the steaks in the marinade about 3 hours, leaving them at room temperature for 1 hour before grilling.
2.   Preheat the grill, and brush the grill with oil just before the steaks are put on. Grill the steaks about 4 or 5 minutes each side for medium doneness (see page 145).
3.   Sprinkle lightly with salt and pepper and remove from the grill. Serve immediately with your choice of a butter sauce (see pages 79-80).

I have found that a combination of cooking methods works well on chicken with the bone in. The chicken is first baked in the oven for 20 minutes and then grilled for the remainder of the cooking time. This will insure that the chicken will be cooked through without being burned on the surface.

GRILLED CHICKEN OREGANO
Serves 3 or 4

a 2½ lb. chicken
2 cloves garlic
¼ cup lemon juice
½ cup olive oil
1 teaspoon dried oregano
salt and pepper

1.   Cut the chicken into quarters (see page 40). Chop the garlic and combine in a bowl with the lemon juice, olive oil, and dried oregano. Marinate the chicken overnight in the refrigerator.
2.   When ready to cook, bring the chicken to room temperature. Preheat the oven to 375°. Arrange the chicken on a baking sheet, sprinkling some marinade over the chicken, and bake for 15 minutes. Preheat the broiler or grill to its highest setting.
3.   Remove the chicken from the oven, arrange on the hot grill or under the broiler, brush with marinade, and grill 5 inches from the heat for 5 minutes each side.
4.   Season with salt and pepper and serve hot or at room temperature.

By cutting the green onions in half, and placing them lengthwise at either end of the skewer, it will look as if the chicken pieces were skewered by the green onions. It makes a very effective presentation.

GRILLED CHICKEN BREASTS ON SKEWERS
Serves 6

6 half breasts of chicken
6 large green onions
Red Wine Marinade
6 skewers

1.   Bone and skin the breasts (see page 42) and cut the fillets into 6 chunks each. Cut off the roots and trim 2 inches of green off the tops of the green onions. Cut each in half crosswise.
2.   Marinate the green onions and chicken in the marinade 2 hours. Soak the skewers in water for 30 minutes if they are wooden. Preheat the grill or broiler for 30 minutes.
3.   Skewer the root end of the green onion first, follow with 6 pieces of chicken, and end with the other half of the green onion. Grill a total of 8 minutes—turning and basting 2 or 3 times. Serve hot or at room temperature.

Any fresh vegetable can be used in this recipe. Select tiny ones to grill whole on skewers, or slice larger vegetables into bite-size pieces. They can be mixed on the skewer, or skewered in groups—all mushrooms together, all zucchini together, and so on.

GRILLED MIXED VEGETABLES
Serves 4

2 medium or 12 tiny
  zucchini
12 medium mushrooms
2 red bell peppers
8 tiny boiling potatoes
4 cloves garlic
1 cup olive oil
salt and pepper
8 skewers

1.   Clean but do not peel the zucchini. Leave the tiny ones whole or cut the larger zucchini into 12 pieces. Brush the mushrooms and leave whole. Seed the peppers and cut into 8 pieces each. Cut the potatoes in half.
2.   Crush the garlic and combine with the olive oil in a container large enough to hold the vegetables. Marinate the vegetables in the oil overnight in the refrigerator.
3.   Soak the skewers in water for 30 minutes if they are wooden. Skewer the vegetables as desired. Preheat the grill for 30 minutes.
4.   Grill the vegetables until tender when pierced with a skewer, turning and basting several times. Sprinkle with salt and pepper.

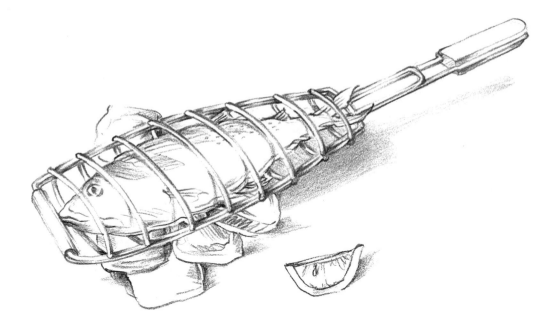

COOKING SEAFOOD

Chapter 9

In my cooking school, I have separate lessons for cooking fish, even though we use the same cooking methods—braising, poaching, grilling, etc.—as with other foods. It has been my experience that it is easier to understand how to cook seafood if it is treated as a separate food group. The little tricks learned about fish in general are repeated often enough so that you quickly see the similarities that occur in methods and techniques among different varieties of fish.

Again, rather than try to learn a hundred recipes, we will first learn about the cooking method and then what kinds of seafood fit that method. Our goal is to really understand the wonder of this abundant food from the sea and then to learn to cook it in a way that will enhance its natural deliciousness.

There is a very important theme running through the cooking of seafood, and that is, DON'T OVERCOOK! Overcooking fish or cooking it until it is "opaque and flaking" as some recipes instruct you to do, gives a dry result or a strong (fishy) taste.

149

Buying and Preparing Seafood for Cooking

Always select fresh fish, avoid frozen fish, and always cook fish the same day you purchase it. If you are interested in gutting or scaling your own fish, I suggest you buy one of the many comprehensive fish encyclopedias available, and follow the step-by-step directions for cleaning fish. The recipes following assume you are purchasing fresh fish at markets that offer seafood for sale in the following ways:

Steaks   Fish steaks are cross sections, usually about 1 inch thick, cut from large round fish such as halibut and salmon. Fish steaks are sold with the backbone and skin intact and need no further preparation before cooking. They are most commonly pan-fried or grilled.

Fillets   Fish fillets are sold boneless and skinless. There is no further preparation necessary before cooking. They are most commonly pan-fried or grilled.

Whole fish   When whole fish are sold in markets, they are sold scaled and gutted. If you wish, you may cut off the fins or have it done for you at the fish market. Whole fish may be baked, braised, or poached. Small whole fish (trout, for instance) can be pan-fried or grilled.

Mussels, clams, oysters   Mussels, clams, and oysters are sold in the shell, alive. A live animal will snap shut when its shell is tapped. Discard any with shells that will not close. A good scrubbing with a stiff brush under cold running water is necessary to remove surface mud or sand. Bivalves can be opened by prying apart the two half shells and severing the muscle that holds the shells together. That is easily accomplished with a tool called an oyster knife. Bivalves can be served raw, steamed, or baked.

Abalone and scallops   Abalone and scallops are usually removed from their shells before they are sold. The fishmonger slices and pounds the abalone to tenderize it so that it is ready to be cooked when purchased. Scallops, too, can be used as purchased. Abalone is most commonly sautéed, and scallops may be sautéed, deep-fried, or poached.

Lobster and crab   Lobster and crab are sold in their shells, alive. They are most commonly poached or steamed as they come from the market.

Shrimp   Shrimp (or prawns, as the larger ones are sometimes called, even though a true prawn is biologically different from a shrimp) are sold in their shells, usually without their heads. They vary in size from 5 to 50 per pound. They may be cooked peeled or unpeeled. With larger shrimp, the vein running down the back of the shrimp is removed at the same time the shrimp is peeled. Shrimp are most commonly poached, steamed, or sautéed.

Squid   It is preferable to buy squid that is already cleaned. If you are unable to do so, follow the step-by-step directions for cleaning below.

   1. Grasp the body (mantle) with one hand and with the other, grasp the head behind the eyes. Pull out the head and tentacles. The viscera and ink sac will come out with the head.

   2. Cut the head off just below the eye and discard the viscera and ink sac. Remove the bony beak from the tentacles by squeezing it out or pulling it out with your fingers.

   3. Remove the thin plastic-like quill from the body. Rinse the body and peel off the purple-spotted skin.

STEWING OR BRAISING
SEAFOOD

The information given in chapter 5 regarding braising or stewing may be applied in this lesson on fish with some exceptions. Fish is not browned before it is braised and, since the flesh is so delicate, fish is never cooked for hours as braised meat or poultry sometimes is. In braised fish dishes, the cooking liquid and vegetables are generally simmered together first, and the seafood is added only long enough to cook through before serving. Sometimes, after the seafood has been gently braised, it is removed from the braising liquid and the sauce is then concentrated or sieved before the stew is served. The fish and shellfish for any stew or braise can be chosen to suit the season and the cook's taste.

Bouillabaisse, the famous dish from southern France, is really a stew, not a soup, as many people think. When properly cooked, there should be only enough broth to moisten the bread you'll be serving with it. (The bread should not be toasted.) For an outstanding bouillabaisse, use the greatest variety of fish possible. When shellfish are included, they should be left in their shells for serving. Bouillabaisse is delicious served with a highly seasoned mayonnaise-like sauce called a rouille.

PACIFIC COAST BOUILLABAISSE

Serves 8 to 10

2 dozen clams or mussels
1 lb. shrimp
3 lbs. fish steaks or fillets*
2 medium onions
2 leeks
1 carrot
4 cloves garlic
1½ lbs. tomatoes (or 1 28-oz. can)
½ cup olive oil
2 tablespoons tomato paste
1½ cups dry white table wine
4 cups Fish Stock
1 bouquet garni
¼ to ½ gram saffron
¼ cup Pernod
Rouille (see recipe below)
2 loaves French bread

1. Scrub the clams or mussels and refrigerate. Rinse the shrimp, leaving them in their shells, and refrigerate. Cut the fish into 1½-inch chunks and refrigerate. Chop the onions. Clean the leeks; discard the dark green tops and chop the whites. Chop the carrot and garlic. Peel and chop the tomatoes—do not remove the seeds. (If using canned tomatoes, use the juice as well.)
2. Sauté the onions, carrots, leeks, and garlic in the olive oil 5 minutes. Add the tomatoes, tomato paste, white wine, and stock. Add the bouquet garni, saffron, and Pernod. Bring to a boil; lower the heat and simmer gently 30 minutes, uncovered. Remove the bouquet garni.
3. Twenty minutes before serving, reheat the sauce, add the clams or mussels and simmer covered until the shellfish open, about 5 to 7 minutes. Add the other fish and shrimp and simmer 1 or 2 minutes uncovered. *Be careful not to overcook the fish.* Serve in large soup bowls. Pass the rouille and sliced French bread at the table.

(*A variety of textures is desirable, so combine a firm fish such as cod with a finer-textured fish such as flounder or sole. Do not use strong-flavored fish like salmon, as those flavors will dominate.)

Rouille

1 cup diced French bread
½ cup Fish Stock
4 cloves garlic
1 small jalapeño pepper
1 egg yolk
¾ cup olive oil

1.   Soak the bread in the stock. Peel the garlic; take the seeds out of the pepper and divide it in half.
2.   In the bowl of a food processor or blender, place the bread, garlic, half the pepper, and the egg yolk. Process until thoroughly blended. Taste and add the other half of the jalapeño pepper if desired.
3.   Add the oil in a slow steady stream, whisking or processing until the oil is incorporated—the rouille will resemble a mayonnaise. If the rouille separates, add a little liquid from the bouillabaisse and continue to stir. Serve the rouille in a sauceboat or bowl. This sauce may be stored 2 or 3 days in the refrigerator.

Here is another hearty fish stew. This one is from Livorno, Italy.

CACCIUCCO
Serves 8

a 2-lb. whole codfish
1½ lbs. tiny squid
2 dozen tiny clams
2 dozen tiny mussels
1 lb. codfish fillets
1 lb. medium shrimp (16 to
  20 to a lb.)

1 large red onion
6 cloves garlic
2½ lbs. ripe tomatoes
½ bunch parsley
¼ cup olive oil
1 teaspoon sugar
cayenne pepper
¼ cup red wine vinegar
4 cups Brown Stock
salt, to taste

1 loaf French or Italian
  bread
olive oil for bread
4 cloves garlic for bread
an 8-qt. soup pot

1. Cut the whole fish into 2-inch chunks. Clean the squid (page 150), and cut the bodies into rings; clean the mussels and clams; peel the shrimp, cut the fish fillets into 2-inch pieces. Refrigerate everything but the chunked whole codfish.

2. Chop the onion and 6 cloves of garlic; chop the tomatoes; chop the parsley.

3. Heat ¼ cup olive oil in the soup pot, and sauté the onion and garlic 5 minutes. Add the tomatoes, sugar, and a pinch of cayenne and simmer gently for 10 minutes. Add the vinegar and the whole fish cut into pieces and simmer covered another 10 minutes. Add the Brown Stock and simmer 20 minutes more with the cover askew.

4. Remove the fish bones and discard; push entire contents of the pot through the coarse grate on a food mill. Return the puréed stew to the pot and taste, adding a little more vinegar, sugar, or cayenne as needed. Add the squid and simmer covered 10 minutes; add the clams and mussels, cover and simmer 5 minutes more or until the clams and mussels open.

5. Slice the bread thickly, brush each slice with olive oil, place on a baking sheet, and toast in the oven 5 minutes. When the toast is crisp, cut the 4 garlic cloves and rub over the surface of the toast.

6. Just before serving, heat the broth. Add the shrimp and pieces of cod fillets, and simmer 1 minute. Stir in the chopped parsley and taste for seasoning. Add salt if necessary. Serve the stew in large soup bowls spooned over the garlic toast.

As a contrast to the bouillabaisse and the Cacciucco, here is another seafood stew, a little fancier and more refined.

A DELICATE SEAFOOD RAGOÛT
Serves 8

6 medium artichokes
1 lemon
16 large shrimp (12 to a lb.)
½ lb. scallops
1 lb. firm white fish fillets
15 fresh basil leaves
4 shallots
4 tablespoons unsalted
    butter
1½ cups dry white table
    wine
½ cup concentrated Fish
    Stock
1 cup crème fraîche
salt and pepper
cayenne pepper

1.   Discard the leaves and prepare the artichoke bottoms (see page 28). Simmer them in water with the juice of a lemon until tender. Cool, and cut the artichoke bottoms into ¼ inch thick slices. Reserve ½ cup of the artichoke liquid.

2.   Peel and devein the shrimp, and cut each into 3 pieces. Rinse any sand from the scallops and cut each one into 3 pieces. Cut the fish into 1½-inch cubes. Cut the basil leaves into thin strips. Chop the shallots finely.

3.   Melt the butter in a deep saucepan. Sauté the shallots for 2 minutes. Add the wine, the artichoke liquid, and the concentrated Fish Stock. Reduce to 2 cups. Drop in the fish, shrimp, and scallops and poach gently 1 minute. Transfer the seafood to a plate.

4.   Add the crème fraîche to the sauce and reduce by at least half, until the sauce is thickened. Season to taste with salt, pepper, and a little cayenne. Combine the sliced artichoke bottoms, the shrimp, scallops, fish, and sauce. Reheat gently to serve, garnishing each serving with thin strips of basil.

BAKING SEAFOOD

Since baking is a dry-heat method of cooking, and seafood is generally lean, you cannot bake a piece of fish as you would a roast beef. You must compensate for the lack of fat by having some stock, butter, or oil as a basting medium, by wrapping the fish in parchment or foil, or by baking it in a water bath. (A water bath is a container filled with about an inch of boiling water in which a mold is baked. The small amount of water diffuses the direct heat around the bottom of the mold, and creates a moist atmosphere so that the food does not become dry as it cooks.) Whichever method you use, always keep the cooking time short.

A finely puréed food that has egg white and cream worked into it is called a mousseline. The following recipe is a mousseline of shrimp and scallops. The mousseline is placed in cylindrical molds called timbales, and baked in a water bath. (A mousseline can also be hand-shaped and poached very gently, as in quenelles, which we will come to later.) Again, note the short cooking time.

SHELLFISH TIMBALES WITH A LIME SABAYON
Serves 8

½ lb. scallops
2 oz. raw shrimp
2 cups water
2 teaspoons tomato paste
unsalted butter for molds
¼ teaspoon salt
¼ teaspoon pepper
1 egg plus 1 egg white,
  chilled
½ cup crème fraîche
8 timbale molds
parchment paper
water bath
Lime Sabayon (see recipe
  below)

1. Clean the scallops and refrigerate. Peel the shrimp. Refrigerate the shrimp and put the shells in a small saucepan. Add the water to the shells and simmer, partly covered, for 20 minutes. Uncover and reduce the liquid to about ½ cup. Strain out the shells, pressing hard to extract all juices. Return the stock to the saucepan, add the tomato paste, and reduce by half. Reserve for the Lime Sabayon.
2. Cut parchment paper rounds to fit the molds (the parchment will be used to cover the timbales). Butter the parchment paper and the timbale molds.
3. In a food processor or blender, combine the chilled shrimp, scallops, salt, and pepper. Process until smooth. Add the egg and egg white and process for 10 seconds. Scrape the sides of the bowl and process for an additional 5 seconds. With the machine running, add the crème fraîche—and pulse 2 or 3 times to fold in the cream.
4. Divide the shellfish mixture among the molds. Smooth the top with wet hands and tap the dishes on the counter to settle the filling. Press the buttered parchment over each mold.
5. Set the molds into a dish that is at least 3 inches deep (for the water bath), and refrigerate until ready to bake—up to 2 or 3 hours. Make the Lime Sabayon.
6. Pour boiling water about 1 inch deep into the water bath and bake the molds in a preheated 375° oven for approximately 15 minutes.
7. To serve, spoon a little sabayon on each plate and unmold the timbale on top of it.

Lime Sabayon

1 egg plus 2 egg yolks
2 tablespoons lime juice
¼ teaspoon salt
¼ teaspoon pepper
reserved shrimp stock
zest of 1 lime, chopped

1. In the top of a double boiler, over simmering water, whisk the egg and egg yolks with the lime juice, salt, and pepper until light and fluffy.
2. Reheat the reserved shrimp stock and whisk into the sauce until hot and slightly thickened. Fold in the chopped zest and more salt and pepper to taste. Remove the double boiler from the heat. The sauce may be used immediately or held for 20 or 30 minutes, in which case it should be stirred occasionally.

Oyster shells are often used for baking and serving. The cooking time for oysters is always short, and in this recipe, ingredients that keep the flesh succulent are added. Once baked, serve the bivalves immediately.

BAKED OYSTERS

Serves 4 as an hors d'oeuvre

8 live oysters
1 slice pancetta, ¼-inch
thick
rock salt
½ bunch flat-leaf parsley
1 stalk celery
1 large leaf Romaine lettuce
3 sprigs fresh thyme
2 tablespoons lemon juice
1 tablespoon softened
unsalted butter
3 tablespoons soft bread
crumbs
½ teaspoon Tabasco
salt and pepper
paprika
oyster plates

1. Scrub and shuck the oysters (see page 150), retaining the liquor in a small bowl. Line a baking pan with rock salt. Place the oysters, each on the curved half shell, on the rock salt. Cut the pancetta into 8 pieces.
2. Cut off and discard the parsley stems and chop the leaves. Chop the celery, Romaine, and thyme leaves.
3. To the bowl of oyster liquor add the lemon juice, butter, bread crumbs, Tabasco, parsley, celery, lettuce, and thyme. Combine well and add salt and pepper to taste.
4. Pat the crumb mixture around and over the oysters. Top each oyster with a piece of pancetta and sprinkle with paprika.
5. Place oysters in a 475° oven for 5 minutes or until bubbly and the edges curl.
6. Serve on oyster plates, if you have them, or on plates spread with rock salt. (The salt will keep the oyster shells from tipping.)

Technically, a fish baked in parchment is steamed rather than baked. The package must be sealed tightly, and it should be large enough to allow the steam to circulate around the fish. As the package heats, the flavors of the vegetables and fish combine to create a delicious dish.

FISH BAKED IN PARCHMENT
Serves 6

4 carrots
1 bunch broccoli
12 large mushrooms
2 zucchini
4 shallots
12 cherry tomatoes
6 fish fillets (salmon, red snapper, cod, halibut, or sole), about 6 oz. each
¾ cup white table wine
6 tablespoons unsalted butter
6 sprigs fresh tarragon (or basil or dill)
salt and pepper
parchment paper
White Wine Butter Sauce (see page 83)

1. Clean and carve the carrots into 12 oval shapes and blanch 3 minutes.
2. Clean and cut the broccoli into 6 florets and blanch the florets 1 minute.
3. Cut each mushroom into 4 pieces and each zucchini into 6 pieces. Chop the shallots finely, and cut the tomatoes in half.
4. Cut 6 pieces of parchment approximately 15 × 12 inches each. Fold each piece in half and cut into a half-heart as if you were making a valentine. This will give a butterfly shape when you unfold the parchment, the classic *en papillote*. Butter half of each piece of parchment, and sprinkle with the shallots. Place a fish fillet over the shallots and surround each fillet with vegetables. (Each package should contain 2 pieces of carrot, 1 broccoli floret, 8 pieces of mushroom, 2 pieces of zucchini, and 4 halves of tomato.) Sprinkle each package with wine, dot with butter, and place an herb sprig over the fish.
5. Preheat the oven to 450°. Fold the fish into the parchment as illustrated below. (At this point, the fish can be refrigerated several hours before baking.) Bake at 450° for 10 minutes until puffed and brown. Serve in the parchment. Pass the White Wine Butter Sauce at the table.

Fold the paper over the fish so the cut edges meet. Starting at the pointed end, fold a short length of the edges together. Hold this section down and fold the next section partly over the first one.

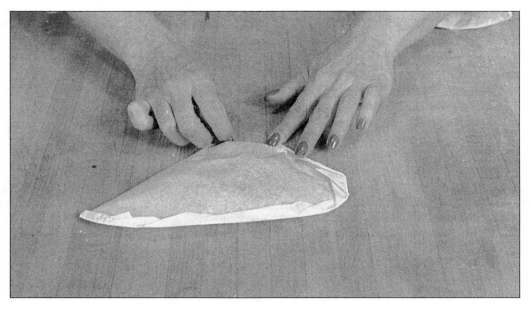

Continue folding until cut edges are completely sealed.

POACHING AND STEAMING
SEAFOOD

Fish and shellfish are poached by a short cooking in simmering liquid. When poaching fish, be very careful that the poaching time is brief and that the water only simmers, never boils. Boiling liquid would break up quenelles or a delicate fish fillet.

Steaming is done by cooking food above simmering liquid. The advantage of steaming over poaching is that the steamed seafood is not immersed in liquid and retains more of its flavor. Fish for poaching or steaming should be fairly lean and firm-fleshed. If a fish is too fat or soft-fleshed, like mackerel or sablefish, it may fall apart when poached or steamed. Salmon, halibut, or sole, whole or cut up, are good fish for poaching and steaming.

Fish steaks, fillets, or small fish can be poached in any dish wide enough and deep enough to hold them. For large whole fish, a "fish poacher" is used. Seafood can be poached in a *court bouillon* or in a fish stock (see page 51).

Rillettes are very rich spreads—French in origin. The classic rillette is made with goose, duck, or pork that is cooked until tender, mixed with fat, and then stored in small stoneware crocks. In this version, poached salmon is combined with smoked salmon and butter. Serve it with bread or crackers as an appetizer or as a first course.

SALMON RILLETTES
Serves 6 as a first course, 12 as an appetizer

a ½ lb. salmon steak (with skin and bone)
1 qt. Fish Stock
10 tablespoons unsalted butter
6 oz. smoked salmon
salt and pepper
1 sprig fresh dill

1. Remove the skin and bone from the salmon steak. Use the skin and bone to make Fish Stock.
2. Poach the salmon in a quart of Fish Stock, or enough to cover, for 2 minutes. Let the fish cool in the stock.
3. Melt 2 tablespoons of the butter in a skillet, add the smoked salmon and 1 tablespoon of Fish Stock, cover and cook gently for 2 minutes. Allow to cool in the skillet.
4. Remove the smoked and poached salmon from the liquids.
5. Shred both salmons with a fork and mix well. Cream the remaining butter and mix it gradually into the salmon, using a fork.
6. Season to taste with salt and pepper. Chop 1 teaspoon of dill and add to the salmon. Pack the mixture into individual ramekins or in a stoneware pot, cover, and chill thoroughly. Serve with crusty French bread, crackers, or toast. The rilletes will keep up to a week if their tops are covered with a layer of clarified butter.

Here is an extremely simple method for poaching fish fillets.

POACHED FISH FILLETS WITH A CREAM CHIVE SAUCE
Serves 8

4 shallots
1 bunch chives
3 tablespoons unsalted
 butter
8 fish fillets, about 6 or 7
 oz. each
salt and pepper
¾ cup concentrated Fish
 Stock
½ cup sherry
1 cup dry white table wine
1½ cups crème fraîche
1 tablespoon tomato paste
½ teaspoon lemon juice
a 12-inch open baking dish
parchment paper

1. Chop the shallots and chives. Spread the bottom of the baking dish with some of the butter and sprinkle with chopped shallots. Season the fish fillets with salt and pepper and lay them over the shallots in a single layer.

2. Preheat the oven to 400°. In a saucepan, bring the concentrated stock, sherry, and wine to a boil and reduce by half. Pour the hot liquid over the fish fillets to barely cover them. Cut a piece of parchment paper the size of the dish, butter it, and press the buttered side down on top of the fish. (This is to keep the part of the fish exposed to the air from drying out.) Poach the fish at 400° for 7 minutes.

3. Remove the fish to a serving dish, pour the poaching liquid into a saucepan and reduce it by half. Add the crème fraîche and tomato paste and reduce the sauce until it is as thick as whipping cream.

4. Season the sauce with salt, pepper, and freshly squeezed lemon juice.

5. Just before serving, warm the fillets in the sauce. Garnish each serving with the chopped chives.

When we made the Shellfish Timbales, we first made a mousseline with the shrimp and scallops (a mousseline, as you recall, is a purée that contains egg white and cream). In that recipe, the mousseline was packed into timbale molds and baked in a water bath. Quenelles are also made with a mousseline, but in this case the mousseline is placed directly into the simmering liquid and poached. Quenelles are very light poached dumplings made from a mousseline or "forcemeat," usually chicken, veal, or lean fish. In making a mousseline of fish, the fish is puréed very finely, the mixture is chilled (put over ice), egg whites are beaten in, and the cream is beaten in—little by little. For a lighter mixture, some of the cream may be whipped before it is combined with the fish. You can use two teaspoons to shape the quenelles, dipping the spoons into hot water after each quenelle to keep the mousseline from sticking to the spoons.

No matter what kind of sauce or finish the quenelles will have, they are first poached in salted water or Fish Stock. It is very important that the poaching liquid simmer very gently. If it boils, the delicate quenelles will fall apart. When the quenelles float to the surface, in about 5 minutes or less, they are done and can be drained on paper towels.

Lean and fairly firm-fleshed fish make the best quenelles. If the fish has a high fat content or soft flesh, the fish will not absorb the cream and egg white very well and you will get a heavy or dry quenelle. Preferred fish are pike, halibut, hake, cod, and winter flounder. Quenelles are usually served as a first course.

QUENELLES
Makes 18 small quenelles; serves 4 to 6

**1 tablespoon unsalted
    butter
2 tablespoons flour
¼ cup Fish Stock
½ lb. firm, lean, fish (see
    above)
pinch of salt
pinch of white pepper
pinch of cayenne pepper
pinch of freshly ground
    nutmeg
2 egg whites
½ cup crème fraîche
about 2 qts. water or Fish
    Stock for poaching
    Quenelles
Fish Sauce Aurore (see
    recipe below)**

1.   Melt the butter in a small heavy saucepan over low heat. Add the flour, blend well and cook, stirring, for 2 minutes to make the roux. Do not let it brown.

2.   Whisk in the Fish Stock, bring to a boil, and cook, stirring, until thick and smooth, about 1 minute. Remove the thickened flour base from the heat and let cool.

3.   In a food processor or blender, purée the fish until it forms a smooth paste, about 1 minute. Add the salt, pepper, cayenne, and nutmeg. Combine gently. Scrape the sides of the bowl, and add the cooled flour base. Mix until well blended.

4.   Turn the fish mixture into a large bowl placed over ice. With a sturdy whisk or large wooden spoon, add the egg whites one by one. Gradually whisk in the crème fraîche and continue to whisk until the mixture is well blended. Refrigerate until well chilled—up to 5 or 6 hours if desired.

5.   In a large sauté pan, bring 3 inches of salted water or Fish Stock to a simmer. To shape the quenelles, dip an oval spoon into hot water and then into the fish mixture. Use a second spoon to shape it into an oval dumpling. Gently slip the quenelles into the simmering liquid. Cook, turning once, until they float to the top, about 5 minutes. Serve with Fish Sauce Aurore.

Fish Sauce Aurore

**1 qt. Fish Stock
3 tablespoons tomato paste
¾ teaspoon salt
¼ teaspoon white pepper
¼ lb. unsalted butter
a 2-qt. saucepan**

1.   In a 2-qt. saucepan, boil the stock over high heat until it is reduced to 1½ cups, about 15 minutes.

2.   Lower the heat and stir in the tomato paste, salt, and pepper. Remove from the heat and gradually whisk in the butter, 2 tablespoons at a time. The sauce will be the consistency of heavy cream.

This dish from Italy is a wonderful first course or light lunch and a good example of poaching and steaming.

MIXED SHELLFISH SALAD
(Insalata di Frutti di Mare)
Serves 8 to 10

½ lb. squid
1 dozen small clams
1 dozen mussels
½ lb. scallops
1 lb. shrimp (30 to a lb.)
1 green bell pepper
1 red bell pepper
1 small red onion
3 stalks celery
6 green olives
6 black olives
½ bunch flat-leaf parsley
4 sprigs fresh oregano
1 cup olive oil
4 tablespoons lemon juice
1 qt. *Court Bouillon* (see page 50)
1 clove garlic
salt and freshly ground pepper
a large glass bowl

1. Clean the squid (see page 150), clams, mussels, and scallops; peel the shrimp. Roast and peel the peppers and cut them into ½-inch strips. Chop the onion; peel the celery and slice thinly. Pit the olives and slice. Remove and discard the parsley and oregano stems and chop the leaves. Combine the oil and lemon juice in a large glass bowl. Make the *Court Bouillon*.

2. Steam the clams and mussels until they open—about 5 to 7 minutes. While they are still warm, remove them from their shells and put them into the glass bowl.

3. Bring the *Court Bouillon* to a boil, drop in the scallops—cook 20 seconds and remove with a slotted spoon. Cut each scallop into 2 pieces and add to the clams. Drop the shrimp into the *Court Bouillon*, poach 1 minute, remove, and add to the bowl. Drop the squid into the liquid and poach until tender—15 to 20 minutes. Drain, slice the squid bodies into rings, and combine with the other shellfish.

4. Put the garlic through a press and add it to the bowl. Add the peppers, onions, celery, olives, parsley and oregano, and mix thoroughly. Taste and add salt and pepper as needed. Allow to marinate at least 2 hours before serving.

Finnan haddie is the colloquial term for Findon haddock, a split, smoked fish named after the Scottish fishing village of Findon. In Scotland, finnan haddie is typically poached in water and milk, and served for breakfast. In this recipe, it is steamed rather than poached, and dressed up with a cream sauce. Adding tea leaves to the steaming liquid and wrapping the fillets in leek greens imparts a wonderful aromatic fragrance and flavor to the smoked fish.

TEA-STEAMED FINNAN HADDIE
Serves 4

3 slices pancetta, ¼ inch
   thick
1 tablespoon unsalted
   butter
1 cup crème fraîche
¼ bunch parsley
salt and pepper
1 lb. finnan haddie fillets
1 leek, greens only
1 tablespoon green tea
   leaves
a pot with steamer basket

1. Chop the pancetta coarsely and sauté in the butter until golden. Drain on towels and discard the fat in the skillet.

2. Combine the pancetta and crème fraîche. Remove and discard the parsley stems. Chop the leaves and add to the crème fraîche. Season with salt and pepper.

3. Rinse the leek greens, wrap the fillets in half of them, and place the fillets in the steamer basket. Chop the remaining leek greens. In the steamer bottom, bring 2 inches of water to a boil and add the tea leaves and chopped leek greens to the water. Cover and simmer 5 minutes.

4. Put the steamer basket with the fish over the simmering tea and cover. Steam the fillets for 6 minutes. Place the crème fraîche mixture in a small saucepan and warm gently.

5. To serve, open the leek wrapping and top the finnan haddie with the pancetta and parsley cream sauce.

Here is another way to "steam"—over a very low heat, without additional water, using the moisture in the fish itself. This is a really good way to trap all the flavor possible.

"PAN-STEAMED" TROUT WITH WALNUTS
Serves 4 to 6

3 trout, deboned and filleted
4 walnuts
4 tablespoons walnut oil
¼ bunch parsley
2 tablespoons Balsamic vinegar
1 tablespoon sweet mustard
1 teaspoon salt
1 teaspoon pepper

1. Have the trout deboned and filleted. Chop the walnuts coarsely and sauté over medium heat in half the walnut oil until browned and toasted—about 1 minute. Remove and discard the parsley stems and chop the leaves.
2. In a nonmetal dish large enough to hold the trout fillets, combine the vinegar, mustard, 1 teaspoon each salt and pepper, and the chopped parsley. Add the walnuts and oil and stir.
3. Heat the remaining oil in a skillet, add the fish fillets, turn down the heat, cover and steam 1 minute.
4. Remove the fillets from the pan and while they are still warm, marinate them in the dressing for 1 hour.
5. Remove the skin before serving.

SAUTÉING (PAN-FRYING) AND
DEEP-FRYING SEAFOOD

Properly sautéed seafood should have a firm exterior and a succulent interior. Fish should be sautéed at a high temperature, much higher than that at which it is poached. The high heat seals the outer surfaces of the seafood so that the inner flesh cooks yet retains its succulence. Sautéing is always done quickly—usually a minute or two each side is sufficient. After the shellfish or fish is cooked, it is removed from the pan, and cream, stock, wines, and herbs may be added to the pan to create a sauce. Lean, firm-fleshed types of fish, fish roe, fish cakes, shrimps, scallops, oysters, and crab sauté very well. Clarified butter is an ideal frying medium. A light coating of flour is used in order to dry the surface of the fish just before frying.

FISH FILLETS WITH A SORREL SAUCE
Serves 6

4 shallots
1 bunch sorrel
5 tablespoons unsalted
  butter
flour
6 fish fillets, about 6 or 7
  oz. each
½ cup concentrated Fish
  Stock
1 cup white table wine
1 cup crème fraîche
1 tablespoon tomato paste
1 teaspoon salt
pinch of cayenne pepper
1 teaspoon paprika

1. Chop the shallots; rinse, dry, and shred the sorrel. Sauté the shallots in 4 tablespoons of the butter for 2 minutes. Remove the shallots from the pan and reserve.
2. Lightly flour the fish fillets and sauté in the shallot-flavored butter 30 seconds each side. Remove to a platter.
3. Pour off any butter remaining in the skillet and add the Fish Stock, white wine, and shallots, and cook until reduced by ⅔. Add the crème fraîche and reduce the sauce until it is thick enough to coat a wooden spoon. Add the tomato paste and salt, cayenne, and paprika and stir. Set aside.
4. In another pan, sauté the sorrel in 1 tablespoon butter for 1 minute, and add to the sauce. Taste the sauce and correct the seasoning.
5. Warm the fillets in the sauce. When serving, spoon the sauce onto the plate first—then place the fish fillet on top.

This dish may be served as a first course or main course. A serving of 2 or 3 shrimps are adequate as a first course, 5 or 6 as a main course.

SAUTÉED SHRIMP ROMAN STYLE

Serves 3 or 4 as a first course

1 lb. large shrimp (8 or 10 to a lb.)
5 shallots
¼ bunch parsley
12 tablespoons unsalted butter (6 oz.)
2 cloves garlic
flour
¾ cup dry white table wine
salt and cayenne pepper

1. Peel and devein the shrimp—leaving the tail shells intact. Chop the shallots finely; discard the parsley stems and chop the leaves.
2. Melt half the butter in a skillet. Add the shallots; add the garlic through a press. Dredge the shrimp in flour, and shake off the excess.
3. Turn up the heat and add the shrimp. Sauté approximately 4 minutes, tossing the shrimp 5 or 6 times during cooking. Remove to a serving dish.
4. Add the wine, and reduce by half to ¼ cup. Add the remaining butter, the parsley, and salt and cayenne pepper to taste. Pour the sauce over the shrimp and serve immediately.

These crab cakes are deep-fried—you may wish to refer to page 140 with any questions you might have on deep-frying.

CRAB CAKES

Makes 12 3-inch cakes

1 lb. cooked crab meat
¼ lb. mushrooms
8 pimento-stuffed green olives
2 tablespoons walnut oil
4 tablespoons unsalted butter, melted
salt and cayenne pepper
3 eggs
2 teaspoons water
3 oz. dry bread crumbs (1 cup)
2 cups vegetable oil
Tartar Sauce II or Rémoulade Sauce (see page 87)
a deep-fryer with basket
a deep-fry thermometer

1. Chop the crab. Clean the mushrooms and chop them finely. Chop the olives.
2. Heat the walnut oil in a skillet and sauté the mushrooms quickly until there is no liquid remaining. In a bowl, combine the mushrooms, crab, melted butter, and olives. Add salt and cayenne to taste.
3. Break 2 eggs into a small bowl and beat well with a fork. Add enough egg to the crab mixture so that it holds together. Mold the mixture into 12 small flat patties each about 3 inches wide.
4. Beat the 2 teaspoons water into the remaining egg. Moisten the patties with the egg mixture and coat them with bread crumbs.
5. Heat oil to 380° in a deep-fryer with a basket. Arrange the cakes without crowding and fry for 3 minutes or until they turn a rich brown color.
6. Drain on paper towels and serve hot on warm plates with Tartar Sauce II or Rémoulade Sauce.

BROILING AND GRILLING SEAFOOD

Broiling or grilling over hot coals is a dry-heat method of cooking and since most fish do not have a lot of fat, cooking times must be short. (See chapter 8 for more general information on grilling.) The fish should be marinated beforehand and basted frequently during cooking with the marinade or some fat. Fatty fish, such as salmon, mackerel, bluefish, or shad are especially good grilled.

This can be your standard recipe for grilled fish steaks—salmon, halibut, tuna, mahimahi, swordfish—any firm-fleshed fish, sold in the fish market as a "steak." Serve with the Parsley-Anchovy Sauce below or any of the butter-based sauces in chapter 3.

GRILLED FISH STEAKS
Serves 4

olive oil for the grill
4 tablespoons unsalted
  butter
4 fish steaks, cut ½ inch
  thick
salt and pepper
Parsley-Anchovy Sauce (see
  recipe below)

1. Preheat the grill or broiler for 30 minutes. Melt the butter.
2. Oil the grill. Brush the fish with butter and grill the fish 4 inches from the heat, 3 to 4 minutes per side; turn once, brushing with butter. Sprinkle with salt and pepper to taste and serve with Parsley-Anchovy Sauce.

Parsley-Anchovy Sauce

1 bunch parsley
1 bunch fresh oregano
4 cloves garlic
6 anchovy fillets
2 tablespoons capers, rinsed
  and drained
¼ cup lemon juice
¾ cup olive oil
pepper

1. Remove and discard the stems from the parsley and oregano. Peel the garlic. Drain the anchovies.
2. In a blender or food processor, combine all ingredients and process until smooth. Add ground pepper to taste.

GRILLED SALMON SALAD
Serves 4 to 6

1½ lbs. boneless salmon
6 fresh mint leaves
2 cloves garlic
½ cup fresh lemon juice
½ cup walnut oil
⅛ teaspoon dry oregano
1 small red onion
½ head Romaine lettuce
½ bunch spinach
12 cherry tomatoes
6 wood or metal skewers

1.   Remove skin from the fish and cut fish into 1½-inch cubes.
2.   Chop the mint leaves and garlic. Combine the lemon juice, oil, mint, oregano, and garlic. Place the fish in a glass bowl and marinate 30 minutes. Drain and reserve marinade.
3.   Cut the onion into quarters and separate the sections. If you are using wooden skewers, soak them in water 30 minutes before skewering fish. Skewer the fish, alternating the onion and fish chunks.
4.   Preheat the grill or broiler 30 minutes. Place skewers on the oiled grill (or under a broiler) 4 to 5 inches from the heat. Grill 3 minutes each side, turning and basting with the reserved marinade.
5.   Wash, crisp, and tear the greens into serving pieces.
6.   Warm the marinade in a small saucepan.
7.   Place greens on each plate, arrange skewered fish on the greens, and spoon the marinade over all. Cut the tomatoes in half and garnish each plate with tomato halves.

Don't be put off by the notion of cooking poultry and shellfish together—the combination is a winner!

SKEWERED CHICKEN BREAST, SHRIMP, AND SCALLOPS
Serves 8

1 cup walnut oil
½ cup raspberry vinegar
1 tablespoon coarsely
  ground pepper
1 teaspoon salt
3 half breasts of chicken
16 medium shrimp (16 to 20
  to a lb.)
16 bay scallops
3 red bell peppers
4 slices pancetta, ⅛ inch
  thick
8 skewers

1. Combine the walnut oil, raspberry vinegar, pepper, and salt in a bowl large enough to hold the chicken, shrimp, and scallops.

2. Remove the bones and skin from the chicken breasts (see page 42) and cut the 3 half breasts into a total of 16 pieces. Place the chicken pieces in the marinade. Peel and devein the shrimp, leaving the tail shells intact, and place the shrimp in the marinade. Rinse the scallops, remove the tough strip of white muscle (if there is one), and drop the scallops into the marinade. Marinate everything for 30 minutes.

3. Cut the bell peppers and pancetta slices into 32 pieces each. If the skewers are wooden, soak them in water for 30 minutes. Preheat the grill or broiler for 30 minutes.

4. For each serving, alternately skewer 2 pieces of chicken, 2 scallops, 2 shrimp, and 4 pieces each of bell pepper and pancetta.

5. Grill or broil 4 inches from the heat for 5 minutes each side, turning once—for a total cooking time of 10 minutes. Brush with marinade when turning. Serve with Wild Rice Salad (see page 102).

Cooking Eggs

Chapter 10

Several years ago, my husband and I found ourselves on a week-long driving trip from Phoenix, Arizona, to San Francisco. We stopped at various cafes and restaurants along the way, and often ordered eggs. By the trip's end, I realized that at few of the places we had eaten, fancy hotel dining room or roadside cafe, did the cooks know how to prepare this basic food. No matter if we ordered the eggs poached, boiled, scrambled, or fried, they were almost always overcooked. That was when I decided to add a lesson on egg cooking to my basic course. When I returned home, I sent to numerous agencies for facts and information about eggs. Soon I began developing recipes to illustrate the proper methods and techniques for cooking eggs.

People who cannot eat eggs know how difficult it can be to eliminate them from the diet. It means giving up a readily available, relatively inexpensive, versatile, and highly nutritious food, one that is practically indispensable in cooking. Whisked egg whites are leavening agents in soufflés and cakes. Whole eggs are stabilizers in sauces like mayonnaise and are also binders in meat loaves or are used as thickening agents in soups, custards, and sauces, and to hold on bread crumbs in breaded, fried foods. They are also brushed over the tops of breads and pastries to insure a shiny surface and are sometimes used like glue to keep foods in place. And, of course, there are endless numbers of recipes in which eggs are the main ingredient, some of which we explore in this chapter. (Also see chapters 14 and 15.)

The eggs we buy in the market are graded for size and quality, from Grade AA to Grade C and from jumbo to peewee. My recommendation is to always buy Grade AA large, as most recipes are written for large eggs. Whether the eggs are brown or white have nothing to do with the flavor or nutritional content of the egg, only with the breed of the hen. Always store eggs in the refrigerator in the egg carton. If they are not covered, they will absorb refrigerator odors.

No matter how you are preparing eggs, the number one rule, as with preparing seafood, is not to overcook them. Always cook eggs carefully over low heat watching the time closely.

BOILED EGGS

Actually, you should never boil an egg. Besides cracking the shell and making the whites rubbery, boiling eggs may cause a chemical reaction between the iron in the yolks and the sulphur in the whites. This reaction can spoil the flavor and turn the yolks green. The following is a method I have used with success:

Put the eggs in cold water in a pot that has a tight-fitting lid. The eggs should lie in a single layer, close enough together to remain steady when the water boils. Bring the water to a boil and immediately remove the pot from the heat. Put on the lid and let the eggs stand until the desired degree of doneness is attained. Immediately immerse the eggs in cold water and let stand at least 1 minute. To peel the eggs, roll them gently on a hard surface to crack the shell and then peel under cold running water, starting at the rounded end. Store the peeled eggs in water (to keep them from drying out) until ready to use.

The following cooking times are for large eggs.

Soft-cooked—3 minutes   *Medium-cooked*—4 minutes
Hard-cooked—12 minutes

HARD-COOKED EGGS WITH A BASIL SAUCE
Serves 8

½ **bunch fresh basil**
½ **bunch flat-leaf parsley**
3 cloves garlic
2 oz. Parmesan
8 hard-cooked eggs
¾ **cup olive oil**
salt and pepper

1.   Remove and discard the stems from the basil and parsley and chop the leaves finely. Chop the garlic finely. Grate the cheese. Peel the eggs and cut in half lengthwise; arrange on a platter.

2.   Combine the garlic, oil, cheese, and herbs. Season with salt and pepper to taste.

3.   Pour the basil sauce over the eggs and allow to marinate 1 hour before serving.

POACHED EGGS

Vinegar helps the white of the egg hold its shape. Do not add salt to the poaching liquid as the salt breaks down the raw egg white and makes it stringy.

Fill an appropriately-sized sauté pan or saucepan half full of water. For every quart of water, add 2 oz. of vinegar. Bring the water to a boil. Crack the egg into a shallow bowl or saucer, lower the heat to a gentle simmer, and slide the egg into the water. Gently poach for 3 minutes. Remove the poached egg with a slotted spoon and trim to a neat shape. (Several eggs may be poached at a time.) If the egg is not to be served immediately, gently place in a bowl of cold water. The egg will stay soft and can be kept in the refrigerator at least a day. When needed, you can warm the egg in two changes of hot tap water for 1 minute each time, and proceed as though it were freshly made.

POACHED EGGS IN A RED WINE SAUCE

Serves 8 as a first course

½ **bunch fresh parsley**
16 **tiny boiling onions**
½ **lb. mushrooms**
10 **tablespoons unsalted butter**
1 **cup Brown Stock**
4 **cups red table wine**
½ **cup concentrated Brown Stock**
16 **poached eggs**
8 **oval gratin dishes**

1. Remove and discard the parsley stems and chop the leaves. Peel and trim the onions; clean and quarter the mushrooms. Warm the gratin dishes in the oven.

2. In a skillet, sauté the mushrooms over high heat in 3 tablespoons of butter for 3 minutes. Transfer to a bowl. In the same skillet, add 3 more tablespoons of butter and sauté the onions 3 minutes. Add the Brown Stock, cover the pan, and simmer until tender. Remove the onions with a slotted spoon and add them to the bowl with the mushrooms.

3. Add the wine and concentrated stock to the skillet and reduce the mixture to a cup. Return the onions and mushrooms to the reduced sauce.

4. Warm the poached eggs in 2 changes of hot tap water for 1 minute each time. Place the warmed poached eggs into the warmed oval gratin dishes. Bring the sauce to a boil, remove from the heat and swirl in the remaining butter to enrich and thicken the sauce. Spoon the sauce over the eggs, sprinkle with chopped parsley, and serve immediately.

The following recipe will be fun for you to try—I think you will be amazed at how professional the results will be.

EGGS IN ASPIC
Serves 6 as an appetizer

1 package gelatin (1 tablespoon)
2 tablespoons cold water
1 qt. Consommé (see page 53)
12 leaves fresh tarragon
6 poached eggs
6 thin slices cooked ham
1 bunch watercress
6 round or oval 4-oz. metal molds

1. Dissolve the gelatin in the cold water. Warm the dissolved gelatin until it liquifies and add it to the Consommé to create the aspic. Pour boiling water over the tarragon leaves and dry on paper towels.
2. Poach the eggs, trim them to neat ovals, and put them in a bowl of cold water. Cut the slices of ham into rounds or ovals so they fit into the molds—reserving the trimmings for another use.
3. Pour a thin layer of liquid aspic into the bottom of each mold. Refrigerate until set—about 15 minutes.
4. Dip the tarragon leaves into the liquid aspic and arrange 2 of them in a design on top of the set jelly in each mold. Chill briefly to set the tarragon leaves.
5. Using a slotted spoon lift the eggs out of the water and place 1 poached egg, yolk side down, in each mold. Cover each egg with a slice of ham. Gently pour in enough of the aspic to fill the mold. Chill the molds, and chill any remaining aspic.
6. To serve, dip each mold into hot water for 3 or 4 seconds. Run a knife around the edge of the jelly and turn upside down on a serving platter. Chop the remaining firm aspic into tiny dice, and arrange around each egg. Garnish with watercress and chill until serving time.

FRIED EGGS

Crack the egg into a shallow bowl or saucer. Melt unsalted butter in a heavy skillet over low heat. When the butter has melted and just begun to brown, gently slide the egg into the skillet. Cover partially and cook 1 minute. After 1 minute begin checking for doneness. The egg is ready as soon as all of the white is just set. The yolk should be soft. Sprinkle with salt and pepper and slide out of the pan.

SCRAMBLED EGGS

Melt unsalted butter in a heavy skillet over medium heat. Break the eggs into a bowl and mix the eggs with a fork until the whites and yolks are blended. When the butter begins to foam, pour in the eggs and turn the heat to low. Season with salt and pepper, and stir the eggs with a wooden spoon, scraping the cooked portions of the eggs into the uncooked portions. Stir constantly and cook until the eggs are thick, soft, and moist.

SCRAMBLED EGGS WITH SHALLOTS AND HERBS
Serves 4

2 shallots
¼ bunch parsley
3 sprigs fresh oregano
¼ lb. unsalted butter
10 eggs
salt and pepper
a 10-inch skillet

1.   Chop the shallots finely. Remove and discard the stems from the parsley and oregano and chop the leaves finely.
2.   Melt half the butter in the skillet over medium heat. Break the eggs into a bowl and mix the eggs with a fork until the whites and yolks are blended.
3.   When the butter begins to foam, add the shallots and sauté 1 minute. Pour in the eggs and turn the heat to low. Season with salt and pepper, add the herbs, and stir the eggs with a wooden spoon, scraping the cooked portions of the eggs into the uncooked portions. Add the remaining butter and, stirring constantly, cook until the eggs are thick, soft, and moist. Serve immediately.

OMELETS

Omelets may be intimidating to some—but in fact, with practice they are not at all difficult to make. They make a perfect meal on those occasions when you do not feel like spending a lot of time and effort cooking and when the refrigerator is quite bare except for eggs and . . .

To prevent omelets from sticking, it is important to season the pan properly. Either follow the manufacturers' instructions for seasoning or follow mine: Pour in enough oil to fill the pan about ¼ inch deep. With a paper towel, spread some oil up the sides of the pan. Place the pan over low heat and allow it to heat until the oil smokes. Remove from the heat and allow the pan to cool. When cooled, discard the oil and wipe out the pan with a paper towel.

Omelets are an exception to the low heat rule, because they are cooked on medium-high heat. However, the basic rule still applies—eggs should never be overcooked. In a well-seasoned omelet pan, melt unsalted butter over medium-high heat. Break the eggs into a bowl and mix the eggs with a fork until the whites and yolks are blended. When the butter begins to foam, pour in the eggs and reduce the heat slightly. Season with salt and pepper and a teaspoon of butter for every egg. Stir the eggs 2 or 3 times, and when the underside of the omelet begins to set, lift the edges so that uncooked egg from the top will run under the cooked egg and set. Repeat until the omelet is firm around the sides but still liquid near the center. Remove from the heat and if the omelet is to be filled, spoon the filling onto one side of the omelet. With a fork, fold the omelet in half. Tilt the pan up against a warmed plate and let the omelet roll onto the plate. Brush the surface of the omelet with butter and serve immediately.

There are almost no limits to the flavorings or fillings that can go into omelets. A mixture of fresh herbs, chopped anchovies, sautéed diced vegetables, smoked fish, sour cream, shredded cheeses, or even a variety of sweet fillings, such as poached fruits or jams, can be added as soon as the edges of the omelet are firm but the top is still moist—just before the omelet is rolled or folded and slid out of the pan. Here is just one idea.

WATERCRESS OMELET
Serves 2

2 shallots
1 bunch watercress
7 tablespoons unsalted
  butter
salt and pepper
6 eggs
a seasoned 8-inch omelet
  pan

1.   Chop the shallots; remove and discard the large stems from the watercress. Reserve 2 sprigs of watercress for garnish.
2.   Melt 2 tablespoons of butter in a skillet and sauté the watercress and chopped shallots for 2 minutes. Chop the watercress finely and season to taste with salt and pepper. Set the filling aside.
3.   Over medium-high heat, melt 2 tablespoons of butter in the omelet pan. Break 3 eggs into a bowl and mix the eggs with a fork until the whites and yolks are blended. When the butter begins to foam, pour in the eggs and reduce the heat slightly. Season with salt and pepper and a tablespoon of butter.
4.   Stir the eggs 2 or 3 times with a fork, and when the underside of the omelet begins to set, lift the edges so that uncooked egg from the top will run under the cooked egg and set. Repeat until the omelet is firm around the sides but still liquid near the center.
5.   Spoon half the filling onto one side of the omelet. With a fork, fold the omelet in half. Tilt the pan at right angles against a warmed plate and let the omelet roll onto the plate. Brush the surface of the omelet with butter and place the reserved sprig of watercress on top. Repeat the procedure for the second omelet and serve immediately.

FLAT OMELETS

Flat omelets, sometimes called pancake omelets, are similar to omelets but differ in two ways: First, they are always flat, not folded, and second, the filling is always mixed in with the eggs. In Spain, they are called *tortillas,* and in Italy, *frittatas.*

POTATO AND ONION OMELET (Tortilla de Patata)
Serves 4 to 6

3 large potatoes
1 medium onion
½ cup olive oil
2 teaspoons salt
4 tablespoons unsalted
  butter
6 eggs
a 10-inch skillet

1. Peel and slice the potatoes into ⅛-inch rounds. Chop the onion finely.
2. Heat the olive oil in the skillet, add the potatoes, sprinkle them with 1 teaspoon of the salt and turn them in the pan to coat well with oil. Continue cooking, until the potatoes brown lightly; then add the onions, reduce the heat, and cook about 10 minutes, stirring now and then—the potatoes should be tender. Transfer to paper towels and drain.
3. Melt the butter in the same skillet. Crack the eggs into a bowl and mix lightly with the remaining teaspoon of salt. Stir in the potatoes and onions. Pour the omelet mixture into the pan, spreading it out with a spatula, and cook over moderate heat 2 minutes. Cover the skillet with a flat plate and, grasping the plate and skillet firmly together, invert them and turn the omelet out onto the plate. Then carefully slide the omelet back into the pan, cooked side up, and cook 2 minutes longer to set the underside. Serve at once.

OMELET WITH HERBS (Frittata aromatica)
Serves 4 to 6

½ bunch spinach (½ lb.)
¼ bunch parsley
¼ bunch basil
4 tablespoons unsalted
  butter
7 eggs
1 teaspoon salt
¼ teaspoon pepper
a 10-inch skillet

1. Clean and chop the spinach, parsley, and basil. Heat the butter in the skillet, and cook the spinach, parsley, and basil over medium heat for 3 minutes.
2. Crack the eggs into a bowl and mix the eggs lightly with the salt and pepper; pour over the herb mixture and cook over medium heat until mixture begins to set—in 5 or 6 minutes. Place a plate upside down over the frittata, and holding the plate and pan together, turn pan quickly upside down over the plate. Slip the frittata, cooked side up, from the plate back into the frying pan and cook about 2 minutes longer to set the underside. Serve immediately.

COOKING WITH CHEESE

Chapter 11

I certainly will not attempt in this chapter to explain and describe all the cheeses of the world. Instead, I will concentrate on the basics of cooking with cheese, and comment briefly on only a few of what cheese books call the "great" cheeses. I would like to suggest that you purchase a comprehensive cheese book and that, along with reading about cheeses, you also purchase small amounts of different cheeses so you can taste them as well. I think you will find learning about cheeses of limitless fascination.

In cooking with cheese, it is important to know that cheese should only be melted, not cooked. Too high a heat or a long cooking time separates the protein in the cheese from the fat, suddenly making the cheese stringy or leathery. For sauces, always shred or break up the cheese into small pieces so that it will melt more quickly; or blend it with other ingredients such as custard, white sauce, or wine to reduce its density. Generally, the longer a cheese has aged, the better the flavor; the younger the cheese, the milder the flavor. Use well-aged cheeses when appropriate, for best results. They may cost a bit more, but they will add a distinctive quality to your dishes that will make them well worth any extra expense. Avoid processed American cheese in cooking since the heating process used in making that type of cheese gives it an unpleasant plastic-rubbery texture. It does not age and remains relatively tasteless.

The following are some of the cheeses most commonly used in cooking.

Swiss Emmenthal is a firm pale cheese with large holes and a wonderful, hazelnut-like flavor. It is made in the Emme Valley in Switzerland and is one of the most difficult cheeses in the world to make. It is aged 4 to 10 months (the United States is shipped the youngest cheeses), and the wheels weigh anywhere from 145 to 220 pounds. Emmenthal has been copied and sometimes faked by every country in the world. There is domestic "Swiss," imported "Swiss," Austrian Emmenthal, Danish "Swiss" (Samsoe), Edam, Jarlsberg, etc. Real Swiss Emmenthal has the words "Switzerland Emmenthaler" etched continuously on the rind.

Swiss Gruyère is in the same flavor family as Emmenthal. The wheels are smaller as are the holes. The color is roughly the same, but the rind of the Gruyère is not smooth and amber colored but brown and wrinkled like an almond skin. Swiss Gruyère tends to be a little sweeter than the French Gruyère—the French has more tang. Gruyère melts beautifully and is often combined with a sharper cheese such as Parmesan.

Italian Fontina is a wonderful delicately savory cheese that has flavor without sharpness. This is the only true Fontina and comes from a rigidly defined zone in the mountains of northern Italy near the Swiss border called the Valley of Aosta. It is warm ivory in color, and the texture is fairly firm and smooth, with tiny holes here and there. There are many imitations such as Fontal, Fontinella, and Fantina which are bland, tasteless, and often rubbery. Italian Fontina melts beautifully and is the cheese used in the famous Piedmontese *Fonduta*—Italian fondue.

Parmigiano-Reggiano is the only *real* Parmesan and is produced under the strictest legal and technical supervision. It is made with milk produced between April 1 and November 11 in the provinces of Parma, Reggio, Modena, Mantua, and Bologna. Any other Italian grating cheese is called simply *grana*. Real Parmesan will have the words *"Parmigiano-Reggiano"* etched in small dots in a continuously repeated pattern over the entire rind. There are "imported" Parmesans from Argentina and elsewhere, as well as domestic Parmesans, all poor imitations of the real thing. *Parmigiano-Reggiano* is an excellent grating cheese, perfect in sauces and soufflés, and wonderful eaten after a meal with fruit. Once you have tasted the true Parmesan it will be very difficult for you to enjoy imitations.

Cheddar cheese originated in England, but is now made all over the world. There is no uniform flavor for a Cheddar, but no matter what part of the world the Cheddar comes from, the criteria for a fine Cheddar remains the same. It is made from whole summer milk of cows, is aged slowly until it is at least 18 months old, has a firm yet porous texture, and is very full in flavor, sharp but not bitter, crumbly but not dry. Cheddars are excellent melting cheeses.

Mozzarella at its best is very tender and drips with its fresh whey as one bites into it. At one time it was made only from buffalo's milk, as it still is in southern Italy. In other parts of Italy, as in the United States, mozzarella is made mostly from cow's milk. Avoid vacuum-packed mozzarella—it is rubbery with virtually no taste. Fresh mozzarella is commonly served as an appetizer, a breakfast cheese, and as a melting cheese.

Mascarpone is an exquisite butter-colored cheese that tastes like whipped cream and is indeed made from fresh cream. It is eaten as is with sugar and fruit, sometimes served beaten with brandy, eggs, and sugar, or used to enrich sauces. It is made all over Italy and may be purchased here in cheese shops or Italian delicatessens. It is not one of the most commonly known cheeses, but is so spectacular, I could not omit it.

Roquefort is made in Roquefort-sur-Sulzon in the province of Rouergue, France. It is made from sheep's milk and is produced by inoculating the cheese curd with *penicillium roqueforti*—a mold-producing substance—and ripening it in the damp, cool, drafty limestone caves peculiar to the rocky country in that district. No other blue cheese of France can legally be called Roquefort. It is the caves' unusual formation and mineral composition that accounts for the fact that even though Roquefort is probably the most imitated cheese in the world, it has never been duplicated. One taste of a really good Roquefort quickly explains why it has been widely recognized as the "king of cheeses."

Cheese Fondue

Cheese fondue is a dish that originated in the French-speaking part of Switzerland. It consists of grated cheese melted in white wine, flavored with a little kirsch. There are Italian, French, Swiss, and German fondues. A recipe follows for Swiss Fondue, the most widely known fondue.

Since eating the dish requires diners to dip into the fondue pot with pieces of bread speared on the ends of long forks—a fondue party is informal and a lot of fun.

Use both Swiss Gruyère and Emmenthaler in making Swiss fondue since the Emmenthaler flavor is necessary but Emmenthaler does not melt well. Gruyère melts to a creamy smoothness and blends well with Emmenthaler. The wine and lemon juice add the necessary acidity which helps the cheeses melt and blend together smoothly. Potato starch thickens the fondue and helps stabilize the cheese. (It doesn't lump and has a greater thickening power than flour.) If your fondue separates, mix a tablespoon of potato starch with 1 teaspoon of lemon juice and 1 tablespoon of wine, add it to the separated fondue mixture, and stir until smooth. If the fondue becomes too thick, add 4 or 5 tablespoons of wine, little by little, stirring until the fondue reaches the desired consistency. If it is too thin, add a little more shredded Gruyère that has been tossed with potato starch. It is always safer to start the fondue on top of the stove, since often a tabletop burner will not get hot enough to initially melt the cheese.

SWISS FONDUE
Serves 4

2 loaves day-old French
  bread
¾ lb. Gruyère
¼ lb. Emmenthal
white pepper
nutmeg
1 clove garlic
2 tablespoons potato starch
1½ cups dry white table
  wine
1 tablespoon lemon juice
4 tablespoons kirsch
a tabletop burner
a ceramic fondue pot and
  fondue forks

1.   Tear (do not cut) the French bread into bite-size pieces and place in a napkin-lined basket. Grate the cheeses and toss in a bowl with 4 grinds of the pepper mill, 2 turns of the nutmeg grinder, and the potato starch.
2.   Cut the garlic clove in half and rub the inside of the fondue pot with the garlic. Discard the garlic.
3.   In a medium-sized saucepan, heat the wine and lemon juice and bring it to a boil.
4.   Lower the heat slightly and toss in a handful of the cheese and stir constantly with a wooden spoon until the cheese melts. Repeat until all the cheese has been added and melted into a light, smooth sauce. Stir in the kirsch and remove from the heat.
5.   Light the tabletop burner and adjust the heat to a low flame. Place the fondue pot on the burner. Transfer the melted cheese to the fondue pot and pass the bread to each guest. The bread is then speared on a long fondue fork and dipped into the fondue pot.

The following mixture has many uses. It can be placed inside pastry to make cheese turnovers. It can be sliced, placed on toast or veal cutlets or chicken breasts, and then broiled. It can be shaped and deep-fried for hors d'oeuvre or croquettes. I suggest you make the recipe in the following quantity, form as many croquettes as needed, and freeze the remainder of the mixture for perhaps another use. Since you begin by making a white sauce, you may want to refer back to chapter 3, page 71 to review that procedure.

CHEESE CROQUETTES
Makes about 24 croquettes

2 oz. Parmesan
6 oz. Gruyère
5 tablespoons unsalted
   butter
10 tablespoons flour (about
   ¾ cup)
1 cup milk
3 egg yolks
salt and pepper
9 oz. bread crumbs (3 cups
oil for frying
a deep-fryer
a deep-fry thermometer

1.   Grate the cheeses. In a 2-qt. saucepan, melt the butter, blend in the flour, cook and stir 3 minutes, then add the milk. Bring to a boil, lower the heat, and stir until thickened.
2.   Turn off the heat, add the grated cheeses, and stir until melted. (You may have to put the mixture back over low heat if it does not readily melt.) Add the egg yolks and stir until well blended. Add salt and pepper to taste, and chill until thick and cool.
3.   Season the bread crumbs with salt and pepper and spread out on a flat surface. Scoop up the cooled cheese mixture a generous tablespoon at a time and place in the bread crumbs. Sprinkle more bread crumbs on top, then roll the croquette over until it is completely coated. Let the croquettes stand at least 30 minutes to set the coating.
4.   Heat enough oil in the deep-fryer to reach halfway up the sides. When the oil is hot—370° on a deep-fry thermometer—place the croquettes one by one in the oil. When the bottoms have browned, turn the croquettes and brown the other sides. Drain on paper towels.
5.   Arrange the croquettes on a folded napkin on a warmed serving plate. Serve immediately.

MELTED CHEESE ON TOAST
Serves 8

½ lb. aged Cheddar
1 tablespoon prepared
   mustard
pepper
paprika
4 tablespoons unsalted
   butter
4 tablespoons milk
8 thick slices bread

1.   Grate the cheese and place in a bowl with the mustard and pepper and paprika to taste. In a small saucepan, heat the butter and milk until the butter melts, remove from the heat, and stir into the cheese until smooth. Allow to cool.
2.   Lightly toast the sliced bread. Spread the cheese mixture on the toast and place under the broiler until the cheese has melted.

These light cheese morsels are ideal with soups or salads or as snacks.

CHEDDAR CHEESE SQUARES
Makes about 5 dozen

3 oz. sharp Cheddar
¼ lb. unsalted butter
½ teaspoon salt
½ teaspoon pepper
10 oz. flour (about 2 cups)

1. Shred the cheese. On a pastry board, combine the butter and cheese until well blended. Combine the salt, pepper, and flour. Gradually combine the flour and cheese mixtures and form into a ball of dough. (The mixture will be crumbly.) Place in a plastic bag and chill 2 hours.
2. Preheat the oven to 375°. Roll the dough out to ½-inch thickness. Cut into ¾-inch squares and place on a baking sheet. Bake in the oven for 20 minutes.

This dessert is one I always make when I only have about 10 minutes preparation time and a big crowd to serve. I don't know if there is another less pretentious yet, at the same time, more exquisite dessert.

MASCARPONE WITH BERRIES
Serves 8 to 10

¾ lb. mascarpone cheese
3 egg yolks
3½ oz. superfine sugar
   (½ cup)
6 tablespoons brandy
1 cup crème fraîche
1 lb. fresh berries
individual long-stemmed
   dessert glasses

1. Whisk the mascarpone until smooth and fluffy. Add the egg yolks, sugar, and brandy and combine well.
2. Whisk the crème fraîche until soft peaks form and gently fold into the cheese mixture.
3. Spoon the cheese into the dessert glasses and garnish with berries.

CRÊPES

Chapter 12

In my cooking school, some students think this is the class that is the most fun because there is a great deal of student participation. Everyone comes up to the stove and makes crêpes by my special foolproof method. As nervous as most people are, standing in front of their classmates, they still make a perfect crêpe!

Crêpes are French in origin and differ from our pancake by their thinness and lightness. There is no other dish that offers as much opportunity for creative cooking as crêpes. They can be stuffed and rolled or shaped into half moons or little "horns of plenty," or they can be stacked with filling in between the layers. They can be sweet or savory. They can be served as hors d'oeuvre, first courses, main courses, or desserts. They are just the thing for a fast and effortless "do-it-ahead" menu since crêpe batter can be made and stored in the refrigerator for 2 days and the finished crêpes can be made in quantity and stored in the refrigerator a couple of days or in the freezer for a month. Once they are filled, they may be refrigerated several hours before being heated through for serving.

Crêpe Batter

Crêpe batter should be the consistency of cream: the thinner the batter, the thinner the crêpes. The batter ingredients, most often flour, eggs, milk, and butter, should be combined thoroughly to eliminate any lumps. The batter, once made, needs to rest at least an hour before it is used.

Crêpe Pans

In making crêpes, it is important to have the right pan, and just as important that it be properly seasoned. There are pans sold specifically for crêpe making. They are generally 5 to 7 inches across the bottom, the smaller being suitable for hors d'oeuvre or dessert crêpes, the larger for a first course or main dish crêpe. Seasoning the pan will create a finish so smooth that the crêpe will not stick to it. Either follow the manufacturers' instructions for seasoning or follow mine: Pour in enough oil to fill the pan about a quarter inch deep. With a paper towel, spread some oil up the sides of the pan. Place the pan over low heat and allow it to heat until the oil smokes. Remove from the heat and let the pan cool. When cooled, discard the oil and wipe out the pan with a paper towel. Once you have seasoned a pan, reserve it for crêpe making only. A well-seasoned pan needs buttering only before the first crêpe.

Making the Crêpe

With my special method for making crêpes, you are guaranteed the thinnest possible crêpe each time.

1. Make the batter, allow it to rest at least 1 hour, and put it into a measuring cup with a good pouring spout.

2. Heat the pan, add a small amount of butter, and when it melts, wipe out the pan with a paper towel. Reserve the buttered paper towel and place the pan back over the heat. Test the pan with a few drops of batter; if they sizzle, the pan is ready.

3. If you are right-handed, hold the pan with your right hand, and with your left, pour some batter into the pan. (The reverse is true if you are left-handed.)

4. Immediately, pour any excess back into the container of batter. (The longer you leave the excess batter in the pan, the thicker the crêpe will be.)

5. Continue until all the batter is used, stacking the crêpes on top of each other so they do not dry out. They are now ready for storing or filling.

Pour some batter into pan.

Pour excess batter back into container.

Cook crêpe until set, no more than 20 seconds.

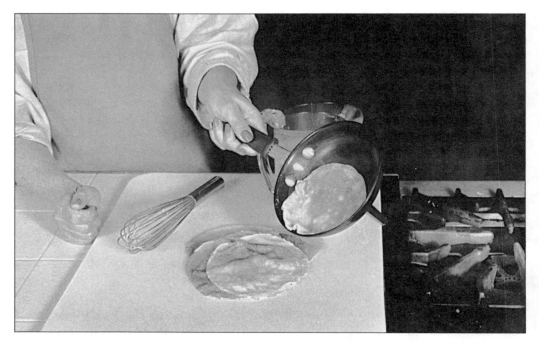

Flip crêpe over, cook another 5 to 10 seconds, and turn out onto plate or work surface.

Storing the Crêpes

If you do not plan to use the crêpes immediately, they may be stored in the refrigerator for 2 days or in the freezer for several weeks. Arrange the crêpes in stacks of 10 or so, wrap each stack in foil, and place in a plastic bag. Be sure to label them before storing them in the refrigerator or freezer.

Remove the crêpes from the refrigerator 20 minutes before you plan to use them. If they are frozen, allow 2 hours for them to defrost.

Heating the Crêpes

Once the crêpes are assembled as called for in the particular recipe you are using, they may stand several hours (in the refrigerator) before heating and serving. When heating the crêpes, always cover the baking dish and be careful not to leave it in the oven too long, since the crêpes will become crisp and dry if they are overbaked.

Crêpe batter can be made in a food processor or blender, or the ingredients can be simply whisked together in a bowl.

BASIC CRÊPE BATTER
About 12 7-inch or 16 5-inch crêpes

2 tablespoons unsalted butter
2 large eggs
¾ cup milk
3 oz. flour (a generous ½ cup)
½ teaspoon salt

1. Melt the butter. Combine the eggs and milk. Add the flour, melted butter, and salt and combine well using a blender, food processor, or whisk.
2. Allow the batter to stand for an hour or longer (if more than an hour, store in the refrigerator).

Variations:

Herbed Crêpes

Add 2 tablespoons chopped fresh herbs to the basic crêpe batter. Herbed crêpes can be rolled into cylinders and cut crosswise to create strips that may be used in soups like noodles. These are particularly good in a clear consommé (see page 53).

Dessert Crêpes

Add 2 tablespoons of sugar and 1 tablespoon of brandy or rum to the basic crêpe batter. Dessert crêpes may be eaten sprinkled with a little powdered sugar or filled with any sweet mixture like poached pears (see page 194).

In the following two recipes, the crêpes are stacked in layers like a cake. Both dishes make wonderful first courses or light suppers. They may be assembled hours ahead, refrigerated, and then heated before serving.

STACKED CRÊPES WITH SPINACH, MUSHROOMS, AND CHEESE
Serves 4 to 6

12 7-inch crêpes
Cheese Filling (recipe
 follows)
Spinach Filling (recipe
 follows)
Mushroom Filling (recipe
 follows)
1½ cups Basic Tomato Sauce
 (see page 78)
an oval or round ovenproof
 platter, lightly buttered

1.   Make the crêpes and set aside. Make the fillings (see below) and spread each filling out onto a plate, ready to assemble.

2.   **Assembly.** Place a single crêpe on the buttered platter. With a spatula, spread a thin layer of Cheese Filling over the entire crêpe, being careful to go out to the edge of the crêpe but not over. Put another crêpe on top and spread on a thin layer of Spinach Filling. Add a crêpe, and a thin layer of Mushroom Filling. Continue alternating layers of crêpe and filling until the last crêpe is used, finishing with a plain crêpe.

3.   Cover with foil and heat in a 350° oven about 20 minutes, or until warm.

4.   To serve, cut into wedges like a cake. Heat the Basic Tomato Sauce, put some on each serving plate, and lay the wedge of stacked crêpes on top of the sauce.

Cheese Filling

¼ lb. cream cheese
¼ lb. Roquefort cheese
2 tablespoons chopped
 fresh parsley
2 tablespoons crème fraîche
salt and pepper

Combine all the ingredients and mix until smooth. Taste for seasoning, and add salt and pepper as needed.

Spinach Filling

1 lb. fresh spinach
2 hard-cooked eggs
2 shallots
3 tablespoons unsalted
 butter
salt and pepper
nutmeg
3 tablespoons crème fraîche

1.   Clean the spinach, cut off and discard about an inch of stems, and cook in the water clinging to the leaves—tossing constantly. (It will take about 3 or 4 minutes.) Drain and chop the spinach coarsely. Sieve the hard-cooked eggs. Chop the shallots finely.

2.   Melt the butter in a skillet, add the shallots, and sauté 30 seconds. Add the spinach, sieved eggs, salt, pepper, and 2 grinds of nutmeg. Stir over a low heat 1 minute. Mix in the crème fraîche, and transfer to a plate to cool.

Mushroom Filling

½ lb. fresh mushrooms
2 green onions
Basic White Sauce
2 tablespoons unsalted
  butter
salt and pepper

1.   Clean and chop the mushrooms finely. Clean and chop the green onions finely. Make Basic White Sauce using 2 tablespoons flour, 2 tablespoons unsalted butter, but only ¼ cup milk, because it needs to be quite thick. (See page 71.)
2.   In a skillet, melt the butter and sauté the mushrooms and onions until softened, about 2 minutes.
3.   Remove from the heat and stir in enough of the White Sauce to hold the mixture together. Season to taste with salt and pepper and transfer filling to a plate to cool.

STACKED HAM CRÊPES
Serves 6

12 7-inch crêpes
1 recipe Cheese Sauce (see
  page 72)
6 tablespoons unsalted
  butter
24 slices Black Forest Ham*,
  ⅛ inch thick
pepper
an oval or round ovenproof
  platter

1.   Make the crêpes and set aside. Make the Cheese Sauce. Melt the butter.
2.   Brush some butter on the platter in the shape of a crêpe. Place a crêpe over the butter and cover with 2 slices of ham. Brush the ham with melted butter, and sprinkle with a little ground pepper. Continue alternating layers of crêpes and ham and melted butter until the last crêpe is used, finishing with a plain crêpe.
3.   Spoon the Cheese Sauce over the stacked crêpes, and heat in a preheated 350° oven 20 minutes, or until sauce is bubbling.
4.   To serve, cut in wedges like a cake.

(*Any preferred cooked ham may be used; I have specified Black Forest Ham because the round shape fits the crêpe perfectly.*)

Folding crêpes into little "horns of plenty" shapes is an interesting way to serve vegetables. Asparagus, cauliflower, green beans, etc., work just as well as the broccoli in this recipe, and a cheese sauce may be substituted for the Hollandaise.

CRÊPES WITH BROCCOLI HOLLANDAISE
Serves 8

16 5-inch crêpes
2 cups Hollandaise Sauce (see page 84)
32 broccoli florets
an ovenproof platter, lightly buttered

1. Make the crêpes. Make the Hollandaise Sauce. Cook the broccoli using JE-H's Special Method (page 96).
2. Fold each crêpe in half, then in half again and place 2 cooked broccoli florets in each crêpe.
3. Place the crêpes on the buttered platter. Cover and place in a 350° oven 10 minutes to warm.
4. Carefully reheat the Hollandaise, and spoon some sauce on each warmed serving plate. Place 2 crêpes on top of the sauce and serve. Pass Hollandaise at the table.

In this dish, the crêpes are rolled around the pears in a conventional manner. This dessert is served warm. Apples, peaches, apricots, etc., may be substituted for the pears.

WARM PEAR CRÊPES WITH CHOCOLATE SAUCE
Serves 8

16 5-inch dessert crêpes
2 cups Wine Syrup (see page 22)
4 Bosc pears
1 cup Chocolate Sauce (see page 212)
an ovenproof platter, lightly buttered

1. Make the crêpes and set aside. Make the Wine Syrup. Peel, core, and quarter the pears, and poach until tender in Wine Syrup. (Use a wooden stick to determine when each pear is done. The riper the pear, the sooner it will be cooked.) Drain the pears and strain and reserve the syrup for another use*. While the pears are poaching, make the Chocolate Sauce.
2. Place one poached pear quarter on each crêpe and roll up.
3. Place the rolled crêpes, seam side down, on the buttered ovenproof platter, cover with foil and heat in a 350° oven for 10 minutes, or just until warmed.
4. Place 2 crêpes with the seam side down on each serving plate. Rewarm the sauce and spoon it in a ribbon over the crêpes letting the sauce make a little "pool" around the crêpes. Serve warm.

(*The syrup may be stored in the refrigerator and used whenever you need it again. Be sure to label the container.)

PASTA

Pasta comes in all shapes and sizes—tiny "pastina" for soups, long pastas like spaghetti, short thick noodles in butterfly and hat shapes, and stuffed pasta like ravioli. The pasta is usually boiled first, and then served with a sauce, or butter, or cheese, or it is mixed with meat, vegetables, or seafood, and then layered into casseroles and baked, like lasagne. In a well-prepared pasta dish, the noodle does not have a lot of flavor but has a chewy, satisfying texture—never soft or mushy. The flavor comes from the sauce, thereby creating a "perfect marriage."

Pasta, quite simply, is a paste made of flour and water, or, especially in northern Italy, flour and eggs. The dough is kneaded, rolled out, and cut (and, in the case of ravioli or tortellini, filled). Homemade pasta can be cooked fresh, or dried and stored in paper bags indefinitely.

I learned to make pasta when I studied cooking in Italy. My first stay there was for six weeks—and we made pasta every day—seven days a week. I returned an expert pasta maker! Most of the shaped pastas like spaghetti, macaroni, shells, spirals, etc., require special machinery and are not often prepared at home. But the flat, rolled pastas—linguini, lasagne, and fettucini, for example—can easily be made at home. Homemade noodles are not difficult to make and are rewardingly delicious. Once you taste homemade pasta, you will find it very difficult to eat any other.

You will need an unobstructed work surface, about 16×30 inches, upon which you can mix, knead, and roll out the dough. (A portable pastry board, wood or plastic, works very well.) I recommend that you purchase a small pasta machine, the kind that works like a hand wringer on an old-fashioned washing machine for rolling out the dough. If you do not have a pasta machine, you will need a rolling pin at least 14 inches long. However you roll it out, you will also need a place to dry the sheets of pasta a little before you cut them into noodles—a plastic clothes hanger, or the back of a kitchen chair with a towel draped over it works well. And you will need a place to dry the cut noodles before they are cooked or stored. Cake cooling racks work well or you can buy racks made especially for drying noodles. If you have a food processor, the pasta dough can be combined and kneaded in the machine.

When I studied cooking in Italy, I learned that an authentic Italian meal is not the huge plate of spaghetti and meat balls many of us think of when we think of Italian food. Pasta is included, but it is usually served in small portions as a separate course just before the main course. All the pasta dishes in this lesson make wonderful first courses, and the servings specified assume the pasta is being served as such, and not as the entrée. A generous handful of cooked pasta (about 4 oz.) is a reasonable first course serving per person. So, for 8 people you would need 2 lbs. of cooked pasta. Pasta doubles its weight when cooked, so to end up with 2 lbs. cooked, you would start with 1 lb. of uncooked pasta.

BASIC EGG NOODLES
Serves 2 to 3 (about 5 to 6 oz. dough)

¼ **lb. unbleached flour**
   (about ¾ cup)
1 large egg

1. Pour the flour onto the work surface, make a well in the center, put the egg into the well and lightly beat it with a fork. Add the flour gradually to the egg, drawing it from the inside of the well.

2. Incorporate as much flour as possible without the mixture becoming stiff and dry. (It is possible that you may need more flour or not use the entire amount.)

3. When the dough is blended and ready for kneading, put it through the pasta machine (follow directions that come with the machine) or knead it by hand until smooth. (If you have a food processor, the dough may be combined and kneaded—steps 1 through 3—in the machine.) Allow the ball of kneaded dough to rest under an inverted bowl for 20 minutes.

4. Cut the rested dough in half, and roll it out until it is about ¹⁄₁₆ inch thick. Let the sheets of pasta dry a little—until firm enough to cut without the noodles sticking together.

5. When the dough is firm, but not dry, cut the dough into the desired shaped noodle by hand or by machine, and cook immediately or spread out to dry and store.

PASTA SHAPES

Since it takes special equipment to make some pastas, (tubes, shells, spirals, etc.) I am not including them below. You can make any of the following, however, even without a pasta machine.

Cannelloni   Flat rectangles of pasta about 4 × 5 inches, to be rolled around a stuffing.

Fettucini   Flat noodles about ¼ inch wide.

Lasagne   Flat pasta, as it is rolled out of the machine (or cut 4 to 6 inches wide), used in baked, layered dishes.

Linguini   Noodles shaped like a flattened spaghetti.

Spaghettini   The thinnest spaghetti.

Tagliarini   Flat noodles about ⅛ inch wide.

COLORED PASTA DOUGH

I can still remember that first day of cooking in Italy, when, without telling us why, our instructor had us make pasta with egg yolks, pasta with spinach, and pasta with beets. I didn't catch on to what we were doing until the teacher spooned a little of all three colors of pasta into each serving bowl and announced, "The Italian flag—welcome to Italy!"

If you wish, you can make green, red, orange, or yellow pasta. Just use the recipe for Basic Egg Noodles, and follow the directions below. To compensate for the extra moistness when coloring pasta with vegetables, you will need to incorporate more flour—about 3 or 4 more tablespoons per egg—when you add the vegetables to the pasta dough. You will also have to allow for a little longer drying time before cutting the dough into noodles.

Green pasta   Add 3 oz. (weighed before it is cooked) fresh or frozen spinach or chard, cooked, drained, and finely chopped.

Red pasta   Add 1 tablespoon cooked, puréed beets.

Orange pasta   Add 1 teaspoon tomato paste.

Yellow pasta   Use 2 egg yolks and 1 tablespoon water instead of the whole egg.

COOKING PASTA

The best way to cook pasta is to start with plenty of boiling salted water. The pot should be tall and deep and have a capacity of at least 8 qts.—a stock pot is ideal.

1. You need 6 qts. of water and 1 tablespoon of salt for each pound of pasta. Bring the water to a boil, and drop in the pasta.

2. After the water returns to the boil, test every minute for doneness. (To test for doneness, remove a noodle from the pot and bite it or pinch it between your thumb and forefinger. When the pasta is tender but still firm, it is done.) If the pasta is fresh (not dried), it will take about 1 minute to cook. If the pasta is dried, it will take about 4 to 5 minutes to cook.

3. Drain and proceed with your recipe.

BASIC CREAM SAUCE FOR PASTA
Serves 8

2 shallots
1 clove garlic
10 canned Italian tomatoes,
  drained
¼ bunch parsley
2 oz. Parmesan
4 tablespoons unsalted
  butter
1 tablespoon flour
¼ cup dry white table wine
2 cups crème fraîche
salt and white pepper
1 lb. fettucini (3 recipes
  Basic Egg Noodles)

1. Chop the shallots and garlic. Seed and chop the tomatoes coarsely. Remove and discard the parsley stems and chop the leaves. Grate the Parmesan cheese.
2. In a saucepan, sauté the garlic and shallots in the butter until softened—about 1 minute. Add the flour and cook another minute. Add the wine and cook another minute over low heat.
3. Add the crème fraîche and the cheese and cook until the sauce thickens slightly. Add the tomatoes, parsley, and salt and pepper to taste.
4. To serve, boil the pasta, drain, place in serving bowls, and spoon the sauce over the noodles.

PASTA WITH CLAM SAUCE
Serves 8

4 dozen tiny clams
1 clove garlic
1½ lbs. tomatoes
½ bunch parsley
½ cup water
½ cup dry white table wine
½ cup olive oil
4 tablespoons unsalted
  butter
1 tablespoon flour
1 teaspoon dry oregano
freshly ground pepper
1 lb. linguini (3 recipes
  Basic Egg Noodles)

1. Clean the clams; chop the garlic; peel, seed, and chop the tomatoes. Chop the parsley leaves and discard the stems.
2. Steam the clams with the water, wine, and garlic until they open, about 5 to 7 minutes. Shuck 2 dozen clams and leave 2 dozen in their shells. Strain the clam liquor through a cheesecloth; reserve the liquor and discard the garlic.
3. In a heavy saucepan, heat the olive oil and butter. Add the flour and cook, stirring with a wire whisk, for 2 minutes. Add the tomatoes, oregano, and freshly ground pepper, and simmer gently for another minute. Add the reserved clam liquor and the shucked clams. Remove from the heat immediately—at this point, be careful not to overcook the clams.
4. Boil the pasta, drain, and place in serving bowls. Place 3 clams still in their shells on top of the pasta in each plate. Reheat the sauce and spoon over the pasta, garnishing each serving with chopped parsley.

GREEN AND WHITE FETTUCINI WITH MUSHROOMS, CREAM, AND PROSCIUTTO
Serves 8

1 small onion
¾ lb. mushrooms
¼ lb. thinly sliced
   prosciutto
¼ lb. Parmesan
4 tablespoons unsalted
   butter
2 cups crème fraîche
salt and pepper
½ lb. green fettucini (1
   recipe Basic Egg Noodles
   made with 3 oz. spinach)
½ lb. white fettucini (2
   recipes Basic Egg
   Noodles)

1.   Chop the onion, clean and slice the mushrooms, and shred the prosciutto. Grate the cheese.
2.   Melt the butter in a skillet, add the onion and sauté 1 minute; add the mushrooms and sauté an additional 4 minutes. Add the prosciutto, crème fraîche, and half the grated Parmesan. Cook 2 more minutes; add salt and pepper to taste.
3.   Boil each pasta separately and drain. Each serving should have two colors of fettucini placed side by side, not tossed together. Spoon the warm mushroom sauce over each serving. Pass the remaining grated cheese at the table.

GREEN PASTA WITH FOUR CHEESES
Serves 8

¼ lb. Parmesan
¼ lb. Italian Fontina
¼ lb. Gorgonzola
¼ lb. Bel Paese
¼ lb. unsalted butter
1½ cups crème fraîche
freshly ground pepper
1 lb. green tagliarini (2
   recipes Basic Egg Noodles
   made with 6 oz. spinach)

1.   Grate the Parmesan, and cut the other cheeses into small cubes.
2.   Combine the butter and crème fraîche in a saucepan. Add the 4 cheeses and stir over a low heat until the cheeses melt. Add freshly ground pepper to taste.
3.   Boil the pasta and drain. Place in serving bowls and spoon the cheese sauce over each portion.

FETTUCINI WITH A BASIL CREAM SAUCE
Serves 8

1 bunch basil
¼ lb. unsalted butter
¼ lb. Parmesan
2 cups crème fraîche
1 lb. fettucini (3 recipes
  Basic Egg Noodles)
salt and pepper

1. Cut off the basil stems and discard. Reserve 8 leaves for garnish and shred the rest. Melt the butter and warm a bowl for tossing the pasta. Grate the cheese.
2. Warm the crème fraîche in a saucepan with the shredded basil leaves.
3. Boil the pasta, drain, and toss it in the warmed bowl with the melted butter. Toss the pasta with the basil-flavored cream. Add salt and freshly ground pepper to taste.
4. Serve the pasta in bowls, each garnished with a fresh basil leaf, and pass the cheese at the table.

The next three dishes fall into the "baked" pasta category. That is, the pasta is boiled first, assembled with sauce(s), and finally baked. These dishes are all well known—especially the first one—my version of Macaroni and Cheese.

BAKED PASTA WITH CHEESE SAUCE
Serves 8

1 lb. penne (or other
  tubular pasta)
4 tablespoons unsalted
  butter
1 medium onion
4 cups Cheese Sauce (see
  page 72)
1 teaspoon freshly ground
  pepper
fresh bread crumbs made
  from 2 thick slices of
  French bread
a 12-inch baking dish

1. Boil the penne in rapidly boiling salted water until tender but firm, about 8 minutes. Drain, transfer to the baking dish, and toss with the butter.
2. Preheat the oven to 425°. Chop the onion finely and toss with the pasta. Mix in the Cheese Sauce and ground pepper. Sprinkle with fresh bread crumbs and bake for 15 minutes—or until crumbs are lightly toasted. Let stand 10 minutes before serving.

The Baked Green Lasagne following is probably a little different from many restaurant or frozen lasagnes. The primary difference is that home-made pasta is rolled much thinner than any commercial variety available. It is rich, hearty, and elegant all at one time, and, like the other dishes preceding, is meant to be served in small portions as a first course. It can be made in several stages—you can make the pasta and sauces one day, and assemble it all the next. At that point it can be refrigerated several hours until you are ready to bake and serve it.

BAKED GREEN LASAGNE
Serves 8 to 10 as a first course

¼ lb. Parmesan
Meat Sauce (recipe follows)
Lasagna White Sauce
  (recipe follows)
1 lb. lasagne noodles
  (recipe follows)
2 tablespoons unsalted
  butter to dot top layer of
  noodles
a 10- or 12-inch rectangular
  baking dish

1. Grate the Parmesan.
2. Make the Meat Sauce.
3. Make the Lasagna White Sauce.
4. Make the lasagne noodles.
5. **Assembly:** Spread a little Meat Sauce over the bottom of the baking dish. Cover with 1 layer of pasta. Spread a little Meat Sauce over the pasta, spread a little White Sauce over the Meat Sauce, sprinkle a little grated Parmesan over all. Continue layering, making 6 layers altogether, ending with White Sauce and cheese.
6. Dot with butter, cover with foil, and heat the lasagne for 30 minutes in a 375° oven before serving. Remove the lasagne from the oven and allow it to rest 15 minutes before cutting and serving from the dish.

Meat Sauce

½ small onion
1 stalk celery
1 small carrot
2 lbs. tomatoes
3 tablespoons unsalted
  butter
3 tablespoons olive oil
¾ lb. lean ground beef
1 cup dry white table wine
½ cup milk
nutmeg
½ teaspoon salt
½ teaspoon pepper

1. Chop the onion, celery, and carrot finely. Peel and coarsely chop the tomatoes.
2. Heat the butter and olive oil in a large saucepan and sauté the onion, celery, and carrot over low heat for 5 minutes.
3. Add the ground beef and cook an additional 2 minutes, stirring to crumble up the meat. Add the wine and milk and simmer gently until reduced by half. Add a dash of freshly grated nutmeg and the salt and pepper.
4. Add the tomatoes, reduce the heat, and cook until the sauce has thickened—about 30 minutes. Check the seasonings and adjust to your taste.

Lasagna White Sauce

5 tablespoons unsalted
  butter
5 tablespoons flour
3 cups milk
salt and pepper

1. Melt the butter in a heavy saucepan. Stir in the flour and cook over low heat for 3 minutes.
2. Add the milk, whisking constantly, and continue whisking until the sauce comes to a boil. Reduce the heat and simmer 15 to 20 minutes, stirring occasionally.

Lasagne Noodles

1. Make a double recipe of the Green Pasta.
2. Roll out the dough as thin as possible, using the #5 or #6 setting on the pasta machine.
3. Cut the pasta sheets crosswise into lengths to fit the baking dish.
4. Drop the fresh sheets of pasta in boiling salted water for 30 seconds. Remove and drop into a bowl of cold water before laying out on paper towels to drain. (If you wish to store the pasta, remove the paper towels, stack the pasta sheets on top of one another, wrap in foil or plastic wrap and place in the refrigerator. You may make them up to 24 hours in advance.)

Well-made cannelloni is a superb dish consisting of four elements—the filling, the fresh pasta that is wrapped around the filling, and the two sauces. The separate parts can be prepared a day ahead, and the dish can then be assembled and heated just before serving.

CANNELLONI
Serves 8

16 cannelloni rectangles (2 recipes Basic Egg Noodles)

Spinach Filling (recipe follows)

Cannelloni Tomato Sauce (recipe follows)

Cannelloni White Sauce (recipe follows)

2 tablespoons unsalted butter

a 10- or 12-inch rectangular baking dish

1. Make the pasta.
2. Make the Spinach Filling.
3. Make the Cannelloni Tomato Sauce.
4. Make the Cannelloni White Sauce.
5. Butter the baking dish with a little of the butter. Lay a cannelloni rectangle flat and spread a tablespoon of filling on it, covering the whole piece except for a ½-inch border. Roll the cannelloni up on its narrow side, and place it in the baking dish, seam side down.
6. Proceed until you have made 16 cannelloni. Dot with the remaining butter, cover with foil and bake in a 350° oven 20 minutes, until heated through.
7. To serve, warm the White Sauce and Tomato Sauce. Place 2 cannelloni on each plate, spoon over some White Sauce, and over that place 2 tablespoons of Tomato Sauce. Serve immediately.

Spinach Filling

2 lbs. fresh spinach
½ small onion
2 thin slices prosciutto
¼ lb. Parmesan
4 tablespoons unsalted
   butter
1 cup ricotta cheese
1 egg yolk
nutmeg
white pepper

1.   Remove and discard the large stems from the root end of the spinach. Clean the leaves and cook them in the water left clinging to them, tossing constantly. (It will take about 3 or 4 minutes.) Drain and chop the spinach coarsely. Finely chop the onion and the prosciutto. Grate the Parmesan cheese.
2.   Melt the butter in a skillet, and sauté the onion and prosciutto 1 minute. Transfer the onion and prosciutto to a mixing bowl and combine the chopped spinach, ricotta, Parmesan and egg yolk. Grate a dash of nutmeg into the mixture and add freshly ground white pepper to taste.

Cannelloni Tomato Sauce

1 2-lb. can Italian tomatoes,
   with juice
½ teaspoon pepper
½ teaspoon sugar

1.   Chop the tomatoes coarsely and place in a heavy saucepan—include the juice. Simmer gently until thickened—about 30 minutes.
2.   Put through a sieve or food mill to remove the seeds. Season with ground pepper and sugar.

Cannelloni White Sauce

5 tablespoons unsalted
   butter
4 tablespoons flour
2 cups crème fraîche
salt and pepper

1.   Melt the butter in a heavy saucepan, stir in the flour and cook over low heat 3 minutes.
2.   Add the crème fraîche, whisking constantly, and continue whisking until the sauce comes to a boil. Reduce the heat and simmer 15 to 20 minutes, stirring occasionally. Season with salt and pepper to taste.

Cannelloni Rectangles

1. Make the cannelloni dough using 2 recipes Basic Egg Noodles.
2. Roll the pasta out as thin as possible using the #5 or #6 setting on the pasta machine.
3. Cut the rolled-out dough into 3 × 4-inch rectangles.
4. Drop the fresh cannelloni rectangles in boiling water and cook 30 seconds. Remove and drop in cold water to stop the cooking before draining on paper towels. (At this point, you may wrap the cannelloni rectangles in foil, and store in the refrigerator along with the Spinach Filling, the white sauce, and the tomato sauce. All these components can be held in the refrigerator for a day before assembling and baking.)

SOUFFLÉS

If I were to take a poll among my students just beginning the basic course as to what dish intimidates them the most, I am certain it would be the soufflé. They think it is mysterious and difficult, when, in reality, nothing could be farther from the truth. I always tell my students that the most important thing to remember about soufflés is this: Don't let the *notion* of soufflé intimidate you; once you understand how and why they work, you will find soufflés extraordinarily easy to make.

Soufflés can be made from almost any food—cheese, fruit, meat, poultry, fish, or vegetables—and are an ideal way to use leftovers. They can be served as a main course for brunch or lunch or light suppers. For more elaborate meals, they can be a first course, an accompaniment to the main course, or dessert. There are so many different possibilities for making soufflés, an entire cookbook could be devoted to them alone.

WHAT IS A SOUFFLÉ?

The one essential component in any soufflé is air. A soufflé will always contain a base (usually a basic white sauce), the flavoring (cheese, meat, fish, vegetables, chocolate, fruit, and so on), and eggs. The eggs are always separated first. The yolks go into the base; the whites are whisked until soft peaks form, and are then folded into the flavored base. This is how air is introduced into a soufflé.

When the soufflé is baked, the bubbles of air trapped inside the egg whites expand on heating, increasing in volume and bringing everything—the base, flavorings, and egg whites—with them. This is what makes a soufflé puff up. This is also why a soufflé has to be served immediately as it comes out of the oven. Just as the air bubbles expand when they get warm, they contract when they cool. In the case of the soufflé, everything the expanding air bubbles brought up with them will fall down as the air bubbles contract.

In order to achieve the greatest volume, egg whites should be at room temperature and free of any trace of yolk. Use a "balloon" type whisk and start whisking slowly. As the whites break up and become foamy, you may increase your whisking speed. Continue to whisk until the whites form firm peaks that bend when the whisk is lifted out of the mass. The whites should not slide when the bowl is tilted.

Use a large flat rubber spatula to fold, always folding the whites into the base. Taking about ⅓ of the whites onto the spatula, cut down with them into the center of the bowl, lifting the mixture gently but quickly in a rolling motion. While folding, turn the bowl around with your other hand. Continue folding in the whites, ⅓ at a time, but only until the mixture is just blended. The less you work on the whites, the less air you will lose, so work quickly and gently.

Egg whites whisked in an unlined copper bowl with a balloon whisk take about ⅓ the whisking time, achieve a volume 6 to 7 times greater than their original volume, and are more stable than those whisked in other equipment, due to a chemical interaction between the egg whites and the copper. This does not mean that a copper bowl is necessary in making soufflés, only that it is a definite aid.

PREPARING THE SOUFFLÉ MOLD

Soufflé molds should always be well buttered. For dessert soufflés, the buttered mold may be sugared if you enjoy a chewy crust. Very light soufflés may require a collar, since they may rise so high out of the mold they could spill over. A collar prevents the soufflé from spilling over before it has a chance to set. To make a collar, cut a length of parchment paper slightly larger than will go around your soufflé mold. Fold it in half lengthwise and butter the upper portion only. Wrap the collar around the soufflé mold and fasten it with string.

MAKING A SOUFFLÉ "AHEAD"

While it is true that soufflés must be served immediately as they come out of the oven, it is not necessary to bake them immediately after the ingredients have been combined. If the basic soufflé method is followed, the entire soufflé may be prepared ahead, put into the mold(s), covered, refrigerated up to 4 hours, and baked just before serving. It may go from the refrigerator right into the oven. Allow 4 or 5 additional minutes' baking time. This method is especially useful at a dinner party when you want to be in the kitchen as little as possible.

BASIC METHOD FOR MAKING
SOUFFLÉS

1. Prepare the mold. (Butter it and sprinkle it with sugar if it is a dessert soufflé. Put a collar on if it is called for.)
2. Separate the eggs.
3. Make the white sauce base, and off the heat, stir in the egg yolks and flavoring (fruit, vegetables, etc.).
4. Whisk the egg whites until they form peaks that softly bend.
5. Carefully fold the egg whites into the base and spoon the soufflé mixture into the prepared soufflé mold.
6. Bake the soufflé for 15 to 18 minutes, depending on whether you like the center of your soufflé runny or more firm.
7. Once the soufflé comes out of the oven, it must be served immediately.

Tips for Successful Soufflé Making
- Don't make the base of your soufflé so thick that you will not be able to fold in the whisked egg whites. And don't add big chunks of meat, vegetables, or cheese since it will be too heavy for the egg whites to lift.
- The soufflé mold must have straight sides, so that the soufflé can climb straight up and the mold should not be too large. The unbaked soufflé mixture should fill the dish $7/8$ full so that the soufflé will rise up to the top of or out of the dish.
- Do not whisk the egg whites too stiff. If they are too stiff, they will break up into chunks and not incorporate smoothly throughout the base.
- Do not overbake the soufflé. A 6- or 8-cup soufflé should be baked at 375° no more than 20 minutes. Individual soufflés may be baked at 375° for 7 to 8 minutes. A perfectly baked soufflé will have risen out of the mold, and will be nicely browned and firm on top, and slightly runny at its center. If it wobbles a little when you take it out of the oven, it is perfect.

CHEESE SOUFFLÉS

The most versatile of all the soufflés is the cheese soufflé. The choice of cheeses or cheese combinations is endless. The best soufflé cheeses are well flavored, with a low moisture content and a firm texture. Gruyère, Jarlsberg, Emmenthal, Edam, Gouda, Cheshire, Cheddar, and Roquefort are all good choices. A cheese soufflé, some crusty bread, and a green salad make a very nice light luncheon or supper.

BASIC CHEESE SOUFFLÉ
Serves 4 to 6

5 oz. cheese
6 egg whites
4 egg yolks
2 tablespoons unsalted
 butter
3 tablespoons flour
1 cup milk
2 teaspoons prepared
 mustard
salt and pepper
a 6-cup soufflé mold or 4
 individual soufflé molds

1.   Shred (or, in the case of a soft cheese like Roquefort, sieve) the cheese. Separate the eggs, reserving the extra yolks for another use. Prepare the soufflé mold(s). Preheat the oven to 375°.
2.   In a heavy saucepan, melt the butter. Stir in the flour and cook 1 minute. Add the milk, stirring with a whisk until smooth and hot. Remove the pot from the heat and stir in the egg yolks, mustard, and cheese. Return the pot to the heat and stir until the cheese is melted. Remove from the heat and season to taste with salt and pepper.
3.   Whisk the egg whites until they form soft peaks. Carefully fold the whisked egg whites into the base, ⅓ at a time.
4.   Spoon the soufflé mixture into the prepared mold(s). Bake 15 to 18 minutes (or 7 to 8 minutes for individual molds) in the preheated oven and serve immediately.

Variations:

Bacon and Cheese Soufflé

Add 3 slices fried and crumbled bacon to a Basic Cheese Soufflé.

Ham and Cheese Soufflé

Reduce the cheese in the Basic Cheese Soufflé by 2 oz. and substitute 2 oz. finely chopped ham.

VEGETABLE SOUFFLÉS

If you like to be a little different, serve your vegetable side dish as a soufflé instead of in the conventional manner. It is very nice to make individual soufflés so that each diner receives his or her own. Asparagus, lima beans, broccoli, carrots, cauliflower, celery root, corn, garlic, shallots, onions, leeks, green onions, peas, potatoes, spinach, and squash are all suitable for making soufflés. In the following two vegetable soufflé recipes, potatoes are used instead of flour to absorb the liquid from the vegetables.

BROCCOLI SOUFFLÉ
Serves 4 to 6

1 bunch broccoli
1 large baking potato
2 oz. Parmesan
4 egg whites
3 egg yolks
4 tablespoons melted
  unsalted butter
salt and pepper
a 6-cup soufflé mold or 6
  individual soufflé molds

1. Preheat the oven to 375° and prepare the soufflé mold(s). Trim the broccoli and peel the potato. Boil each until soft enough to purée. Purée the broccoli and potato. Grate the cheese and separate the eggs.
2. Combine the puréed vegetables, grated cheese, egg yolks, and butter. Season to taste with salt and pepper.
3. Whisk the egg whites until soft peaks form and fold them gently into the vegetable mixture.
4. Spoon into the prepared mold(s) and bake 18 to 20 minutes (or 7 to 8 minutes for individual molds) in the preheated oven. Serve immediately.

Variation:

Carrot Soufflé

Substitute 1¼ lbs. of carrots for the broccoli and proceed as directed.

SPINACH SOUFFLÉ
Serves 4 to 6

1 bunch spinach
7 egg whites
5 egg yolks
3 tablespoons unsalted
  butter
4 tablespoons flour
1 cup milk
salt and pepper
a 6-cup soufflé mold or 4
  individual soufflé molds

1. Clean, cook, drain, and purée the spinach. Prepare the soufflé mold(s). Separate the eggs. Preheat the oven to 375°.
2. Melt the butter in a saucepan. Add the flour and cook 1 minute. Add the milk and cook and stir an additional minute. Add the puréed spinach and the egg yolks and stir. Add salt and pepper to taste.
3. Whisk the egg whites until soft peaks form. Fold the egg whites into the spinach mixture.
4. Spoon into the prepared soufflé mold(s) and bake 18 to 20 minutes (7 to 8 minutes for individual molds). Serve immediately.

DESSERT SOUFFLÉS

Dessert soufflés are generally lighter than savory soufflés and require a collar to keep them from spilling over the top of the dish before they set. There are many dessert soufflés; the few recipes following have been the most popular among my students. Notice that there is no flour in the chocolate and orange soufflés. For information on cooking with chocolate see pages 14-15.

CHOCOLATE ALMOND SOUFFLÉ
Serves 4

¼ lb. bittersweet chocolate
5 egg whites
3 egg yolks
3½ oz. sugar (½ cup)
2 teaspoons almond extract
a 6-cup soufflé mold or 4
   individual soufflé molds

1. Preheat the oven to 375° and prepare the soufflé mold(s), including a collar. Melt the chocolate in a double boiler and separate the eggs.
2. Whisk the egg yolks and sugar until light in color. Add the almond extract and fold in the melted chocolate.
3. Whisk the egg whites until soft peaks form, and carefully fold the egg whites into the chocolate. Spoon into the prepared mold(s) and bake 15 minutes (7 to 8 minutes for individual molds). Serve immediately.

FRESH ORANGE SOUFFLÉ
Serves 4 to 6

zest of 6 oranges
juice of 6 oranges
7 egg whites
6 egg yolks
3½ oz. sugar (½ cup)
2 tablespoons Grand
   Marnier
a 6-cup soufflé mold or 4
   individual soufflé molds

1. Zest the oranges and chop the zest finely. Squeeze the orange juice and separate the eggs. Prepare the soufflé mold(s), including a collar. Preheat the oven to 375°.
2. In a small saucepan, reduce the orange juice to ¼ cup. Add the orange zest, egg yolks, sugar, and Grand Marnier.
3. Whisk the whites until they form soft peaks and fold into the orange mixture.
4. Spoon into the prepared soufflé mold(s), and bake 16 to 18 minutes (7 to 8 minutes for individual molds). Serve immediately.

APRICOT SOUFFLÉ

Serves 4 to 6

½ lb. dried apricots
4 tablespoons sugar
7 egg whites
4 egg yolks
3 tablespoons unsalted
 butter
3 tablespoons flour
1 cup milk
2 tablespoons apricot
 brandy
a 6-cup soufflé mold or 4
 individual soufflé molds

1. Soak the dried apricots in water to cover for 2 hours. In a small saucepan, combine the sugar and apricots with enough water to cover and cook over medium heat until soft. Purée in the food processor or blender adding a little water if necessary to make a creamy purée. (If the apricot purée is too stiff, it will be difficult to fold.)
2. Prepare the soufflé mold(s). Separate the eggs. Preheat the oven to 375°.
3. In a saucepan, melt the butter; add the flour and cook 1 minute. Add the milk and cook another minute, stirring until smooth. Off the heat, combine the white sauce with the egg yolks, apricot brandy, and apricot purée.
4. Whisk the egg whites until they form soft peaks. Fold into the apricot mixture and spoon into the prepared mold(s). Bake for 15 to 18 minutes (7 to 8 minutes for individual molds). Serve immediately.

MODEL SOUFFLÉS

The following "model" recipe is for you to use once you feel you understand how to make soufflés and want to start creating your own. Before attempting this, however, you should practice on some of the preceding soufflé recipes.

SOUFFLÉ MODEL FOR SERVING 4 TO 6

¾ cup flavoring (cheese,
 cooked meat, cooked
 vegetables, etc.)
2 tablespoons unsalted
 butter
3 tablespoons flour
1 cup milk
4 egg yolks
6 egg whites
4 tablespoons sugar for
 dessert soufflés
a 6-cup soufflé mold or 4
 individual soufflé molds

1. Prepare the soufflé mold(s). Purée or chop finely the cooked meat, vegetables, fruit, etc. Preheat the oven to 375°.
2. Melt the butter in a saucepan. Stir in the flour and cook 1 minute. Add the milk and cook, stirring continuously, 1 minute more. Remove from the heat and stir in the egg yolks, the sugar, if you are making a dessert soufflé, and the flavoring.
3. Whisk the egg whites until soft peaks form. Fold the whites into the base, ⅓ at a time.
4. Spoon the soufflé mixture carefully into the prepared soufflé mold(s).
5. Place the soufflé(s) on the bottom rack of the oven. Bake 15 to 18 minutes (7 to 8 minutes for individual molds) in the preheated oven. Serve immediately.

"SOUFFLÉ PUDDINGS"

In between a soufflé and a sponge cake, is the "soufflé pudding." It contains fewer egg whites than a soufflé, but less flour than a sponge cake. It is cooked in a water bath (page 295) and does not expand as much as a soufflé. Because of the starch it contains, it does not contract very much when it cools, so, it can be served hot or cold. A soufflé pudding is heavier and denser in texture than a soufflé.

CHOCOLATE SOUFFLÉ PUDDING WITH CHOCOLATE SAUCE
Serves 8

5 oz. bittersweet chocolate
6 egg yolks
4 egg whites
¼ lb. unsalted butter
4 tablespoons sugar
2 teaspoons vanilla extract
4 tablespoons flour
2 tablespoons potato starch
Chocolate Sauce (see recipe below)
a 4-cup pudding mold

1. Prepare the mold. Melt the chocolate in a double boiler. Separate the eggs. Preheat the oven to 350°. Boil water for the water bath.
2. Cream the butter and sugar, add the vanilla, and beat until light and fluffy. Beat in the egg yolks, one at a time, then add the melted chocolate. Add the flour and the potato starch and combine well.
3. Whisk the egg whites until they form soft peaks and fold into the chocolate mixture. Pour the pudding into the prepared mold, place in a water bath, and bake 35 minutes.
4. Allow the pudding to stand 10 minutes before unmolding. Serve hot or cold with Chocolate Sauce (see recipe below).

Chocolate Sauce

½ lb. semisweet chocolate
¾ cup crème fraîche
4 tablespoons unsalted butter
1 teaspoon vanilla extract

In a double boiler, melt the chocolate with the crème fraîche, stirring occasionally. Off the heat, whisk in the butter and vanilla extract. Stir until smooth.

RICE PUDDING
Serves 6 to 8

4 eggs
2 qts. water
3½ oz. long grain rice
   (½ cup)
4 cups milk
1 tablespoon unsalted
   butter
3½ oz. sugar (½ cup)
½ cup crème fraîche
1 tablespoon vanilla extract
a shallow 8-cup baking dish
3 tablespoons sugar

1.   Prepare the baking dish. Separate the eggs.
2.   Bring 2 qts. of water to a boil in a medium-sized pot and drop in the rice. Boil 5 minutes, drain in a sieve, and rinse in running water to remove the starch.
3.   In a saucepan, bring the milk, butter, and sugar to a boil and add the preboiled rice. Lower the heat, cover, and cook gently until the rice has absorbed all the liquid.
4.   Beat the egg yolks, crème fraîche, and vanilla together. Allow the rice to cool a little and add the egg yolk mixture, stirring gently.
5.   Preheat the oven to 350° and boil water for the water bath. Whisk the egg whites until soft peaks form and fold into the rice. Pour into the prepared baking dish. Sprinkle 3 tablespoons sugar over the pudding and bake it in a water bath, uncovered, for 20 minutes.
6.   The pudding may be put under the broiler for 1 minute to brown the top. Serve directly from the dish.

BREAD PUDDING
Serves 8

3 eggs
½ lb. bread
2 cups milk
5 oz. sugar (⅔ cup)
1 tablespoon vanilla extract
2½ oz. raisins (½ cup)
2½ oz. walnuts halves
   (½ cup)
a shallow 8-cup baking dish

1.   Butter the baking dish. Separate the eggs. Break the bread into 1-inch pieces and soak them in milk until softened. Preheat the oven to 350°. Boil water for the water bath.
2.   In a large bowl, combine the egg yolks, sugar, and vanilla. Mix well and add the raisins and walnuts. Stir into the bread and milk.
3.   Whisk the egg whites until soft peaks form. Fold into the bread mixture and pour into the prepared baking dish. Bake in a water bath, uncovered, until firm and brown—about 30 minutes.

CUSTARDS, GELATIN DESSERTS, AND MOUSSES

Chapter 15

There are two kinds of custards: baked custards (often referred to as "molded" custards), and soft cooked custards (sometimes called "pouring" or "English" custards). Well-made custards, baked or soft, should be perfectly smooth. The texture will vary slightly according to the method used in preparing them. A custard cooked on top of the stove will have a soft, creamy texture and a custard baked in the oven will be firm.

The most important fact you need to know about making custards is that *they must never be overheated.* All custards are basically a mixture of milk and eggs and both react to heat. When heated, the proteins thicken, but if they get too hot, soft custards will curdle (the proteins shrink); baked custards will "weep" and turn grainy. So whether you are cooking them on top of the stove or in a water bath in the oven, be sure to monitor the temperature.

Baked Custards

To make a baked custard, the eggs, sugar, flavorings, and milk are combined and poured into the mold. For smoothness, the custard mixture is always strained as it is poured into the mold. The custard is then baked in a water bath (see page 295) until firm around the edges. Baked custards should be removed from the oven while the center still quivers rather than when they are firm in the center, because they will continue to cook before they cool. Baked custards include all custards molded and baked like Caramel Custard.

The following two recipes are examples typical of baked custards. The "little pots" of chocolate custard is the richest possible baked custard and should only be served in small portions, no more than 2 or 3 oz. per serving. The dish takes its name from the traditional small pots in which it is baked and served.

LITTLE POTS OF CHOCOLATE CUSTARD
(Petits Pots de Crème au Chocolat)
Serves 8

6 oz. semisweet chocolate
2 cups whipping cream
6 egg yolks, lightly mixed
1 tablespoon vanilla extract
8 tiny custard pots with lids

1. Preheat the oven to 325°. Carefully melt the chocolate in the cream in a double boiler.

2. Add the egg yolks and vanilla and stir until smooth. Strain the mixture into the custard pots.

3. Set the pots in a water bath (see page 295), cover the pots with their lids, and bake in the preheated oven until the custards are barely set—about 25 minutes for pots containing about 3 oz. This custard is not unmolded but served in the pots either chilled or warm.

CARAMEL CUSTARD
Serves 8

7 oz. sugar (1 cup)
½ cup water
1 cup whipping cream
1 cup milk
1 tablespoon vanilla extract
3 eggs
2 egg yolks
3½ oz. sugar (½ cup)
a 4-cup, straight-sided, deep ovenproof mold

1. In a small, heavy saucepan, combine the 7 oz. sugar and ½ cup water. Cook the syrup until it is a light coffee color. (Watch this caramel carefully, since it can burn very easily.) When it is ready, pour the caramel into the mold, turning the mold around and around until the caramel coats it evenly. Allow the caramel to cool while you make the custard.

2. Preheat the oven to 350°. In a small saucepan, warm the cream and milk, and add the vanilla extract. Remove the milk mixture from the heat.

3. Beat the eggs, egg yolks, and the remaining sugar until well mixed. Combine the warm milk mixture and the egg mixture; stir until well mixed.

4. Strain the custard into the prepared mold and cover the mold with foil. Place the mold in a water bath and bake in the preheated oven about 45 minutes, or until the custard around the sides of the mold is firm and the center barely quivers.

5. Chill before turning out onto a plate. The custard will have caramel on the top, and some around the bottom for a sauce. Serve at room temperature or chilled.

Soft Custards

Soft cooked custards are made by combining egg yolks, sugar, flavorings, and milk, cream, or wine in a saucepan. The ingredients are then stirred and cooked over a gentle heat until they thicken into a rich custard that may be served alone or used as a dessert sauce. A soft cooked custard may also be topped with sugar and broiled to make "Burnt Cream," have poached meringues added to create "Floating Islands," or can be thickened with flour and cornstarch and used as a filling for tarts, or as a base for soufflés. Soft custards are often combined with gelatin for molded desserts, mixed with butter for buttercreams (cake frostings) or custard cakes, or combined with cream and frozen to make ice cream. If the milk or cream is replaced by wine, the custard becomes Zabaione.

Soft Vanilla Custard is a "base" custard, used often in desserts just as White Sauce is used often in savory dishes. Use it alone as a sauce over fruits and other desserts, or as a base for the Bavarian Cream.

SOFT VANILLA CUSTARD
(Pouring Custard or English Custard)
Makes about 3 cups

2½ cups milk
3½ oz. superfine sugar
   (½ cup)
6 egg yolks
2 teaspoons flour
1 tablespoon vanilla extract

1. In a saucepan over medium heat, bring the milk and half the sugar to a boil. Turn off the heat.
2. Whisk the egg yolks, remaining sugar, flour, and vanilla together.
3. Whisking constantly, add the egg mixture to the hot milk.
4. Over a medium-low heat, stir the custard constantly until it is like thick whipping cream.
5. Pour through a fine sieve into a bowl and continue to stir the custard until it cools a little. If the custard is not to be used immediately, press waxed paper on the top to keep a skin from forming.

This dessert is a good example of a cooked or soft custard that uses wine instead of milk. It is traditionally served warm in stemmed wine glasses. It can also be used as a filling for cakes, or as a sauce over poached fruits and ice cream.

ZABAIONE
Serves 8 to 10

8 egg yolks
7 oz. superfine sugar (1 cup)
1 cup imported Marsala
10 strips of lemon zest for
   garnish
a 6-cup zabaione pot or
   double boiler

1. In a copper zabaione pot or the top of a double boiler, whisk the egg yolks and sugar until the mixture is thick and creamy.
2. Set the pot over another pot of hot water, and over a medium-low heat whisk the Marsala into the egg mixture.
3. Continue to whisk until the mixture froths to double or triple its original volume. Remove the pan of custard from the heat and continue whisking 30 seconds more.
4. Pour into individual stemmed glasses, garnish each with a strip of zest, and serve at once. (If you are using the zabaione as a sauce, allow it to cool, stirring occasionally.)

The following pastry cream is a form of custard, but it is not meant to be served alone. It has starch added to it so that it will make a firm filling for tarts and other pastries—cream puffs for instance.

PASTRY CREAM
Makes about 2 cups

5 egg yolks
3½ oz. sugar (½ cup)
2 tablespoons flour
2 tablespoons cornstarch
1½ cups milk
1 tablespoon vanilla extract

1. In a small saucepan, off the heat, whisk the egg yolks and sugar together until light colored. Gradually work in the flour and cornstarch until well mixed.
2. Warm the milk and pour it over the egg mixture. Bring to a boil, whisking constantly, and boil about 1 minute. Add the vanilla and strain into a bowl. The consistency should be thick and slightly runny. After it cools, the custard will thicken further.
3. Press a piece of waxed paper on top of the cream to keep a skin from forming, and cool before using. You may store Pastry Cream up to 3 days in the refrigerator.

GELATIN DESSERTS

Add gelatin and fruits, fruit purées, cakes, or cake crumbs to the Soft Vanilla Custard and a group of desserts called gelatins or molded custards is created.

When working with gelatin, remember to soften the gelatin in cold water before warming it. Any other ingredients should be added after the gelatin has thickened the custard slightly but before it has set. Because a gelatin custard is so delicate, refrigerate immediately after unmolding and leave it refrigerated until serving time.

VANILLA BAVARIAN CREAM WITH RASPBERRY SAUCE
Serves 8

1 package gelatin (1 tablespoon)
2 tablespoons cold water
2½ cups warm Soft Vanilla Custard (see page 218)
1 cup whipping cream
1 tablespoon Vanilla Sugar (see page 20)
a well-defined 6-cup metal mold

1. Soften the gelatin in the 2 tablespoons cold water, then warm gently until the gelatin becomes clear.
2. Add the gelatin to the warm custard, stir, and allow to cool slightly at room temperature.
3. Whisk the cream and Vanilla Sugar together until it holds soft peaks, then fold it into the cooled gelatin custard.
4. Pour into the mold and chill 8 hours.
5. Unmold by dipping into hot water and turning upside down on a serving plate. Serve with Raspberry Sauce (recipe follows).

Raspberry Sauce

¼ cup red table wine
½ cup water
7 oz. sugar (1 cup)
1 basket raspberries

1. Make a wine syrup by combining the red wine, water, and the sugar in a heavy saucepan. Bring to a boil, lower the heat, and simmer 5 minutes.
2. Combine the raspberries and the syrup and purée in a blender or food processor. Eliminate the seeds by passing the purée through a sieve or the fine blade of a food mill.

A cold soufflé is fun to serve because it has the appearance of a perfectly baked soufflé, but will never fall since the gelatin, once set, will hold it up.

COLD LEMON SOUFFLÉ
Serves 8 to 10

3 lemons
5 eggs
1½ packages gelatin (1½ tablespoons)
½ cup cold water
10½ oz. sugar (1½ cups)
1½ cups whipping cream
candied violets for garnish (available in fancy food shops)
a 6-cup soufflé dish

1. Prepare the soufflé dish, adding a collar (see page 206). Remove the zest from the 3 lemons and chop the zest finely. Juice the lemons. Separate the eggs. Dissolve the gelatin in the cold water.
2. Whisk the egg yolks and sugar together. Add the chopped zest and the lemon juice. Continue whisking until thick.
3. Warm the gelatin over low heat just until it becomes clear and liquid. Stir the gelatin into the egg mixture.
4. Whisk the cream until it stands in soft peaks. Fold the cream into the lemon mixture.
5. Whisk the egg whites until they form soft peaks. Fold the egg whites into the lemon mixture. Spoon into the prepared soufflé dish and allow to set in the refrigerator for at least 4 hours.
6. Remove the paper collar and decorate the soufflé with the candied violets.

MOUSSES

In texture and consistency, mousses come somewhere between the creamy richness of a custard and the airy lightness of a gelatin dessert. If the egg whites are left out, the mousse will be heavier, richer, and denser. Egg whites and whipped cream must be folded into the base very carefully, as with a soufflé (see page 206), in order to produce a light mousse.

CHOCOLATE MOUSSE
Serves 8 to 10

½ lb. bittersweet chocolate
6 tablespoons unsalted
  butter
1 tablespoon rum
4 egg yolks
1 cup whipping cream
1 tablespoon vanilla extract
6 tablespoons superfine
  sugar
4 egg whites (optional)
a pastry bag with a #8 star
  tip

1. In a double boiler, melt the chocolate with the butter and rum, and allow to cool 10 minutes. Add the egg yolks, whisking gently.
2. Whisk the cream with the vanilla and sugar until it holds soft peaks, then fold it into the chocolate mixture.
3. Whisk the egg whites until soft peaks form and fold them into the chocolate-cream mixture.
4. Chill until firm enough to put through a pastry bag. Using a star tip, fill serving glasses. Chill well before serving.

APRICOT MOUSSE
Serves 8 to 10

½ lb. dried apricots
3½ oz. sugar (½ cup)
2 eggs
4 tablespoons unsalted
  butter
2 tablespoons brandy
1 cup whipping cream
a pastry bag with a # 8 star
  tip

1. Soak the dried apricots in water to cover for 2 hours. In a small saucepan, combine the sugar and apricots with enough water to cover and cook until soft—about 20 minutes. Purée the apricots and the cooking water in a food processor or blender, adding more water if necessary to make a creamy purée. (If the apricot purée is too stiff, it will be difficult to combine with the other ingredients.)
2. Separate the eggs. Melt the butter and combine it in a large bowl with the egg yolks, puréed apricots, and brandy.
3. Whisk the cream until it forms soft peaks, and fold it into the apricot mixture. Whisk the egg whites until they form soft peaks, and fold them into the mousse.
4. Chill until firm enough to put through a pastry bag. Using a star tip, fill serving glasses with the mousse. Chill well before serving.

The following mousse is a "show stopper." Be extra careful in melting white chocolate since it is even more heat-sensitive than dark chocolate (see page 14). Notice that the egg whites have been left out and that the mousse is served frozen. The result is a confection extremely rich, dense, and almost chewy.

FROZEN WHITE CHOCOLATE MOUSSE WITH DARK CHOCOLATE SAUCE
Serves 8

½ lb. white chocolate
¾ cup whipping cream
¼ lb. unsalted butter
4 egg yolks
2 teaspoons vanilla extract
Dark Chocolate Sauce (see recipe below)
8 4-oz. molds
parchment paper

1. Line the bottom of each mold with parchment paper. Carefully melt the white chocolate with half the whipping cream in a double boiler.
2. Off the heat, combine the white chocolate, butter, egg yolks, and vanilla. Stir until smooth and allow to cool 20 minutes.
3. Whip the remaining cream and carefully fold it into the white chocolate mixture.
4. Pour the mixture into the prepared molds, and freeze 8 hours.
5. To serve, unmold the frozen mousses, peel away the parchment paper, and serve them surrounded by Dark Chocolate Sauce (recipe follows).

Dark Chocolate Sauce

6 oz. bittersweet chocolate
½ cup whipping cream
1 teaspoon vanilla extract

1. Combine the chocolate and cream and warm gently until melted using the double boiler or oven method (see pages 14-15).
2. Add the vanilla and stir. Cool before using.

CAKES

Remember the song, "If I Knew You Were Coming, I'd Have Baked A Cake"? Cakes are expressions of love and friendship, joy and celebration. Whether you are making a cake for a six-year-old's birthday party or an elaborate Christmas Log, you have the greatest opportunity in cake baking for creative expression—the closest cooking comes to painting or sculpture. In my cooking school, I always look forward to the section on cakes, since, as the mystery of cake making unravels for the student, I hear some wonderful stories of pleased friends and relatives—the lucky recipients of the students' efforts.

This lesson on cakes deals with the methods of making the most often used basic or "foundation" cakes. No effort will be made to learn special presentations such as tiered wedding cakes or fancy petits fours, although I would like to point out that even the most elaborate cake will have as its base one or the other of the foundation cakes we will learn in this chapter.

I have divided cakes into two categories: the sponge or "egg foam" cakes—those leavened only with air; and baking powder-baking soda cakes—those that have the addition of chemical leaveners.

CAKE MAKING

Measuring   In cake making, unlike other areas of cooking (soup making, for instance), it is important that ingredients be measured accurately. Liquid should be measured in cups that are marked for fluid measure, and all dry ingredients—nuts, sugar, flour, etc.—should be weighed on a scale. If you do not have a scale, I have given cup equivalents where possible. However, please realize that dry ingredients, measured in a cup, will never yield the same quantity twice because there will always be some slight differences in volume.

Preparing cake pans   Melt butter, and with a brush, butter the bottom and sides of the cake pan. Place about a tablespoon of flour on the bottom of the pan, then tilt it to spread the flour. Both the bottom of the pan and the sides should be coated with flour. Turn the pan upside down to get rid of any excess flour. An alternative is to cut a round of parchment paper to fit, and place it in the bottom of the pan. In this case, only the sides need butter and flour.

Mixing   A heavy-duty electric mixer with a beater and a whisk is essential for efficient regular cake baking. The cake recipes in this lesson assume a mixer is being used.

Folding   The same rules apply to these cakes as apply to hot soufflés. The lightness of the cakes come from whisking air into the eggs and not losing the air when folding the eggs into the other ingredients. Use a large rubber spatula, fold in two or three stages, quickly and lightly, to avoid losing air.

Ovens   It is a good idea to have an oven thermometer in order to be sure your oven is heating accurately. Do not bake more than two cakes at a time in a single oven, as the heat needs to be able to circulate in the oven. Generally, the oven should be preheated, and the cake baked in the center of the oven.

Doneness   A cake is done when it shrinks slightly from the sides of the pan and has a "springy" feel when touched lightly in the center, or when a cake tester (a toothpick or skewer) put into the cake comes out clean.

Cooling   Always wait 5 minutes before turning a baked cake out of its mold onto the cooling rack (a hot cake may fall apart). Allow the cake to cool completely before icing.

INGREDIENTS

Flour   Cake flour produces the finest textured cakes and should be used when called for. Flour should always be sifted to remove any lumps. Oftentimes, in a cake recipe, you will be instructed to sift four or five times. This aerates the flour and is important in very light cakes. It is also a good idea to add the flour to the batter through a sifter, rather than plopping it in all at once.

Sugar When cake recipes call for powdered or superfine sugar, it is usually so that the sugar will dissolve more easily. Both those sugars are available in food stores or can be made from granulated sugar in a food processor. (In the bowl of the food processor with the metal knife in place, pulse 10 times and check the texture of the sugar. It should be finer than granulated but not quite a powder for superfine.)

Butter Always use fresh, unsalted butter for the best flavor.

Eggs Eggs provide the network within which the air is trapped to give lightness to a cake. They also provide some of the moisture in the batter. All of the recipes in this chapter are written for large eggs. Cold eggs will separate better than room temperature eggs. Eggs at room temperature or eggs that have been warmed in hot tap water, will whisk to a greater volume than cold eggs.

SPONGE OR "EGG FOAM" CAKES

Cakes in this category are somewhat like soufflés. They acquire their volume from the air bubbles that are whisked into the eggs and that expand as the cake bakes, and from the steam created in the baking process. However, the ratio of flour in a cake is greater than in a soufflé, and once baked, the gluten in the flour maintains the delicate structure of the cake. Soufflés, on the other hand, always tend to contract as they cool.

The large amount of sugar and the butter, if there is any, prevent the gluten from toughening the texture of the cake. The very lightest cakes in this category, such as the Angel Food Cake, use cake flour and a lesser amount of fat than do the denser-textured cakes like the Genoise. Chemical leavening agents like baking powder or soda are not used in sponge cakes.

The sponge category is a large one, going from the simplest, a meringue with only two ingredients, to the Genoise, with seven or eight ingredients. Sponges are delicate; every ingredient added, each different method used, changes the taste, texture, and appearance of the finished product.

Meringues have two ingredients—sugar and egg whites—and that's all. The proportion of sugar to egg white is what determines how crisp or soft the cooked meringue will be. Meringues can be baked or poached and served as they are, or be folded into mousses, spread over pies and baked, as in Lemon Meringue Pie, or even spread over ice cream and cake and broiled, as in a Baked Alaska.

When ground nuts are added to a meringue, the texture changes into something more substantial and cake-like. Traditionally, almonds or hazelnuts are used in nut meringues.

The following meringue recipe has a high proportion of sugar, and is ideal for piping into individual shapes. This type of meringue is "dried" in the oven, rather than baked, to evaporate the moisture. The oven temperature should be low and the meringues left to dry at least 2 hours—a little longer should the weather be rainy. To practice, you can use a spoon to put the meringues onto a baking sheet. Properly done, you will have a very crisp meringue "cookie."

MERINGUE
Makes about 6 large or 12 small meringues

4 egg whites
½ lb. powdered sugar
  (2 cups)
2 baking sheets
parchment paper

1. Cut a piece of parchment paper to fit each baking sheet.
2. Whisk the egg whites until soft peaks form, then sift in the sugar, little by little, whisking all the time. Continue whisking until the meringue holds soft peaks, about 5 minutes, and is firm enough so that it could be piped through a pastry bag.
3. Using a pastry bag and a #8 star tip (or a spoon), put small amounts of the meringue on the prepared baking sheet. Dry in a 200° oven for 2 hours, until firm and dry.

Here are two cakes made from nut meringues. This type of meringue is always combined with frostings, fillings, or creams to create some kind of cake or pastry. For both cakes, the nuts should be toasted in the oven, and ground finely (in a nut grinder or food processor) without making a paste.

"HEAVENLY" CAKE
(An Adaptation of Fernand Point's Marjolaine)
Serves 8 to 10

¾ lb. blanched almonds (2¼ cups)
4 tablespoons flour
10½ oz. sugar (1½ cups)
8 egg whites
1 lb. semisweet chocolate
1 cup crème fraîche
6 oz. sugar (¾ cup)
¼ cup water
8 egg yolks
1 tablespoon brewed espresso coffee
½ lb. unsalted butter, softened

a 13 × 17-inch jelly roll pan
parchment paper
a cake board*

1.   Preheat the oven to 350° and toast the almonds 10 minutes, until lightly browned. Allow to cool and combine the almonds and flour in a food processor, and grind as fine as possible without making a paste. In a medium-sized bowl, combine the nuts with 3½ oz. (½ cup) of the sugar and set aside.
2.   Cut a sheet of parchment paper to fit the jelly roll pan. Preheat the oven to 325°.
3.   In an electric mixer, whisk the egg whites until they form soft peaks. Slowly add the remaining sugar in a steady stream, whisking until the meringue holds soft peaks, about 1 minute more.
4.   Fold the nut mixture into the meringue and gently spread onto the prepared baking sheet. Bake 1 hour, or until the cake is light brown, crisp on top but still pliable. Turn the cake out onto a cooling rack, peel off the parchment, and cut the cake into 4 strips, each 3 inches wide.
5.   Melt the chocolate and the crème fraîche together. Mix well and allow to cool.
6.   Boil the 6 oz. (¾ cup) of sugar and the ¼ cup water to 235° on a candy thermometer. Combine the egg yolks and coffee and whisk in an electric mixer at medium speed for 1 minute. Slowly add the syrup, whisking constantly for approximately 2 more minutes until the cream is cooled. Add the softened butter and whisk at low speed until the buttercream is fluffy—about 3 more minutes.
7.   **Assembly:** Place 1 layer of cake on the cake board and spread with some of the coffee butter cream. Add the second layer and spread with the chocolate cream. Continue, finishing with the chocolate cream, covering the entire cake, including the sides, but not the ends. Cut off a slice from each end, exposing the fillings. Chill before serving.

(*Cake boards are cardboard rounds or rectangulars that are placed under the cake for easy handling. They may be purchased in gourmet shops or you may make your own by cutting heavy cardboard to the shape of your cake.)

HAZELNUT MERINGUE CAKE
Serves 8 to 10

Apricot Cream Filling (see below)
5 oz. blanched hazelnuts
2 tablespoons flour
5 oz. superfine sugar (¾ cup)
4 egg whites
powdered sugar
2 8-inch round cake pans
parchment paper

1.   Make the Apricot Cream Filling and chill it.
2.   Preheat the oven to 350° and toast the hazelnuts 10 minutes, until lightly browned. Allow to cool, and combine the nuts and flour in a food processor or nut grinder. Grind as fine as possible without making a paste. Mix the hazelnuts with 3½ oz. (½ cup) of superfine sugar and set aside.
3.   Butter and flour the sides of the cake pans and line the bottoms with parchment paper.
4.   In an electric mixer, whisk the egg whites until they form soft peaks. Slowly add the remaining superfine sugar, whisking until the meringue holds soft peaks, about 1 minute more.
5.   Fold the ground hazelnut-sugar mixture into the meringue.
6.   Preheat the over to 350°. Pour the batter into the prepared cake pans and bake approximately 30 minutes until delicately browned. Allow the meringues to cool 5 minutes, then turn out of the pans, peel off the paper, and place on cake racks until completely cool.
7.   **Assembly:** Spread the apricot filling generously on 1 layer of the cake. Add the top layer and through a coarse sieve, cover the top layer with powdered sugar. The remaining filling can be served on the side. Chill at least 1 hour before serving.

Apricot Cream Filling

¼ lb. dried apricots
4 tablespoons sugar
juice of ½ lemon
1 cup crème fraîche

1.   Soak the apricots in water to cover for 2 hours. In a small saucepan, combine the sugar, lemon juice, and apricots with enough water to cover, and cook until soft, about 20 minutes. Purée the apricots and the cooking water in a food processor or blender, adding more water if necessary to make a creamy purée. (If the apricot purée is too stiff, it will be difficult to combine with the crème fraîche).
2.   Whip the crème fraîche and carefully fold into the cooled, puréed apricots.
3.   Store in the refrigerator until ready to use.

With the addition of flour, a meringue becomes an Angel Food Cake. The traditional tube pan works best in baking these and other light "egg foam" cakes, since the heat comes from both the center and the outer sides of the pan and bakes the cakes a little faster. This prevents loss of volume. *Never* grease the pans. The batter needs to cling to the sides of the pan as it rises. When the cake comes out of the oven it must cool upside down to keep it from sinking. If your pan does not have "feet" to rest on, invert the tube onto a bottle, and allow it to hang until cooled.

ANGEL FOOD CAKE
Serves 8 to 10

7½ oz. cake flour (1½ cups)
14 oz. superfine sugar
  (2 cups)
14 egg whites
2 teaspoons cream of tartar
½ teaspoon salt
2 teaspoons vanilla extract
a 9- or 10-inch tube pan

1. Preheat the oven to 400°. Sift the flour, add 5½ oz. superfine sugar (¾ cup), and sift the flour-sugar mixture 5 times—set aside.
2. Using an electric mixer, whisk the egg whites. When foamy, add the cream of tartar and the salt. Then add the remaining superfine sugar in a very slow steady stream, whisking constantly until the whites are thick and form soft peaks.
3. With a large rubber spatula, fold the flour-sugar mixture into the egg whites in two stages, as quickly and gently as possible to avoid losing air. Fold in the vanilla.
4. Pour batter into the *ungreased* tube pan and bake the cake in the hot oven for 10 minutes. Reduce the heat to 350° and bake an additional 30 minutes. Reduce heat again to 300° and bake until the cake is done, approximately 10 minutes more.
5. Remove the cake from the oven, and immediately turn it upside down to "hang" until cooled.
6. Remove the cake from the pan after it is cooled. To cut the cake, without flattening it, "saw" it carefully with a serrated knife.

Ladyfingers are used to line molds or as a part of other desserts. They are seldom served on their own. In order to form perfectly-shaped ladyfingers, a special mold and a pastry bag and tip are necessary. If you cannot obtain the proper mold, just pipe the batter onto a baking sheet—the ladyfingers will not be uniform in shape, but will not be otherwise affected. These sponge ladyfingers include egg yolks, which produce a different texture from our last sponge, the Angel Food Cake.

LADYFINGERS
Makes 36

½ **lemon**
5 oz. flour (1 cup)
5 oz. sugar (¾ cup)
5 eggs
powdered sugar
ladyfinger molds or a
  baking sheet with
  parchment paper
a pastry bag with a ½ inch
  round plain tip

1.   Grate and chop the zest from the half lemon. Squeeze the juice. Combine the flour and 2½ oz. (⅓ cup) of the sugar and sift 3 times. Separate the eggs. Butter and flour the molds or line the baking sheet with parchment. Preheat the oven to 350°.
2.   Whisk the yolks until they are thick and pale—about 3 minutes in an electric mixer. With a large rubber spatula, fold the lemon juice, zest, and flour-sugar mixture into the egg yolks in two stages.
3.   Using the electric mixer, whisk the egg whites until they begin to form soft peaks. Add the remaining sugar in a slow steady stream, whisking constantly. Continue whisking until the whites are thick and hold soft peaks. Fold the whites into the yolk mixture.
4.   Place the batter in the pastry bag. Fill each "finger" of the mold with batter, lifting up the tip and moving it forward slightly to stop the flow of batter as you complete each ladyfinger.
5.   Sprinkle powdered sugar through a coarse sieve over the ladyfingers and bake for 10 minutes, until they begin to brown. Remove from the oven and transfer each ladyfinger to a cooling rack while still warm.

Here is a cake made out of a soft cooked custard. Notice that butter and chocolate are added to half the custard so that the cake will have body when chilled and that the remaining half of the custard is used as a sauce over the cake. You will need ladyfingers, (see above) and since this dessert needs to be served well chilled, you should make it a day ahead of time.

CHOCOLATE CUSTARD CAKE

Serves 8 to 10

12 egg yolks
2 cups milk
2 oz. sugar (⅓ cup)
1 tablespoon vanilla extract
½ lb. semisweet chocolate
½ lb. unsalted butter
3 dozen ladyfingers
a 6-cup charlotte mold or
** loaf pan**

1. In the top of a double boiler over hot (not boiling) water, combine the egg yolks, milk, and sugar. Stir constantly until the mixture thickens, and add the vanilla. Divide the custard in half. Refrigerate half the custard to be used later as a sauce and pour the other half into a bowl.
2. Melt the chocolate and butter together and stir until smooth. Combine with the custard in the bowl, mixing well.
3. Lightly butter the mold, and line the mold with the ladyfingers. Pour in the chocolate custard and cover the top of the mold with the remaining ladyfingers.
4. Chill for at least 12 hours. Unmold, slice, and serve each portion with a little of the reserved custard sauce.

This sponge contains egg yolks and is made using a technique called the Italian Meringue Method. That is, instead of granulated sugar, a hot sugar syrup, is whisked into the egg whites. The heat of the sugar syrup "cooks" the egg whites, producing a very stable meringue, perfect for adding to fillings, Bavarian creams, whipped cream, or for topping off pies. This cake is plain and delicious, and making it is a good way to practice another cooking technique.

ORANGE SPONGE CAKE
Serves 8 to 10

10½ oz. sugar (1½ cups)
5 oz. water
1 cup egg whites
½ teaspoon salt
7 egg yolks
zest of 2 oranges, chopped
¼ cup orange juice
5 oz. cake flour (1 cup)
a 9- or 10-inch × 4-inch tube
  pan
a candy thermometer

1. Boil the sugar and water until the syrup reaches 235° on the thermometer. Remove from the heat.

2. In an electric mixer, whisk the egg whites and salt until they form soft peaks. Pour the hot syrup slowly into the egg whites, whisking constantly and continue whisking until the meringue is thick and shiny, about 1 minute. Reduce the speed to low and continue whisking an additional minute to cool the meringue.

3. In a clean bowl, whisk the egg yolks, zest, and juice at high speed until light colored and thick. With a spatula, fold the cooled meringue into the egg yolk mixture.

4. Preheat the oven to 350°. Sift the flour 5 times. Sift and fold it into the batter in three stages, folding lightly and quickly.

5. Pour the mixture into the *ungreased* tube pan and bake about 45 minutes, until risen and very lightly browned.

6. Remove from the oven and turn upside down to "hang" (see Angel Food Cake) until completely cooled.

7. Carefully remove the cake from the pan and "saw" gently with a serrated knife to serve.

The next cake in the sponge category is the Genoise. This light butter cake has a slightly denser, moister texture than the other sponges, and is the foundation of dozens of cakes. What distinguishes a Genoise or Light Butter Cake from other sponges is that it contains egg yolks and butter. The method is also different: in a Genoise, the eggs are not separated when the air is whisked into them. To compensate for the fat in the egg yolks, the eggs are warmed before they are whisked. Warming the eggs can be done by putting the room temperature eggs (still in their shells) into several changes of hot tap water before they are whisked to triple their volume.

For a different texture, substitute 2 oz. potato or corn starch plus 3 oz. cake flour for the 6 oz. of cake flour called for in the recipe. The cake flour gives a more velvety crumb and the corn starch or potato starch tightens the crumb for a moister cake. Sift the flour when you add it to the batter instead of plopping it into the eggs and deflating the batter. Be sure to fold in the flour mixture quickly but thoroughly—any lumps of flour will become hard during baking.

Allow the cake to cool at least 1 hour before slicing or frosting. If you are going to brush it with syrup or sprinkle it with spirits, the top and bottom crusts are sliced away first. To make a chocolate Genoise—replace 1 oz. of corn starch/flour with 1 oz. unsweetened cocoa.

GENOISE (Light Butter Cake)
Makes 2 layers

5 eggs, warmed (see page 234)
5 oz. superfine sugar (¾ cup)
6 oz. cake flour (1 cup plus 3 tablespoons)
1 tablespoon vanilla extract
3 oz. melted clarified butter
2 8-inch round cake pans
parchment paper

1. Preheat the oven to 350°. Butter and flour the sides of the pans, and line the bottoms with rounds of parchment paper.
2. Combine the warmed eggs and sugar and whisk in an electric mixer at high speed for 3 minutes, or until the eggs have tripled in volume. Lower the speed to medium and whisk another minute.
3. Sift the flour 5 times, and fold carefully into the eggs in two stages, folding quickly until all the flour has been incorporated.
4. Combine the vanilla and cooled but still liquid clarified butter in a small bowl and fold in about a cup of the flour-egg mixture. Return all to the larger bowl of batter and fold to combine*.
5. Pour the cake batter into the prepared pans and bake in the preheated oven approximately 30 minutes, or until the cake pulls away from the sides of the pans.
6. Remove the cakes from the oven and let stand 5 minutes before unmolding onto cooling racks.

(*This is an important step. It is too difficult to fold in the melted butter and vanilla without first lightening it with the flour-egg mixture.)

Madeleines are small cakes baked in shell-shaped molds. Their foundation is the Genoise batter. They are perfect for you to practice your Genoise technique on.

MADELEINES
Makes 24

5 eggs, warmed (see page
234)
5 oz. superfine sugar
(¾ cup)
6 oz. cake flour (1 cup plus
3 tablespoons)
2 tablespoons orange juice
zest of 1 orange, chopped
3 oz. melted clarified butter
madeleine molds (for 24)
powdered sugar

1. Preheat the oven to 350°. Butter and flour the madeleine molds.
2. Combine the warmed eggs and superfine sugar and whisk in an electric mixer at high speed for 3 minutes or until the eggs have tripled in volume. Lower the speed to medium and whisk another minute.
3. Sift the flour 5 times, and fold carefully into the eggs in three stages, folding quickly until all the flour has been incorporated.
4. Combine the orange juice, the chopped zest, and the cooled but still liquid clarified butter in a small bowl and fold in about a cup of the flour-egg batter. Return all to the larger bowl of batter and fold to combine.*
5. Pour the cake batter into the prepared madeleine molds and bake approximately 8 to 10 minutes.
6. Remove from the oven and let stand 2 minutes before unmolding onto cooling racks. Sprinkle with powdered sugar.

(*Note: This is an important step. The melted butter, orange juice, and zest are too difficult to fold in without first lightening it with the flour-egg mixture.)

The last cake in the sponge category is the Pound Cake. True pound cakes are made without baking powder or soda, as is this one. Traditionally, pound cakes were made with one pound of each of the main ingredients—flour, sugar, eggs, and butter. My version comes a bit short by weight, but not in any other sense. All the sponge cake rules apply.

POUND CAKE
Makes 1 loaf

5 eggs
1 lemon
½ lb. unsalted butter
7 oz. sugar (1 cup)
½ teaspoon salt
½ teaspoon cream of tartar
10 oz. cake flour (2 cups)
a 5 × 8-inch loaf pan

1. Preheat oven to 350°. Butter and flour the cake pan. Separate the eggs. Grate and chop the zest of the lemon and squeeze the juice.
2. Cream the butter and half the sugar until the mixture is light and fluffy. Add the egg yolks, one at a time, beating well after each addition. Beat in the zest and lemon juice.
3. Add the salt to the egg whites and whisk in an electric mixer until they begin to form soft peaks. Add the cream of tartar and the remaining sugar in a slow steady stream, continuing to beat until the meringue is thick and holds soft peaks.
4. Sift the flour 4 times. Gently fold the flour and egg whites alternately into the butter mixture.
5. Pour the batter into the prepared pan and bake until lightly browned, about 40 minutes.

CHEMICALLY LEAVENED CAKES

Baking powder was first produced commercially in the 1850s in Boston, and it revolutionized baking methods. Up until then, the only way to make baked goods light was to beat air into the eggs or to add yeast. Using baking soda or baking powder saves time and energy and is more economical since you can use far less eggs and butter and still produce a distinctive feathery, light-textured cake.

Baking soda is sodium bicarbonate. Once it is activated with an acidic ingredient such as buttermilk or lemon juice, it immediately begins to release carbon dioxide and the batter containing it should be baked as soon as possible. Most recipes call for baking powder. Baking powder is a combination of baking soda and cream of tartar. Add moisture of any kind to this mixture and again, carbon dioxide is produced. In the oven, the heat helps release additional carbon dioxide from the baking powder. It expands the trapped carbon dioxide gas and air and creates steam. The resulting pressure swells the air bubbles, which in turn expand the food being baked. If too much baking powder is used, the result can be a bitter taste in the cake. The biggest advantage to using chemical leaveners is that most cakes can be mixed in one bowl. All the general rules for cake baking given at the beginning of this lesson apply to chemically leavened cakes.

This cake is a good one for you to practice on.

PECAN FUDGE CAKE
Serves 10 to 12

5 oz. pecans
2 eggs
¼ lb. unsweetened
  chocolate
¼ lb. unsalted butter
14 oz. superfine sugar
  (2 cups)
10 oz. cake flour (2 cups)
¼ teaspoon salt
2 teaspoons baking powder
1½ cups milk
1 tablespoon vanilla extract
2 8-inch round cake pans
parchment paper
Pecan Fudge Frosting (see
  recipe below)

1. Preheat the oven to 350°. Butter and flour the sides of the pans, and line the bottoms with rounds of parchment paper. Toast the pecans in a 350° oven for 10 minutes, cool and chop finely. Whisk the eggs lightly. Melt the chocolate in a double boiler.
2. In an electric mixer, cream the butter, gradually add the sugar, and beat until fluffy. Beat in the eggs and melted chocolate.
3. Sift the flour, salt, and baking powder, and beat it into the creamed mixture alternately with the milk. Add the nuts and vanilla and stir just until combined.
4. Pour the batter into the prepared pans. Bake for 25 to 30 minutes or until the center of the cake springs back when you touch it and the sides have begun to shrink away from the pan.
5. Remove from the oven and let stand 5 minutes before unmolding onto cooling racks. Cool completely before filling and frosting.

Pecan Fudge Frosting

¼ lb. unsalted butter
2 oz. unsweetened chocolate
1 teaspoon lemon juice
1 teaspoon vanilla extract
¾ lb. powdered sugar
  (3 cups)
5 oz. pecan halves

Melt the butter and chocolate together in a double boiler. Blend in the lemon juice, vanilla, and powdered sugar. Beat at high speed until the frosting is fluffy and light. Mix in the pecan halves.

BREADS

I don't think there is a better food smell than the aroma of bread baking in the oven, or that anything could taste better than a piece of warm home-baked bread. Even if you don't intend to become a regular bread baker, I urge you to bake some of the basic breads described in this chapter, just so you will know what good bread should taste like. It will help you in selecting a good commercial bakery bread and besides, you might get addicted to the smell!

Just like cheeses, or cakes, there are so many different breads that a whole book could be devoted to breads alone. The chapter on breads here, however, will be short and will only cover some of the most common basic or foundation doughs—the basic French baguette, basic American white and whole wheat breads, an egg-and-butter bread called brioche, a bread dough suitable for pizza, and a sourdough loaf.

INGREDIENTS

Before you start baking, you need to understand something about the ingredients and methods used in making bread. You can mix any amount of flour, water, yeast, and salt, bake it, and get something called bread. But in bread making, the methods used to combine the ingredients play a large part in the end result. And likewise with ingredients—each ounce more or less of flour, whether or not you add butter and eggs, or if you use milk instead of water will all give you a different result. In order to understand that concept let's talk about each element.

Flour   Flour is the crushed or finely ground meal of cereal grains like rice, barley, rye, corn, and wheat.

White wheat flour   The whole wheat kernel is made up of three parts—the endosperm, the germ, and bran. The milling process transforms the wheat kernel or berry into white (wheat) flour. It involves breaking apart the kernel and grinding the starchy portion, called the endosperm, to a fine meal. This meal is in turn passed through fine sieves to extract the bran and wheat germ. White flour, therefore, is made only of endosperm. Freshly ground white flour is a pale yellow color. As it ages, it becomes white naturally, and is referred to as "unbleached" white flour. It can also be chemically bleached.

Whole wheat flour   In whole wheat flour, the kernel is ground *without* removing the germ and bran. Whole wheat flour has better flavor but because the germ has not been removed, the flour does not keep as well as white flour (the germ is the part of the wheat berry that contains fat which can become rancid with age). In bread making, when whole wheat flour is used without the addition of white flour, it makes a very dense, heavy loaf.

Gluten   The endosperm part of the wheat kernel is made up of starch and gluten. It is because of the gluten in the flour that bread can be made. The gluten stretches and holds in the gases of the fermenting yeast, allowing the dough to rise. The amount of gluten in flour depends on the kind of wheat used. It is estimated that there are about 30,000 existing varieties of wheat from which white flour is produced. They in turn can be divided into two groupings—hard wheats and soft wheats. Hard wheat varieties are those high in gluten and relatively lower in starch. Soft wheat varieties are lower in gluten and relatively higher in starch. When you are shopping for flour to use in bread making, purchase the flour marked "best for bread." That simply means that the gluten content of the flour is proper for home bread making.

Measuring flour   Flour proportions in baking are important. For this reason the volume (cup) method is very unsatisfactory. Flour should be weighed on a scale with all other dry ingredients.

Yeast   Baker's yeast contains a mass of tiny, one-celled plants that belong to the group of plants called fungi. Yeasts increase very rapidly if placed in a warm, moist environment and if given their favorite foods, sugar or starch. In a bread dough, as yeast ferments, enzymes from the yeast cells attack the starch in the flour and change it to sugar. The sugar is then changed to alcohol and carbon dioxide gas. The gas bubbles formed in the dough make it porous and light. When the bread is baked, the alcohol evaporates and the yeast plants are destroyed, but, of course, by then the yeast has done its job.

Activating yeast There are two forms of commercial yeast—dry and compressed. To activate dry yeast, you will need to dissolve it in a warm liquid—100° to 115°. If the liquid is too hot, the yeast may be destroyed. If you feel you are unable to judge the temperature, use an "instant read" thermometer. Compressed yeast is fresh and active and is crumbled directly into the other ingredients. It will only last approximately a week in the refrigerator. One cake of compressed yeast, or 1 envelope of active dry yeast, or 1 scant tablespoon of bulk dry yeast are all equivalent and are interchangeable in any recipe.

"Proofing" yeast If you have had your dry yeast on hand for two months or more, you may want to "proof" it, that is, see if it is still alive. This may be done by dissolving the yeast in warm water with ½ teaspoon of sugar. Within 15 minutes, you should see some action—lots of bubbles on the top of the liquid. That will let you know your yeast is alive. If there is no action, discard it and buy some new yeast.

Leavening with yeast Mixing yeast with dough to ferment it is called leavening the dough. Temperature has everything to do with what happens with yeast. To retard the action of a yeast dough, it may be refrigerated; freezing suspends the action; warmth accelerates the action; and high heat destroys the action completely.

Eggs Eggs enrich bread, add color, and help make the bread rise higher. The eggs should be at room temperature, or, for greater volume, slightly warmed.

Sugar Sugar aids in retaining moisture in the dough and helps promote a good crust color. Sugar added to the yeast quickens the action of the yeast, although in large amounts (1 cup or more), sugar retards the yeast action. Sugar, honey, or molasses are interchangeable in any recipe.

Salt Salt brings out the flavor of the dough and prevents yeast from working too fast, therefore allowing a good-flavored dough to develop. Salt also helps in strengthening the gluten. Never add salt directly to the yeast.

Fats Butter and oil contribute taste, help make a tender loaf with a smooth crust, and lubricate the gluten—helping the dough to rise.

Milk Milk allows flour to absorb more liquid, therefore milk doughs tend to use less flour than water doughs. Milk will give bread a softer and finer, more delicate texture and taste. Dry skim milk may be substituted and need not be reconstituted. Instead of milk, substitute an equivalent amount of warm water and add the dry milk powder to the flour.

BREAD-MAKING METHODS

Sponge method A sponge is a batter consisting of half the flour, the dissolved yeast, and the liquid called for in a recipe. In this method, the sponge is allowed to rise several hours before the rest of the ingredients are added. It is thought that because of the extra rising time, the flavor of the bread is enhanced. We use the sponge method in the brioche recipe.

Starter method A starter consists of a mixture of water, flour, and yeast which is mixed together, placed in a crock, and allowed to stand in a cool place several days before being used the first time. A cupful or so of the starter is used instead of yeast for each bread recipe. The starter needs to be used regularly and "replenished" regularly by the addition of more flour and liquid. Before the invention of dry yeast or compressed yeast, a starter was the only way to make bread. It is still the only way of making sourdough bread and is more fully explained in the section on sourdough.

Quick method   The quick method consists of dissolving the yeast in liquid and adding it to the remaining ingredients—probably the most common method used today.

Kneading   Kneading dough not only develops the gluten but evenly distributes the fermenting yeast cells throughout the dough, trapping them inside the strands of gluten, causing the dough to rise. A heavy-duty electric mixer or food processor is recommended for kneading bread. If you prefer to hand knead, here is the kneading technique: Sprinkle a little flour on a wooden breadboard or countertop and turn the mixed dough out onto it. With floured hands, fold the back of the dough toward you and with your palms, push the dough away from you with a rolling motion. Repeat, folding toward you and rolling away, adding a little flour only if the dough seems too sticky. Continue to knead until the dough is smooth and elastic. Bread is adequately kneaded when the indentation formed by sticking the knuckle of a bent finger into the dough springs back—usually about 10 to 15 minutes of hand kneading or 2 to 3 minutes by machine. One minute of machine kneading is generally equal to 5 minutes kneading by hand.

Rising   Rising or "proofing" the yeast dough is done to allow the yeast cells to infuse the dough with carbon dioxide, stretching the strands of gluten, thereby giving the resulting bread a finer texture. Most recipes will call for at least two risings, each allowing the dough to roughly double in bulk, each taking about 1½ hours at 70°. In between risings, the dough is "punched down" (with your fist) to compact it in the bottom of the bowl, ready to rise again. Yeast dough can rise in temperatures between 40° and 85°. The cooler it is, the slower the bread will rise. By slowing down the rising time, the flavor of the bread will develop more fully. Always grease or cover the dough to keep it from forming a dry crust as it rises. On the last rising before the dough goes into the oven, allow the dough to rise only about 1½ times its own bulk—about 30 minutes in a warm place. This will allow for the last expansion in the hot oven which is called "oven spring."

Baking   Preheat the oven to the desired temperature for at least 15 minutes before putting the loaves in to bake. Yeast breads should be baked at 400° for the first 10 minutes. Then the temperature is reduced to 350° for the last 30 or 40 minutes. Bread doughs that have lots of sugar and butter will brown quickly, and a cooler oven should be used, starting at 375° and reducing the heat to perhaps 350°. Bake on the middle shelf, with the pans 2 inches from each other or from the sides of the oven. Place them on the diagonal for better heat circulation. Do not crowd the oven. Unless the oven is very large, two large loaf pans or four small ones are capacity.

Do not open the oven door for the first 10 minutes. It is during this period that the final rising (oven spring) takes place. When the bread is done, remove yeast breads from the pans immediately and cool them on their sides on wire cooling racks.

Crust The outer surfaces of bread is called the crust, the inner part is called the crumb. For a darker, crisper crust, use dark metal pans and brush the loaf with cold water before baking. You may also spray the oven with cold water, or place a pan of hot water on the floor of the oven, or throw in some pieces of ice to create steam. Brushing the dough with butter gives the bread a softer crust, and brushing with egg gives a shiny crust. If you want a softer crust, cover the bread with a cloth while it is cooling.

Doneness When you begin to smell that wonderful bread aroma, your bread is approaching doneness. A yeast bread is done when it is a pale brown and has begun to shrink from the sides of the pan, though it will not pull away as much as a cake will. Turn the bread out of the pan and thump the bottom of the bread with your fingers. If it sounds hollow, it is done; if it doesn't, return the loaf to the pan and bake a little longer. If the loaf seems too soft when taken out of the pan, it may be placed on a baking sheet and baked another 5 minutes, or until it feels firm to the touch. If the top is already brown enough, cover with a piece of foil. If you are undecided whether the loaf has been baked long enough, insert a wooden skewer into the center of the loaf. If it comes out clean, the bread is done. If not, return it to the oven for another 5 minutes.

Freezing Yeast doughs freeze well, and can be frozen at any stage of the bread-making process. If you freeze the dough in the middle of the recipe, just bring the dough back to room temperature and proceed where you left off with your recipe. To freeze baked bread, cool the bread and wrap well in either foil or plastic wrap, then place in a plastic freezer bag. Baked bread should not be frozen for more than 2 months, as it will become dry.

Equipment

Ovens Commercial bakers' "hearth" ovens differ from home ovens because they are lined with stoneware tiles which absorb and hold the heat, providing continuously higher and more even temperatures. Should you wish to simulate this type of oven, I recommend you purchase a baker's stone, (see page 5).

Electric mixers A heavy-duty electric mixer or food processor for mixing and kneading bread dough is a big timesaver and is highly recommended.

Bread-baking pans For our purposes, I shall define a standard loaf pan as a rectangular shape, 8½ inches to 10 inches long, by 3 inches to 4½ inches wide, by 2 inches to 3 inches deep. There are also baguette pans or "French bread frames" that come in racks of 2 or 4 for baking a softer dough that needs to be held in a particular shape while it is baked. Many bread doughs are shaped and baked on ordinary baking sheets. And finally, you may be quite creative and experiment with any shape ovenproof container for some interesting results.

Scales Because exact proportions in bread making are so important, a scale should be used to weigh all dry ingredients.

The best bread for you to start out with is my Basic American White Bread. It is relatively foolproof, but will take you through the entire basic bread-making process. It is made by the quick method (the yeast is dissolved in liquid first), and will take about 3 hours from start to finish (not all supervised time) since it only has one rising. Remember that you may put your bread "on hold" at any time by making use of the refrigerator or freezer. Refer to the sections on method, terms, or equipment with any questions you might have.

BASIC WHITE BREAD
Makes 2 loaves

1 teaspoon vegetable oil
1½ level tablespoons dry
   yeast
13 oz. warm water (100° to
   115°)
2 tablespoons sugar
2 teaspoons salt
2 tablespoons soft unsalted
   butter
1½ lbs. unbleached "best-
   for-bread" flour (4¾
   cups)
2 standard loaf pans

1. Grease the pans well with the vegetable oil. Dissolve the yeast in ½ cup of the warm water.
2. In the bowl of an electric mixer, or a large mixing bowl, if you are making the bread by hand, combine the remainder of the water with the sugar, salt, butter, and half the flour. Mix well. Add the dissolved yeast and the rest of the flour and mix until combined.
3. Knead the dough until smooth, about 5 minutes in an electric mixer or 15 minutes by hand.
4. Place the ball of dough in a greased bowl, cover, and let rise until it is double its original bulk—about 1½ hours at room temperature.
5. Punch the dough down, and shape into loaves. Place in the prepared pans, cover and allow to rise until they are 1½ times their original bulk—about 45 minutes.
6. Preheat the oven to 400°. With a razor blade make 2 diagonal slashes in the tops of the loaves, brush with butter, and bake at 400° for 10 minutes, until the loaves begin to brown, then reduce the heat to 375° and finish baking—approximately 25 to 30 minutes more.
7. Remove from the oven; remove the bread from the pans and cool at least 1½ hours before slicing.

This is the second loaf you should try. It is also made by the quick method.

BASIC 100% WHOLE WHEAT BREAD
Makes 2 loaves

1 teaspoon vegetable oil
2 tablespoons dry yeast
½ cup honey
2¼ cups warm water
¼ cup melted unsalted butter
1 lb. 14 oz. whole wheat flour (6 cups)*
1 tablespoon salt
2 standard loaf pans

1. Grease the pans well with the vegetable oil. Dissolve the yeast and honey in the warm water.
2. In the bowl of a heavy-duty electric mixer or a large bowl, if you're making the bread by hand, combine the dissolved yeast and honey, the melted butter, and half the flour; add the salt and the remainder of the flour and mix until combined.
3. Knead the dough until smooth and shiny, about 5 minutes in the mixer or 15 minutes by hand.
4. Place the ball of dough in a greased bowl; cover and let rise until doubled in bulk—about 1½ hours at room temperature.
5. Punch the dough down, knead lightly (2 or 3 turns) and place the ball of dough back into the bowl. Cover and let rise a second time until double in bulk—about 1 hour at room temperature.
6. Punch the dough down and shape into loaves. Place in the prepared pans, cover, and allow to rise until they are 1½ times their original bulk—about 45 minutes.
7. Preheat the oven to 425°. With a razor blade make 2 diagonal slashes in the tops of the loaves, and bake for 10 minutes at 425°; lower the oven temperature to 375° and finish baking—about 25 to 30 minutes more.
8. Remove from the oven; remove the bread from the pans and cool at least 1½ hours before slicing.

(*For a lighter-textured loaf, substitute unbleached white flour for half the whole wheat flour.)

BASIC SOFT ROLL DOUGH
Makes about 2 dozen small rolls

¼ cup + 1 teaspoon
  vegetable oil
2 tablespoons yeast
2 cups warm water
6 tablespoons sugar
1 tablespoon salt
1 egg
1 oz. powdered skim milk
  (¼ cup)
2 lbs. unbleached flour
  (6¼ cups)
2 baking sheets

1. Grease the baking sheets with 1 teaspoon vegetable oil. Dissolve the yeast in 1 cup of the warm water and set aside.

2. In the bowl of an electric mixer or a large bowl if you are making the bread by hand, combine the other cup of warm water with the sugar, salt, egg, powdered milk, and ¼ cup oil. Mix well. Add half the flour and mix; add the yeast-water and the remainder of the flour and mix until well combined.

3. Knead the dough until shiny and smooth, about 5 minutes in an electric mixer or 15 minutes by hand.

4. Place the ball of dough in a greased bowl, cover, and let rise until it is double in bulk—about 1½ hours at room temperature.

5. Punch the dough down, knead lightly (2 or 3 turns), and place the ball of dough back into the bowl. Cover the dough and let it rise a second time until double in bulk—about 1 hour at room temperature.

6. Punch the dough down and divide into 16 to 24 pieces, depending on the size rolls you wish. Shape the pieces into balls, adding a little flour to your hands if the dough gets too sticky. Place the balls of dough about 2 inches apart on the prepared baking sheets. With the palm of your hand, flatten the balls slightly. For a crisper crust, mist the rolls with water. For a soft crust, brush with melted butter. Let rise 30 minutes at room temperature.

7. Preheat the oven to 400° and bake the rolls 15 to 20 minutes.

Now we come to that classic crusty European loaf—the French baguette. Because the dough is so moist, steam will develop during baking and will produce large holes in the bread unless the kneaded dough is given two risings before shaping. After shaping, the dough is too soft to hold its form unless supported by the baguette pan. The baguette pan is designed to create and maintain the familiar cylindrical shape of the loaves. Don't rush this bread—it tastes best with long, slow risings to fully develop the flavor.

BASIC FRENCH BAGUETTE

Makes 4 to 6 loaves

2 tablespoons dry yeast
2½ cups warm water (100°
to 115°)
1 lb. 14 oz. unbleached
white flour (6 cups)
1 tablespoon salt
1 tablespoon warm water
4 to 6 baguette pans

1.   Dissolve the yeast in 2½ cups warm water.
2.   In the bowl of an electric mixer, or a large mixing bowl if you are making the bread by hand, combine half the flour and the yeast and water. Mix the batter on low speed for 5 minutes. Dissolve the salt in the tablespoon of warm water and add it to the batter, mixing well. Add the rest of the flour and mix until combined.
3.   Knead the dough 8 minutes in the electric mixer or 20 minutes by hand—it will be very elastic, smooth, and shiny.
4.   Place the dough in a large greased bowl, cover tightly, and allow to rise in a cool place overnight.
5.   Punch the dough down, knead lightly for 3 minutes by hand, and place the dough back into the bowl for its second rising which can be another long (8- to 10-hour) rising in a cool place.
6.   Oil the baguette pans. Preheat the oven to 450°. Turn the dough out onto the work surface. Punch it down and divide it into 4 or 6 pieces. Allow the pieces to rest 5 minutes before shaping into loaves. Shape into long thin loaves the length of the pans, and place in the baguette pans. Allow the loaves to rise, uncovered, for 30 minutes in a warm place.
7.   Spray with water, slash each loaf twice diagonally with a razor blade, and place in the preheated oven. After 10 minutes, turn the oven down to 400°, mist the loaves once again with water, and bake until lightly browned, about 20 minutes more.

The following bread is one I learned to make in Italy. It is a coarse country dough, perfect for pizza and for another wonderful dish, Chicken in Bread.

TUSCAN BREAD DOUGH

1 scant tablespoon dry yeast
1 tablespoon sugar
about 2 cups warm water
 (100° to 115°)
1½ lbs. unbleached flour
 (4¾ cups)
2 teaspoons salt

1. Dissolve the yeast and sugar in ½ cup of warm water.
2. In the bowl of an electric mixer, or a large mixing bowl if you are making the bread by hand, combine the dissolved yeast and flour. With the electric mixer at medium speed, add as much of the water as necessary to make a dough. Add the salt.
3. Knead in the machine or by hand until the dough is shiny and smooth—about 5 minutes in the machine or 15 minutes by hand.
4. Cover and allow to rise until double in bulk—about 1½ hours at room temperature.
5. Proceed with either Onion Pizza or Chicken Baked in Bread (see below).

ONION PIZZA
Serves 6 to 8

1 recipe Tuscan Bread
 Dough
2 medium red onions
6 tablespoons olive oil
1½ lbs. tomatoes
½ lb. Italian Fontina
¼ lb. Parmesan
4 tablespoons tomato paste
salt and pepper
dry oregano
a baking sheet

1. Slice the onions and sauté in 4 tablespoons olive oil for 2 minutes. Slice the tomatoes. Grate the cheeses. Oil the baking sheet with 1 tablespoon olive oil.
2. Roll out the dough into a circle or rectangle and place on the oiled baking sheet. Using your fingers, make a little rim of dough so that the topping ingredients will not slide off. Spread the tomato paste over the dough with a brush. Cover the tomato paste with the sliced onions. Sprinkle with salt, pepper, and oregano. Cover the onions with the sliced tomatoes and sprinkle again with salt, pepper, and oregano. Sprinkle with a little olive oil and let stand 15 minutes before baking. Preheat the oven to 425°.
3. Bake the pizza in the preheated oven for approximately 30 minutes. Lower the oven temperature to 350°. Remove the pizza from the oven, sprinkle with both cheeses, and return to the oven for 5 minutes more—to melt the cheeses.
4. Remove from the oven and let the pizza rest 10 minutes before serving.

The fun of the next dish is the surprise of cutting into what appears to be a large loaf of bread and then being overwhelmed by the vision of the chicken and vegetables appearing like magic inside the loaf.

CHICKEN BAKED IN BREAD
Serves 8 to 10

1 recipe Tuscan Bread
  Dough
2 medium red onions
2 stalks celery
4 carrots
2 cloves garlic
3 oz. prosciutto
2 small fryers (2½ lbs. each)
2 chicken livers
4 fresh sage leaves
1 small sprig fresh
  rosemary
1 tablespoon olive oil
4 tablespoons unsalted
  butter
salt and pepper
¾ cup red table wine
freshly grated nutmeg
1 egg
2 tablespoons milk
a large baking sheet

1. Make the bread dough, proceeding through step 4.
2. Chop the onions; chop the celery, carrots, and garlic. Cut the prosciutto into matchstick-sized julienne. Cut the fryers into 8 pieces each (see page 40), and chop the livers. (Reserve the neck, giblets, and wing tips for stock.) Chop the sage leaves and sprig of rosemary. Oil the baking sheet.
3. Melt half the butter in a large skillet and sauté the onions, celery, carrots, garlic, and prosciutto gently for 10 minutes. Transfer to a plate. Add the rest of the butter and the chicken pieces, sprinkle with salt and pepper and sauté 5 minutes (you may have to do this in two batches). Add the chopped chicken livers and the wine to the chicken in the skillet, and simmer over high heat until the wine has reduced to a tablespoon—about 2 minutes. Allow the chicken to cool.
4. When the dough has risen, punch it down and roll it out into a large circle with a thickness of about ½ inch. Pick the dough up with the rolling pin and place it on the oiled baking sheet. Sprinkle the dough with salt and pepper. Place the 4 half-breasts in the center of the dough, sprinkle with salt, pepper, a little rosemary, sage, nutmeg, and ⅓ of the vegetables and livers. Next, place the thighs on top of the vegetables, sprinkle with seasonings and another ⅓ of the vegetables, and repeat the procedure with the legs and wings.
5. Fold the dough with the chicken inside in such a way as to look like a large oval loaf of bread. Preheat the oven to 375°. Beat the egg together with the milk. Brush the bread with the egg mixture and allow to rise at room temperature 30 minutes. Bake about 1 to 1½ hours—until the bread is browned.
6. Let rest 30 minutes before serving. To serve, make a cut in the bread all the way around about a third from the top. Lift off the bread top and, with a large spoon, serve the chicken and vegetables. Tear the bread with your hands, and serve with the chicken. (The bottom crust will be saturated with juices from the chicken, vegetables, and herbs—serve it too.)

The next dough is rich with butter and eggs—the classic brioche. Note that the sponge method is used to make the brioche. This involves a first rising with only part of the ingredients mixed into the dough, followed by a second rising of the complete dough. The finished brioche dough must always be chilled before you work with it. Because of the high egg and butter content, it becomes too sticky to work with if it warms up.

BRIOCHE DOUGH
Makes about 2½ lbs. of dough

¼ cup warm milk
¼ cup warm water
1 tablespoon dry yeast
4 tablespoons sugar
1 lb. 2 oz. unbleached flour
  (3½ cups)
6 eggs
1½ teaspoons salt
½ lb. unsalted butter,
  softened

1.   Warm the milk and water to 100° to 115°. In the bowl of an electric mixer, or large mixing bowl if you are making the bread by hand, dissolve the yeast and 2 tablespoons of sugar in the warm milk and water. Add 5 oz. (1 cup) of the flour and 2 beaten eggs and beat 30 seconds in the mixer, or about 3 minutes by hand. Sprinkle the remaining flour over the yeast batter (do not mix it in), cover, and let stand at room temperature about 2 hours. (After that time, you will see the batter breaking through the flour.)

2.   Add the 2 remaining tablespoons of sugar, the salt, and the 4 remaining eggs, and beat at medium speed until the eggs are well incorporated into the dough.

3.   Add the softened butter, bit by bit, and beat until the dough is shiny and smooth—about 1 minute. Cover and allow the dough to rise until doubled in bulk, 3 hours at room temperature.

4.   Turn the dough out onto a floured board and press into a rectangle. Fold over into thirds, turn, press into another rectangle, and fold into thirds again. This procedure (see Puff Pastry page 268) redistributes the yeast and helps build body into the dough. Sprinkle the dough with flour, wrap in plastic, and refrigerate 8 hours (or up to 2 days) before using.

5.   After the dough has been refrigerated 8 hours, remove it from the refrigerator, cut off the amount of dough needed for your recipe and proceed—remembering to work quickly as the dough will get sticky when warm.

Brioche Parisienne is commonly served at breakfast in France. It is baked in a fluted mold. Traditionally it is made with an extra piece of dough that forms a little topknot.

Brioche molds come in numerous sizes. You need to know just how much dough (by weight) the mold will hold. The following table can serve as a guide. Using a scale will take the guesswork out of this step.

A mold that holds 2 oz. of water will hold 2 oz. of dough.

A mold that holds 4 oz. of water will hold 3 oz. dough.

A mold that holds 6 oz. of water will hold 5 oz. dough.

A mold that holds 1½ qts. of water will hold 1¼ lbs. dough.

A mold that holds 2 qts. of water will hold 1½ lbs. dough.

BRIOCHE PARISIENNE

1 to 1½ lbs. Brioche Dough
butter to grease molds
1 egg + 1 tablespoon water
brioche Parisienne molds

1. Cut off pieces of dough (check by weight) to fit your molds. Divide the pieces of dough in two—a larger piece for the base and a smaller piece for the topknot.

2. Butter the molds. Form each piece of dough quickly into a ball and drop the larger piece into the mold. Cut a cross in the dough and press the smaller ball of dough down into the cross. Repeat until all the molds have been filled. Let rise 1 hour at room temperature.

3. Preheat the oven to 400° for 20 minutes. Beat the egg with the water and brush each brioche with the egg wash. If the molds are small, set them on a baking sheet. Bake in the preheated oven for 5 minutes. Lower the oven temperature to 350° and bake 8 to 10 minutes more (or 25 to 30 minutes more for large molds), until delicately browned.

4. Remove the brioches from the oven, unmold, and cool on a rack 30 minutes before serving.

As you bite into the soft, buttery brioche wrapped around the firm, spicy sausage, the rich Madeira-mushroom sauce enhancing each morsel, you will be unable to think of a better way to begin an elegant meal! In this dish, the sausage is brushed with egg and rolled in flour to keep the dough from shrinking away and leaving a space between the sausage and dough after it is baked.

SAUSAGE IN BRIOCHE WITH MADEIRA MUSHROOM SAUCE
Serves 8

¾ lb. Brioche Dough
1½ cups Basic Brown Sauce
   (see page 75)
1 large sausage (1 lb.)
½ lb. mushrooms
¼ bunch parsley
1 egg
2 tablespoons milk
flour
¾ cup Madeira
salt and pepper
a standard loaf pan

1. Make the Brioche Dough. Make the Brown Sauce.
2. If the sausage you are using is not cooked, prick the casing and simmer it for 30 minutes. Allow the sausage to cool in the liquid and remove the casing. Slice the mushrooms thinly. Remove and discard the parsley stems and chop the leaves. Beat the egg and combine with the milk.
3. Roll the Brioche Dough into a rectangle large enough to enclose the sausage. The dough should be about ½ inch thick. Brush the dough with the egg mixture.
4. Brush the sausage with the egg mixture and roll in flour. Place the sausage on the dough and roll the dough around the sausage, brushing the edges of the dough with the egg mixture so they stick together. Roll out the dough at each end so that when the two ends are folded over the seam, they meet.
5. With the seam side down, place the dough in a well-oiled loaf pan, brush the top with egg and decorate with leaf shapes cut from the dough trimmings; use the egg to stick on the leaves. Let the dough rise for 20 minutes at room temperature and then bake in a preheated 400° oven for 30 minutes, or until nicely puffed and browned. Remove from the loaf pan and cool for 30 minutes before slicing.
6. While the sausage is baking, simmer the mushrooms in the Madeira until the wine is reduced to ¼ cup. Add the Brown Sauce and taste for seasoning—adding salt and pepper as needed.
7. To serve, slice the Sausage in Brioche into 8 pieces, ladle Madeira sauce over each slice. Garnish with chopped parsley.

Many years ago, before commercial yeast production (and before super-markets), all breads were made from starters. Commercial yeasts are rather mild in flavor, so if you prefer a stronger taste to your bread, you might consider a home-grown yeast-and-flour mixture called sourdough starter.

Starters are simple to make, but must be used and renewed to keep active. You need to use your starter at least once a week. In between times, keep the crock covered and in the refrigerator. When you use your starter for breads, always leave some starter in the crock, and add enough flour and water in equal amounts to the leftover starter to bring it back to its original level. For example, if you were to take out a cup of starter, you would want to replenish the starter with ½ cup water and ½ cup flour. Stir, cover, and let stand overnight before refrigerating once again.

SOURDOUGH STARTER

1 tablespoon dry yeast
2 cups warm water (100°
  to 115°)
10 oz. unbleached flour
  (2 cups)
a 2-qt. stoneware crock with
  cover

1. Combine the yeast and water in the crock, and stir until the yeast is dissolved. Add the flour and stir until well mixed.

2. Cover, and set aside for 3 days at room temperature. The mixture will foam up and eventually the flour will settle to the bottom, leaving a clear liquid on top. You should smell a fermenting odor when you lift the cover. Stir before using.

You must always replenish the starter with an amount equal to whatever you have used. Use half water and half flour to replenish the starter, and add to the crock. Stir to combine and leave at room temperature overnight.

We are using a starter and the sponge method to make the next bread.

SOURDOUGH FRENCH BREAD
Makes 2 loaves

1 cup Sourdough Starter
1 cup warm water (100° to
    115°)
10 oz. unbleached flour
    (2 cups)

1 tablespoon dry yeast
1 cup warm water (100° to
    115°)
1 lb. 4 oz. unbleached flour
    (4 cups)
1 tablespoon salt
1 egg
2 tablespoons water
a baking sheet

1. In the bowl of an electric mixer, or a large mixing bowl if you are making the bread by hand, combine the sourdough starter, 1 cup warm water, and 10 oz. (2 cups) of flour. Mix until well combined, cover, and let stand overnight.
2. Dissolve the yeast in 1 cup warm water. With the machine on low, add the remaining flour, the dissolved yeast, and salt to the sponge and mix well.
3. Knead until the dough is smooth and shiny, about 5 minutes by machine or 15 minutes by hand.
4. Put the dough in an ungreased bowl, cover, and let rise until tripled in bulk—about 2 hours at room temperature.
5. Punch the dough down, and allow it to rise one more time until tripled in bulk, about 1½ hours at room temperature.
6. Punch the dough down, form into 2 loaves, and allow to rise 30 minutes on the baking sheet at room temperature.
7. Preheat the oven to 450°. Beat the egg with the water. Slash the tops of the loaves diagonally, and brush with the egg wash. Bake about 10 minutes at 450°, turn the oven down to 400°, and bake about 20 minutes more until delicately browned.

PASTRIES

The art of arousing your guests' appetites begins with delighting their eyes. Ripe fruits nestled in a crisp crust, shimmering through a clear glaze, will do just this—setting pastries apart as a particularly exciting area of cooking.

A certain mystique surrounds the whole subject of pastries—a belief that there are closely guarded recipes and tricks known only to a few lucky people. Not so! You'll discover that making good pastry is amazingly simple once you learn the proper techniques. Soon, not only will you be making a variety of Fresh Fruit Tarts, but dishes like Roquefort in Puff Pastry, *Gougère*, Cornish Pasties, or Mixed Ground Meats in Pastry, will become part of your standard repertoire.

In this chapter we will cover the three basic pastry doughs: short pastry (primarily used to make crusts for pies and tarts); chou paste (used to make cream puffs and eclairs); and puff pastry (mainly used to make turnovers, tarts, and patty shells). The methods and techniques you need to know are discussed preceding each basic recipe.

INGREDIENTS

Flour   Unless otherwise specified, use all-purpose flour. (See page 240 for more information on flour.)

Butter   Butter is probably the most important ingredient in pastry dough. It is what makes the pastry rich and tender, and it lubricates the gluten in the flour so that the pastry rises and puffs and appears light. Butter also gives pastry its flavor. For the lightest and most tender pastry possible, keep the butter cold. If the butter melts, the final baked result will have a brittle, cardboard-like consistency. (The exception is chou paste.) Always use unsalted butter.

Eggs   In chou paste, eggs act as a leavening agent. The additional fat contained in egg yolks makes any pastry with eggs richer.

Salt   Salt brings out the flavor of other ingredients in pastries.

EQUIPMENT

In addition to your regular kitchen equipment, you will need some special items that you will use primarily for baking.

Electric food processor   A heavy-duty food processor makes excellent pastry dough—quickly and easily.

Pastry board   You will need a special work surface—a 24 × 30-inch area of counter space with a Formica, maple, or marble surface (tile won't do). Otherwise, portable boards of that size are widely available in kitchenware shops.

Pastry brushes   You will need two brushes that you can reserve exclusively for pastry making. One, about 2 inches wide, will be used for brushing off excess flour when rolling out pastry doughs. This one should never be washed. The other, about 1 inch wide, will be used for brushing pastries with an egg wash or a fruit glaze.

Rolling pin   For rolling out pastries, you will need a rolling pin. Purchase a pin that is at least 14 inches long and as heavy as possible. Avoid pins that you fill with ice.

Tart and pie pans   If a tart or pie is not taken from the pan shortly after it comes from the oven, the steam from the pastry will be trapped between the bottom of the pastry and the pan bottom, and in a short time will create a soggy crust. I suggest you purchase removable-bottomed tart and pie pans, since they make for easy removal of the pastry.

Cooling rack   You will need at least one large wire rack (about 12 × 15 inches) that allows the air to circulate evenly around the pastries.

SHORT PASTRY

"Short" pastry is a rich dough used to make crusts for pies, tarts, quiches, and dishes that require a pastry wrap. The term "short crust" comes from the large amount of shortening required to make it. While the butter used is the most important ingredient in short pastry, the method used to blend the ingredients is equally important.

Measuring   Like cake batters and bread doughs, pastry doughs require exact measurements. Weigh all dry or solid ingredients (like butter) on a scale and use a measuring cup for liquids.

Combining butter and flour   The butter is always combined with the flour first, very lightly and quickly, and then just enough liquid is added to make the pastry hold together. It will take you approximately 13 seconds to combine the butter and flour in a food processor and should not take more than 2 minutes by hand. Combine only until mixture becomes crumbly.

Adding liquid   Insufficient liquid will make the pastry crumbly and hard to manage, whereas too much liquid will make the dough sticky and hard to handle, and will produce a baked pastry that is tough. Pastry that is just right will easily form a smooth, pliable ball of dough that is easy to handle. After the liquid is added, it will take an additional 30 to 40 seconds for the dough to begin to gather together in a food processor, and about 3 or 4 minutes by hand. Work as quickly as possible. Excessive handling develops the gluten in the flour which is fine when you're making bread, but will result in a tough pastry. If you are making the pastry by hand, use the tips of your fingers to work the dough, as the palms of your hands are inclined to be warmer.

Resting   After the dough is combined, wrap it in plastic and allow it to rest in the refrigerator. Short pastries should be refrigerated for at least 1 hour before rolling out, preferably more. Resting firms up the butter and relaxes the gluten, making the dough much easier to roll out.

Rolling out the dough   Unwrap the chilled, rested dough and place it on a lightly floured surface. Hit the dough a few times with the rolling pin to make it more pliable. Roll out the dough from the center, turning it around a little after each pass of the rolling pin, until it forms the shape you want.

Transferring the dough   Lay the rolling pin on top of the dough and roll the dough lightly around the pin. Lift up the rolling pin, hold it over the tart tin, pie pan, or baking sheet, and unroll the dough. Cut off any excess with the rolling pin or a knife.

This basic short crust pastry may be used for sweet and savory pies and tarts.

BASIC PASTRY
Makes about 1 lb. dough, enough for 1 11-inch crust or 2 8-inch crusts

½ lb. all-purpose flour
   (1½ cups)
½ teaspoon salt
5 oz. unsalted butter,
   chilled (10 tablespoons)
¼ teaspoon vinegar or
   lemon juice
4 to 5 tablespoons ice water

1.   Combine the flour and salt. Cut the butter into 8 pieces and work the butter into the flour until the mixture is crumbly (see **Combining butter and flour,** above).

2.   Mixing the dough lightly, add the vinegar or lemon juice and then add the water gradually (you may not need it all or you may need a little more), until the dough gathers together (see **Adding liquid,** above).

3.   Flatten the dough, sprinkle with a little flour, wrap in plastic, and allow to rest in the refrigerator at least an hour before rolling out (see **Resting,** above).

Because it has sugar in it, this pastry should only be used for sweet dishes. Baked, it has a cookie-like texture.

SWEET PASTRY
Makes about 1 lb. dough, enough for 1 11-inch crust or 2 8-inch crusts

½ lb. all-purpose flour
(1½ cups)
4 tablespoons superfine
sugar
½ teaspoon salt
4 oz. unsalted butter,
chilled (8 tablespoons)
¼ teaspoon vinegar or
lemon juice
1 egg

1.   Combine the flour, sugar, and salt. Cut the butter into 8 pieces and work the butter into the flour until the mixture is crumbly (see **Combining butter and flour,** above).
2.   Mixing the dough lightly, add the vinegar (or lemon juice) and egg, and mix until the dough just holds together (see **Adding liquid,** above).
3.   Flatten the dough, sprinkle with a little flour, wrap in plastic, and allow to rest in the refrigerator at least an hour before rolling out (see **Resting,** above).

This is an all-purpose pastry. Because it contains a large amount of crème fraîche or sour cream, the dough is extremely pliable and easy to work with, and is perfect for recipes that call for a "wrapping" of pastry.

CREAM PASTRY
Makes about 1½ lbs. pastry, enough for 2 11-inch crusts or 3 8-inch
crusts

¾ lb. "best-for-bread" flour
(2¼ cups)
½ teaspoon salt
6 oz. unsalted butter,
chilled (12 tablespoons)
1 egg
½ cup crème fraîche or sour
cream

1.   Combine the flour and salt. Cut the butter into 8 pieces and work the butter into the flour until the mixture is crumbly (see **Combining butter and flour,** above).
2.   Mix the egg and crème fraîche or sour cream together and lightly mix with the butter-flour until the dough holds smoothly together (see **Adding liquid,** above).
3.   Flatten the dough, sprinkle with a little flour, wrap in plastic, and allow to rest in the refrigerator at least an hour before rolling out (see **Resting,** above).

The best way to get started in pastry making is to make a fresh fruit tart. As the name implies, the fruit in the tart is not cooked. The pastry, of course, cannot be eaten raw, so it must be baked first without the filling. The term for baking an empty pastry is baking it "blind."
If you were to simply place the pastry in the pan and bake it in the oven, the sides would fall down and shrink, the bottom would bubble up, and you would be unable to use it. Follow these directions for a perfectly shaped pastry case. You will need a removable-bottomed tart tin for this method.

Baking a Pastry "Blind"

1. Roll the pastry out to a size slightly larger than the tart tin. Roll the pastry around the rolling pin and unroll the pastry into the tin. With the knuckles of your fingers, gently ease the pastry into the tin, allowing for shrinkage. Roll the pin over the edges of the tin to cut off excess pastry.

2. Line the pastry with parchment paper, and fill to the brim with pie weights. (You may use rice or beans for that purpose. Best results, however, come from ceramic or metal "pie weights," available in kitchenware shops.)

3. Bake the pastry in a preheated 375° oven about 20 minutes, or until you see the edges begin to brown.

4. Remove from the oven, take out the weights and parchment, and return to the oven for an additional 5 minutes to brown the bottom crust.

5. Place the baked tart in its tin on a bowl and let the sides drop. Place a large spatula between the metal bottom of the tin and the pastry and transfer the pastry to a cooling rack.

Fresh fruit tarts are a welcome dessert at any meal, formal or informal, and a wonderful way to practice your pastry-making skills. You may use an 8-, 9-, 10- or 11-inch removable-bottomed tin, or, if you wish, 6 individual tart tins.

FRESH FRUIT TARTS
Serves 6 or 8

1 cup light-colored fruit jam
2 tablespoons water
1 recipe pastry (any kind)
1 cup Pastry Cream (see page 219)
selected firm, ripe fruit (any single fruit or combination of bananas, nectarines, strawberries, blueberries, raspberries, oranges, kiwis, apricots, grapes, papayas, mangos etc.)

1. Press the fruit jam through a sieve to eliminate any large pieces of fruit. Add the water and warm in a small pot, stirring until smooth. Remove from the heat. This glaze will be brushed over the fruit in the tart.

2. Roll out your preferred short pastry, line the tart tin with it, and bake it blind. Unmold it and allow it to cool completely.

3. Make the Pastry Cream and allow it to cool.

4. Select and prepare the fruits, i.e., peel and slice the bananas, cut the grapes in half, peel and section the oranges, peel and slice the kiwi, etc.

5. Spread a layer of Pastry Cream over the bottom of the baked tart shell.

6. Arrange the fresh fruit in an attractive pattern over the Pastry Cream.

7. Reheat the jam glaze and, with a brush, lightly cover the fruit with the warm melted jam. Tarts may be assembled up to 4 hours before serving.

Here is a very easy cooked apple tart. You may use an 8-, 9-, 10-, or 11-inch removable-bottomed tin, or, if you wish, 6 individual tart tins.

SIMPLE COOKED APPLE TART
Serves 6 or 8

1 cup light-colored fruit jam
2 tablespoons water
1 recipe pastry (any kind)
4 large tart apples, Pippin or Granny Smith

1.   Press the fruit jam through a sieve to eliminate any large pieces of fruit. Add the water and warm the jam in a small pot, stirring until smooth. Remove from the heat. This glaze will be used for brushing over the pastry before it is baked and then over the fruit in the tart.
2.   Roll out the pastry and line the tart tin. Brush the unbaked pastry with the warm jam glaze.
3.   Preheat the oven to 425°. Peel, core, and slice the apples about ¼ inch thick. Arrange in an overlapping, concentric pattern on top of the pastry.
4.   Bake the tart 10 minutes at 425°, lower the heat to 375° and bake an additional 25 to 30 minutes, until the sides of the pastry are browned and the apples are soft. Remove from the oven and unmold onto a cooling rack.
5.   Reheat the remaining jam glaze and brush it over the apples.

This savory tart can be served as a main dish at brunch or lunch, or as an hors d'oeuvre or first course at dinner.

CHEESE AND HAM TART
Serves 6 to 8

1 recipe pastry
  (unsweetened)
3 oz. cooked ham
5 oz. Italian Fontina
1 oz. Parmesan
2 eggs plus 2 egg yolks
1½ cups crème fraîche
salt and pepper
freshly grated nutmeg
a 10-inch removable-
  bottomed tart pan

1.   Roll out the pastry and line the tart tin.
2.   Cut the ham into matchstick-sized julienne and sprinkle over the pastry.
3.   Preheat the oven to 425°. Grate both cheeses and sprinkle over the ham.
4.   Combine the eggs, egg yolks, and crème fraîche. Season with a little salt, pepper, and nutmeg, and pour over the cheese and ham.
5.   Bake the tart on the floor of the oven for 10 minutes to brown the bottom crust. (If you have an electric stove, place the tart pan directly over the coils of the stovetop burner at medium-low heat for the first 10 minutes of baking.)
6.   After 10 minutes, lift the tart to the oven rack, reduce the oven heat to 350°, and finish baking, approximately 10 minutes more, until nicely puffed and slightly browned.
7.   Unmold and cool on a rack at least 20 minutes before cutting and serving.

For variety, meats can be wrapped in pastry. Care needs to be taken though, not to overcook or undercook the food inside the dough, and, in turn, not to overcook or undercook the dough itself. For example, tough cuts of meat, suitable for braising, will take a much longer time to cook than the pastry that covers them. Therefore, the meat will need to be precooked so that the meat will be done at the same time as the pastry. On the other hand, delicate foods that do not require much cooking should not be encased in pastry as they will be overcooked by the time the pastry is baked. Pastry-wrapped foods are often one-dish meals and always make dramatic presentations.

MEAT LOAF IN PASTRY
Serves 8 to 10

1 recipe Cream Pastry
¼ lb. mushrooms
½ bunch parsley
1 small onion
¼ lb. Gruyère
1 egg
2 tablespoons milk
2 tablespoons unsalted
  butter
¾ lb. ground beef
¾ lb. ground pork
¾ lb. ground veal
½ cup milk
salt and pepper
1 cup crème fraîche
2 cups chutney
a baking sheet

1.   Make the pastry dough and allow it to rest in the refrigerator while preparing the other ingredients.
2.   Clean and chop the mushrooms. Remove and discard the parsley stems and chop the leaves. Chop the onion, and grate the cheese. Beat the egg together with the 2 tablespoons milk to make an egg wash.
3.   Sauté the mushrooms in the butter and transfer to a large bowl. In the same skillet, sauté the ground meats until they lose any pink color—about 3 or 4 minutes. Add the cooked meats to the bowl, draining the fats as you go.
4.   Add the onions, parsley, grated cheese, and milk to the meat, combine well, and season to taste with salt and pepper.
5.   Cut the rested pastry dough in half and roll out each half into a 6 × 14-inch rectangle, reserving any scraps.
6.   Lift one sheet of pastry over the rolling pin and onto the baking sheet. Place the meat mixture in a narrow loaf down the center of the dough, patting it to keep it firm.
7.   Place the second sheet of pastry on top of the meat loaf and press the edges together with the tines of a fork.
8.   Preheat the oven to 400°. Roll out the scraps and cut them into strips that may be crisscrossed over the top of the loaf or cut into stars or crescents to decorate the top. Brush the pastry with the egg wash, decorate with the pastry strips or shapes, and brush with the egg wash a second time.
9.   Bake approximately 45 minutes or until the loaf has turned a golden brown. Allow to rest 30 minutes before slicing.
10. Serve thick slices of the hot loaf, accompanied by a bowl of crème fraîche and a side dish of chutney.

I grew up in Grass Valley, California, where there lived a large group of people that had emigrated from Cornwall, England. I still remember the distinctive, delicious aroma of Cornish Pasties floating out of our neighbor's kitchen window, and my mother's delight when they would send some over. The meat pasty following is a recipe given to my mother by our Cornish neighbors.

CORNISH MEAT PASTY
Serves 2

1 recipe Cream Pastry
1 medium onion
¾ lb. beef sirloin
2 large russet potatoes
¼ bunch parsley
1 egg
2 teaspoons milk
2 tablespoons unsalted
butter
salt and pepper
a baking sheet

1. Make the pastry, divide it, and reserve half for another use. Allow it to rest in the refrigerator while the other ingredients are being prepared.
2. Chop the onion finely. Cut the beef into ½-inch cubes. Peel the potatoes and cut them into ½-inch cubes. Remove and discard the parsley stems and chop the leaves. Combine the egg and milk.
3. Melt the butter in a large skillet and sauté the onion 1 minute; add the meat and potatoes and sauté 10 minutes more over a medium heat. Remove from the heat and season to taste with plenty of salt and freshly ground pepper. Add the parsley and mix well. Let the filling cool.
4. Preheat the oven to 350°. Roll out the pastry into a round shape ¼ inch thick and 10 to 12 inches across. Place the pastry on a lightly greased baking sheet and place the filling on one half of the pastry. Brush the outer edges of the dough with the egg mixture and fold over the other half of the pastry so that you have a half-moon shape. Crimp shut with a fork, and poke 3 holes in the top of the pasty for the steam to escape. Brush the pasty with the egg mixture.
5. Bake 45 minutes or until nicely browned.

CHOU PASTE

Chou paste, sometimes called "cream puff" dough or "twice-cooked" dough, has the same ingredients as the short pastries, but yields entirely different results because the ingredient ratio is different and the method of combining the ingredients is different. When chou paste is made, it is a soft batter that can be mixed with other ingredients like puréed potatoes, (and then fried to make tiny potato puffs) or Gruyère cheese (and then baked to make *Gougère*), or it can be shaped with a pastry bag or spoons and baked to make cream puffs that can be filled with sweet or savory fillings. Or it can be combined with other pastries to create elaborate desserts like a Saint-Honoré Cake (see page 266) or the French creation, a *Croquembouche.*

Method
In making chou paste, the butter and water are brought to a boil, and the flour is added all at once and stirred until it becomes a dough that leaves the sides of the saucepan. The pot is then removed from the heat and the eggs are added, one at a time, and beaten until they are incorporated into the dough. The final paste is thick and shiny and is easily formed into the desired shapes through a pastry bag. Here is the basic recipe for chou paste.

CHOU PASTE
Makes about 1 lb. of dough, or 20 small pastries

1 cup water
1 teaspoon sugar
½ teaspoon salt
¼ lb. unsalted butter (8 tablespoons)
5 oz. all-purpose flour (1 cup)
4 large eggs

1. In a heavy saucepan, combine the water, sugar, salt, and butter and heat to a full boil.
2. Immediately add the flour all at once and stir vigorously until the dough comes away from the sides of the pan.
3. Remove from the heat and add the eggs, one at a time, beating well after each egg, making sure it is incorporated into the dough before adding the next one. The paste will be thick, creamy, and shiny.
4. Proceed with your recipe.

Deep-frying chou paste (See page 140 for basic information on deep-frying, temperatures of oil, etc.) Drop teaspoonfuls or strips of chou paste through a pastry bag into hot fat and deep-fry 4 or 5 minutes, turning once, until pastries are golden brown. Drain on paper towels.
To make cream puffs Cover a baking sheet with parchment paper. Drop mounds of paste onto the baking sheet with a teaspoon or through a pastry bag, leaving an inch or so in between each pastry to allow for expansion. Once in the oven, hollows form inside each pastry as the moisture in the paste turns to steam and expands. Bake in a preheated 400° oven 20 minutes until firm and lightly browned. If the pastries are underbaked, they may collapse when they come out of the oven. Pierce each pastry to allow the steam to escape, and return to the oven for 5 more minutes to dry the interiors. Cool on racks before filling.

Savory fillings Cooked chopped shrimp, crab, scallops, chicken, or vegetables, bound with Cream Sauce (page 71) and spooned inside each cream puff, make wonderful hors d'oeuvre and first courses.

Sweet fillings Sweetened whipped cream, ice creams (spooned into the cream puff at the last minute and served immediately), and sweet custards are the most common dessert fillings for cream puffs.

The following savory pastry has its origins in France. It is nice served with wine as an hors d'oeuvre.

GOUGÈRE
Serves 6 to 8

1 recipe Basic Chou Paste
¼ lb. Gruyère
1 egg
2 tablespoons water
a 9-, 10-, or 11-inch pie pan
parchment paper

1. Make the Chou Paste. Grate the cheese. While the Chou Paste is still warm, stir in the grated Gruyère. Preheat the oven to 400°. Line the bottom of the pie pan with parchment paper. Beat together the egg and water.
2. With a tablespoon, transfer egg-sized portions of dough to the prepared pie dish, one against the other in a circle. Smooth the circle on top with the back of the spoon. Brush with the egg wash.
3. Bake for 35 to 40 minutes in the preheated oven or until the pastry is firm and lightly browned. Serve warm or cooled.

The following confection is a wonderful way to show off the pastries you have learned so far. A round of short crust supports an edging of cream puffs. The cream puffs as well as the center of the cake are filled with a rum-flavored pastry cream. It is a very elaborate and beautiful dessert to present. I suggest you make this a two-day project. Make the custard and bake the pastries on the first day. On the second day, fill the cream puffs, make the caramel, and assemble the Saint-Honoré.

SAINT-HONORÉ
Serves 10 to 12

1 recipe Sweet Pastry
1 recipe Chou Paste
1½ recipes Pastry Cream
  (see page 219)
1 egg
2 tablespoons milk
9 oz. sugar (1¼ cups)
½ cup water
1 package gelatin (1
  tablespoon)
2 tablespoons cold water
2 tablespoons dark rum
6 egg whites
16 candied cherries
a pastry bag with a #7 tip
  and a nozzle tip
2 baking sheets
parchment paper

1.   Make the Sweet Pastry and allow it to rest. Make the Chou Paste and set aside. Make the Pastry Cream, strain into a bowl, press a piece of waxed paper onto the surface, and set aside. Combine the egg and milk in a small bowl to make an egg wash.
2.   Preheat the oven to 400°. Roll out the short pastry into a large square, ¼ inch thick. Using a 10-inch round tart tin as a guide, cut out a round of pastry. Place it on a baking sheet, and prick it several times with a fork. Using a pastry bag with the largest plain tip (a #7), pipe a rim of Basic Chou Paste around the outer edge of the 10-inch pastry round. Brush with some egg wash and bake for 25 minutes or until the whole pastry is browned. Transfer to a cooling rack.
3.   Using two spoons, form 14 walnut-sized puffs from the remaining Basic Chou Paste onto a parchment paper-lined baking sheet. Brush with the egg wash and bake in a preheated 400° oven for 20 minutes or until puffed and browned. Make a small hole near the bottom of each puff to allow the steam to escape. Put them back into the oven for a few minutes to dry out. Cool.
4.   Fill the puffs with Pastry Cream using a pastry bag and long (nozzle) tip. Set aside. (The remaining Pastry Cream will be combined with the gelatin and egg whites.)
5.   In a small, heavy saucepan, make some caramel by combining 7 oz. (1 cup) of sugar and ½ cup of water. Dissolve the sugar over low heat, then turn up the heat and boil the syrup until it thickens and turns golden. Dip the filled puffs in the caramel syrup and arrange them around the edge of the cake, attaching them with more caramel.
6.   Soften the gelatin in the cold water and warm it in a small saucepan until it is clear and liquid. Add the warm gelatin and the rum to the remaining pastry cream. Whisk the egg whites until they form soft peaks, adding the remaining sugar the last minute of the whisking. Fold the egg whites into the Pastry Cream. Fill the center of the cake with the pastry cream mixture. Place the candied cherries in between each puff for garnish. Refrigerate until serving time. (It is best to serve this cake within 4 to 6 hours after it is made.)

PUFF PASTRY

My favorite story concerning the origins of puff pastry is the one about a young Parisian bakers' apprentice who was assigned the daily task of making a batch of ordinary short pastry that the bakers needed to make tarts and other pastries. One day, the apprentice combined the flour, water, and salt, kneaded the dough as always, and then put it to rest, forgetting to incorporate the butter called for in the recipe. Later, it suddenly dawned on him what he had done. Fearing that the bakers would find out, he softened the butter by kneading it, and quickly buried it in the ball of resting dough, rolling and folding the dough as best he could to hide his mistake. When the bakers used the pastry, it puffed and rose miraculously. Delighted, they called for him in order to discover his wonderful secret. Of course, the boy, thinking they were angry, ran away in terror. Eventually though, he was found, and with great relief, he shared his secret with the bakers.

This story illustrates perfectly the object in rolling in the butter in making puff pastry—that is, to create a series of tissue-thin layers of dough, butter, and air, so that each layer puffs up as it bakes and raises the pastry to 10 or 12 times its original thickness. The story also illustrates that making puff pastry really consists of a two-stage process. First, the base (a short pastry) is made and rested. Then, the butter is "rolled-in"—a process of folding and rolling the dough a total of 6 times. This creates hundreds of tissue-thin layers of pastry, which when baked, will "puff" because of the moisture (turned to steam) trapped within the layers—somewhat the same concept as a soufflé.

Allow at least an hour unsupervised time for the dough to rest between each folding and rolling. I recommend that you spread out the making of puff pastry over a two or three-day period at your convenience. It only takes about 2 minutes to make and complete each turn—a total of 12 minutes for 6 turns—but the dough must rest from 30 minutes to an hour between times when it is handled. It will keep well in the refrigerator an additional 2 days before baking. You may also store it in the freezer, although I have noticed that frozen puff pastry does not rise as beautifully as the refrigerated variety.

When you bring the gorgeous Roquefort in Puff Pastry or the spectacular Apple Cream Turnover to the table, (which will inevitably evoke a chorus of "Ahs"), and as the buttery, crisp, tender layers of pastry melt in people's mouths, the quiet will be followed by frantic inquiries of "What bakery. . . ." Your family and friends will be amazed when you tell them, "Oh, I made it myself this afternoon!"

PUFF PASTRY

Makes about 2½ lbs. dough

1 lb. "best-for-bread" flour
   (3⅛ cups)
¼ lb. cake flour (¾ cup)
1¼ teaspoons salt
1¼ lbs. unsalted butter,
   chilled
½ teaspoon vinegar or
   lemon juice
1¼ to 1½ cups ice water
flour for rolling out dough
a 3-inch pastry brush

1.   Combine both flours and the salt. Cut ¼ lb. of butter into 8 pieces and work the butter into the combined flour until the mixture is crumbly.
2.   Mixing the dough lightly, add the vinegar or lemon juice and the cold water and mix until the dough holds together. (You may not need all of the water.)
3.   Gather the dough into a ball, flatten it slightly with your hand, and with a knife, slash it in a crisscross fashion (this speeds the resting of the dough). Sprinkle the dough with a little flour, wrap it in plastic, and allow it to rest in the refrigerator at least an hour before rolling the butter into the dough.
4.   Take the remaining butter from the refrigerator, dust the work surface and the butter with a little flour and hit the butter with your rolling pin to make the butter flat and pliable, using more flour if necessary. This will make it easy to roll the butter into the base. Return the kneaded butter to the refrigerator so that it remains cold.

Rolling in the butter   Dust the work surface with flour and roll the rested dough into a rectangle about 8 × 16 inches. Lay the flattened butter on top of the dough. Bring up the lower third of the pastry so that it covers half the dough. Fold down the top third. The butter will be concealed inside the dough and you will have 3 layers of dough. Wrap the dough in plastic and refrigerate at least 30 minutes before folding and turning.

First turn   Place the dough on the pastry board with the closed fold on the right. Hit the dough with the rolling pin to make it pliable and roll it out into another rectangle 8 × 16 inches, always rolling in the same direction. If the dough begins to stick to the pin or the pastry board, sprinkle with flour, using a dry pastry brush to brush away any excess. Fold the dough again into thirds. Wrap the dough in plastic and let rest in the refrigerator at least 30 minutes before rolling out again. You have completed 1 turn.

Remaining turns   Remove the dough from the refrigerator and give it 2 more turns, following the directions from the 1st turn. After the 2nd and 3rd turns, return the dough to the refrigerator to firm up the butter. Give the dough its last 3 turns before rolling out and baking.

   Note: If the butter begins to break through, patch it with some flour and return the dough to the refrigerator to chill.

Cutting and shaping   After completing all 6 turns, let the dough rest in the refrigerator 1 hour. Then cut off the dough needed and roll into a sheet. The sheet in turn is cut into the shapes desired. The thinner the sheet is rolled, the less rise there will be after the pastry is baked.

Baking.   Always start puff pastry in a preheated 425° oven the first 15 minutes of baking. The oven should be reduced to 375° for the following 10 minutes and then reduced to 325° for the remainder of the baking time, to help avoid a doughy center. Puff pastry should be served the same day it is baked.

The following puff pastry dessert is a fairly easy one to make, so it's a good one for your first try at puff pastry dough. To make it you need to have on hand a pound of Puff Pastry and 1 recipe of Pastry Cream.

APPLE CREAM TURNOVER
Serves 8

1 lb. Puff Pastry
1½ cups Pastry Cream (see page 219)
6 tart apples
2 tablespoons sugar
6 tablespoons unsalted butter (3 oz.)
1 egg
2 tablespoons water
powdered sugar
1 cup crème fraîche
1 teaspoon vanilla extract
a baking sheet

1.   Make the Puff Pastry and refrigerate it.
2.   Make the Pastry Cream and refrigerate it.
3.   Roll out the Puff Pastry into a 16 × 12-inch rectangle. Transfer to a baking sheet that has been sprinkled with a few drops of water and chill the pastry on the baking sheet until ready to fill—at least 30 minutes.
4.   Preheat the oven to 425°. Peel and core the apples and cut them into wedges about ¼ inch thick. Place the apples in an ovenproof dish and toss them with the granulated sugar and butter. Bake the apples 15 minutes. Remove from the oven and cool. In a small bowl, beat the egg together with the water.
5.   Remove the pastry from the refrigerator and spread Pastry Cream over half the dough, staying about an inch from the edge of the pastry, and arrange the apples in rows on top of the cream.
6.   Brush a little egg around the edges of the pastry, fold over the other half of the dough, and seal the edges with a fork. Brush the top of the pastry with some more beaten egg. Refrigerate 1 hour or more before baking.
7.   Preheat the oven to 425° and bake the turnover 20 minutes. Reduce the oven heat to 375° and bake an additional 10 to 15 minutes, reduce the heat to 325° and bake an additional 5 minutes—until puffed and golden brown. Once out of the oven, sprinkle the turnover with powdered sugar.
8.   Whip the crème fraîche with the vanilla and serve with thick slices of the warm turnover.

Puff pastry always makes a stunning beginning to a meal. This is one of the dishes I serve when I want to impress a guest and I always cut and serve it at the table. To make it you need to have on hand about a pound of Puff Pastry.

ROQUEFORT IN PUFF PASTRY
Serves 8

1 lb. Puff Pastry
¼ lb. Roquefort cheese
2 tablespoons unsalted
  butter
white pepper
paprika
2 large eggs
2 teaspoons arrowroot
(about) ½ cup crème fraîche
a 10-inch fluted removable-
  bottomed tart tin

1.   Roll out half the Puff Pastry to a thickness of ⅛ inch and line the bottom and sides of the tart tin. Cut off and discard excess pastry and chill the tart bottom.

2.   In a small saucepan, over low heat, warm the Roquefort cheese and butter; season with ½ teaspoon each of pepper and paprika or to your own taste. Add 1 of the eggs and mix well.

3.   In a small bowl, dissolve the arrowroot in half the crème fraîche, then add it to the cheese mixture, stirring over low heat until thickened. (If the mixture becomes too thick, thin it with a little more cream.) Spread the cheese filling out onto a plate and cool it in the refrigerator.

4.   Spread the chilled filling over the bottom of the chilled pastry, leaving a ½-inch border all around.

5.   Roll out the remaining dough to a thickness of ¼ inch, and place on top of the filling. Mix the remaining egg with 2 tablespoons water to create an egg wash. Use a little egg wash to seal the edges of the pastry—cut off any overlapping scraps of dough.

6.   Prick the pastry with a fork and cut the top in a swirl pattern. Refrigerate the tart until ready to bake—or at least 30 minutes.

7.   Preheat the oven to 425°. Brush the top of the tart with the egg wash and bake at 425° for 15 minutes. Reduce heat to 375° and bake another 10 minutes; reduce the heat to 325° and bake another 10 to 15 minutes, until browned and puffed. Unmold and let stand 15 minutes before cutting and serving.

Here's another light luncheon dish or first course. In order to make this, you will need 6 poached eggs. You will also need to have 6 baked puff pastry shells on hand. Using a fluted round puff pastry cutter (available in kitchen shops), cut out and then bake 6 pastry shells.

POACHED EGGS IN PUFF PASTRY
Serves 6

½ lb. fresh peas or ¼ lb. frozen
4 shallots
4 leaves butter lettuce
½ lb. mushrooms
¼ bunch parsley
4 sprigs fresh tarragon (½ teaspoon dry)
6 eggs
4 tablespoons unsalted butter
1 tablespoon flour
¼ cup white table wine
½ cup concentrated Brown Stock or White Stock
1 cup crème fraîche
6 baked puff pastry shells

1. Shell the peas, boil and reserve. Peel the shallots and chop finely. Cut the lettuce into fine shreds; clean and slice the mushrooms. Remove and discard the parsley and tarragon stems and chop the leaves.
2. Poach the eggs (see page 175) and reserve in water.
3. Melt the butter in a skillet, and sauté the shallots and mushrooms 1 minute. Sprinkle in the flour and stir in the wine, stock, and crème fraîche. Cook, uncovered, over low heat for 5 minutes or until the sauce is thickened. Add the shredded lettuce and the reserved peas.
4. When ready to serve, warm the eggs in hot water (see page 175). Place a baked pastry round on each plate, place a poached egg on each pastry; reheat the sauce and spoon some sauce over each egg.

As in the previous dishes using puff pastry, you need to have the dough on hand before you can make the dish. These charming fan-shaped cookies can be made with leftover scraps of puff pastry. If you wish to do this, gather the scraps together, then roll them out and fold them several times. Wrap in plastic and chill 30 minutes before proceeding.

PALMIERS (Palm Leaves)
Makes about 20

½ lb. Puff Pastry
sugar
parchment paper
baking sheet

1. Sprinkle the work surface with sugar and roll the dough into a rectangle ⅛ inch thick. Sprinkle some sugar over the dough and press it into the dough lightly with the rolling pin.

2. Fold both the right and left edges of the dough to meet in the center. Sprinkle more sugar on the dough and press in lightly with the rolling pin.

3. Now bring both the right and left folded edges in to meet in the center and sugar again.

4. Fold the dough now as you would a book; you should have 8 layers. Wrap in plastic and refrigerate.

5. When the dough is firm, slice the dough crosswise into ¼-inch slices. Cover a baking sheet with parchment paper, and place the pastries on the paper about 2 inches apart, to allow for expansion. Pinch the bottom of each palmier together to achieve a nice leaf shape. Chill 30 minutes before baking.

6. Bake in a preheated 425° oven 15 minutes. Reduce the oven to 375°, turn the cookies over, and bake another 10 minutes, until lightly browned.

HORS D'OEUVRES

Chapter 19

In France, the hors d'oeuvre is the first part of a meal, leading on to the other courses—the soup, main course, the salad, etc.,—and it is generally served at the table. For Americans, it more often means a choice selection of tidbits or "fingerfood," served before dinner. Quite often it constitutes the entire fare at a cocktail party.

The cocktail party had its beginnings as a kind of celebration of the repeal of Prohibition. Since then, it has developed into an American institution, and along with it has evolved a whole class of portable fingerfoods designed to go with the cocktails or wine. Some of these foods have been borrowed from Europe and Asia, but many are distinctly our own.

Knowing how to make a variety of appetizers has always been a priority with the students in my cooking school. Now that you have familiarized yourself with the basics of cooking, you may enjoy applying them to a sampling of treats from the hors d'oeuvre classes. Following are some of the best!

VEGETABLES WITH DIPS

Fresh vegetables, blanched or raw, make stunning presentations. Select vegetables that are absolutely fresh and unblemished. Small vegetables can be served whole, large ones made bite-sized. They may be prepared in advance and kept refrigerated for several hours before serving. A full, abundant arrangement always looks best, and may be displayed on attractive serving platters, or in rustic wooden bowls or baskets.

There are a myriad of dips made from mayonnaise, creamed cheese, puréed vegetables, sour cream, crème fraîche, or yogurt, that may be served with the vegetables. It just depends on your personal taste. Always serve thinly sliced baguette with the vegetables so that your guests may have the option to either dip the vegetables or spread the mixture on the bread.

A nice way of presenting any dip is in a hollowed out purple cabbage, or a yellow, red, or green bell pepper. If you use a cabbage, you can line the vegetable basket with some of the outer leaves.

AVOCADO DIP
Makes about 2 cups

1 clove garlic
¼ jalapeño pepper
¼ bunch parsley
¼ bunch cilantro
1 large ripe avocado
1 cup mayonnaise
3 tablespoons crème fraîche
1 tablespoon wine vinegar
2 tablespoons tarragon
  mustard
salt and pepper

1. Chop the garlic; remove the seeds and stem from the jalapeño and chop finely. Remove and discard the stems from the parsley and cilantro and chop the leaves finely. Peel and seed the avocado.
2. Combine all ingredients (except salt and pepper) in the bowl of a food processor or blender and process only until the mixture is smooth. Taste and add salt and pepper.
3. Store in the refrigerator until needed.

FRESH HERB AND SPINACH DIP
Makes about 2 cups

½ bunch flat-leaf parsley
½ bunch dill
½ bunch watercress
1 bunch spinach
2 green onions
1 cup mayonnaise
1 cup crème fraîche
salt and pepper

1. Remove and discard the stems from the parsley, dill, and watercress. Remove and discard the stems from the spinach. Clean the spinach and steam 2 minutes. Clean the green onions.
2. In a food processor or blender, process the parsley, dill, watercress, green onions, and spinach until finely chopped.
3. Add the mayonnaise and crème fraîche to the processed mixture and combine. Add salt and pepper to taste. Refrigerate until needed.

STUFFED VEGETABLES

You can use firm-textured raw vegetables as edible containers for fillings. Celery ribs, mushroom caps, Belgian endive, cherry tomatoes, cucumbers, summer squashes, and carrots (slivered and coiled) all work well. Other vegetables, too firm to be eaten raw, like beets, potatoes, and Brussels sprouts or turnips, may be cooked and hollowed out to form containers for an endless variety of fillings.

Celery stalks   Use the inner tender stalks. Rinse, dry with paper towels, and cut into 2- to 3-inch lengths.

Mushroom caps   Brush with a mushroom brush; carefully remove the stems.

Belgian endive   Cut off 1 inch from the root end; carefully separate each leaf.

Cherry tomatoes   Cut off tops; scoop out seeds and juice; sprinkle with salt and turn upside down to drain for 1 hour.

Cucumbers   Peel the cucumbers so that you will have an unpeeled strip next to a peeled strip, and cut them across into 1-inch slices. Take out the center of each slice with a large melon baller, leaving enough cucumber at the sides and bottom to make a little cup.

Zucchini   Prepare the same as cucumbers.

Carrots   Peel large carrots and cut them lengthwise into broad strips ⅛ inch thick. (Use the 2mm blade on your food processor.) Coil each strip around your finger, slide it off, and secure the curl with a tooth pick. Refrigerate in water for 1 hour. When ready to fill, drain, dry, and place a piece of lettuce inside each of them to form a cup.

Sweet pepper rings   Select nicely shaped small green, red, or yellow bell peppers. Cut around the top of each pepper and remove the stem and seeds. Reach inside and remove any remaining seeds. Pack a firm filling into the peppers. Wrap in foil and refrigerate to firm the filling. Slice the pepper into thick slices to serve.

Beets   Use small beets; boil for 30 minutes (or until tender) and peel. Scoop out the center with a melon baller.

Brussels sprouts   Trim the stems so each sprout will stand upright for serving. Boil for 4 minutes. Drain and hollow out a small cavity with a paring knife.

Eggplant   Select tiny eggplants. Halve lengthwise; sprinkle with salt and invert on paper towels for 30 minutes. Pat dry, brush with oil, and bake in a 350° oven until tender, 8 to 10 minutes. Hollow out a small cavity with a paring knife or curved serrated knife.

Potatoes   Select small boiling potatoes. Scrub, but do not peel, and boil until tender, but still firm. Cool and hollow out a cavity; take a thin slice off the bottom, so that the potato will stand upright for serving.

Turnips   Select small turnips and boil until barely tender—about 5 minutes. Cool, peel, and hollow out a cavity for the filling at one end, and take a thin slice from the other so that the turnip will stand upright for serving.

The fillings suitable for vegetables vary with the shapes of the containers. You can use soft mixtures based on cream cheese, yogurt, sour cream, or mayonnaise when your container is a cup. Rings and sandwiches need firmer fillings like flavored butters and blended cheeses. Blended cheeses with nuts and garlic, and herbed butters or cream cheeses spiced with dill, basil, and horseradish, all make good combinations.

SHRIMP AND CHEESE FILLING

Fills about 18 to 24 vegetables

2 oz. cooked shrimp
¼ lb. cream cheese
2 tablespoons crème fraîche
salt and pepper
paprika

Chop the shrimp finely. Combine the cream cheese, crème fraîche, and the chopped shrimp. Season to taste with salt, pepper, and paprika.

CRAB MEAT FILLING

Fills about 24 vegetables

1 2-oz. can whole pimentos
1 green onion
1 shallot
½ lb. cooked crab meat
1 teaspoon prepared
  mustard
2 teaspoons lemon juice
2 to 4 tablespoons
  mayonnaise
salt and pepper
paprika

Chop 1 pimento (reserve the remainder for another use), the green onion, and the shallot. Combine the crab meat, mustard, lemon juice, green onion, shallot, and 2 tablespoons of the mayonnaise, adding more if needed. Add the pimento and season to taste with salt, pepper, and paprika.

EGG AND CHEESE FILLING

Fills about 24 vegetables

3 hard-cooked eggs
2 oz. Roquefort cheese
2 to 4 tablespoons
  mayonnaise
salt and pepper

Chop the eggs and place in a bowl. Add the Roquefort cheese and about 2 tablespoons of mayonnaise. Combine well, and, if needed, add more mayonnaise to bind the mixture. Season to taste with salt and pepper.

STUFFED MUSHROOMS
Makes 24

24 large mushrooms
1 small onion
2 cloves garlic
1 small green bell pepper
2 slices French bread
2 oz. Parmesan
3 tablespoons olive oil
1 teaspoon salt
1 teaspoon pepper

1. Clean the mushrooms and carefully remove the stems. Chop the mushroom stems, onion, and garlic. Remove the stem and seeds from the pepper and chop the pepper. Make bread crumbs from the French bread (see page 13); grate the Parmesan.
2. Heat the olive oil in a large skillet and sauté the onion, garlic, green pepper, and mushroom stems for 5 minutes. Remove from the heat and add the salt, pepper, and grated Parmesan. Add enough of the bread crumbs to hold the mixture together.
3. Preheat the oven to 375°. Stuff the mushrooms; place in an oiled baking dish, sprinkle with a little olive oil; bake 15 minutes or until the mushrooms are soft.
4. Serve hot or at room temperature.

COOKED VEGETABLES

The following dish will keep for weeks in the refrigerator. If you keep some on hand, you'll always have an hors d'oeuvre or first course ready when unexpected guests drop by.

CAPONATA
Makes about 1 quart

1 medium eggplant
coarse salt
3 medium onions
½ bunch parsley
3 stalks celery
2 cloves garlic
½ cup olive oil
1½ cups tomato purée
¼ cup Balsamic vinegar
2 tablespoons sugar
2 tablespoons capers
salt and pepper
10 large green olives

1. Peel the eggplant, cut into ½-inch cubes, sprinkle with coarse salt, and allow to drain on paper towels 30 minutes. Slice the onions thinly. Remove and discard the parsley stems and chop the leaves. Slice the celery thinly. Chop the garlic.
2. Blot the eggplant with paper towels. Heat all but 4 tablespoons of the olive oil in a large skillet and sauté the eggplant until tender. Add the remaining oil, if needed and add the onions and celery. Sauté an additional 3 minutes. Add the garlic and the tomato purée, bring to a boil, lower the heat, and simmer gently, covered, for 20 minutes.
3. Add the vinegar, sugar, capers, and salt and pepper to taste. Add the olives and refrigerate the Caponata until serving. Serve with crusty French or Italian bread.

NUTS AND OLIVES

Of all the cocktail "accessories," nuts and olives are the most popular. The texture of nuts and the rich flavor of olives, complement wines and spirits of all kinds. Salted or spiced nuts, and marinated olives, are superior when prepared at home.

Note: Remember to watch the time and temperature whenever you brown or toast nuts, because nuts burn easily.

SALTED MIXED NUTS
Makes 3 lbs.

½ lb. raw almonds
½ lb. raw hazelnuts
½ lb. raw cashews
½ lb. raw brazil nuts
4 tablespoons unsalted
  butter
4 tablespoons olive oil
½ lb. raw walnuts
½ lb. raw pecans
coarse salt

1.   Mix the almonds, hazelnuts, cashews, and brazil nuts with the butter and olive oil in a large baking dish and put them in the oven at 300°. Roast for 10 minutes, tossing occasionally.
2.   Add the walnuts and pecans, sprinkle with salt and roast for another 20 minutes, stirring occasionally.
3.   Remove from the oven and drain on paper towels. Sprinkle with more coarse salt if desired, and store in airtight jars.

SPICED NUTS
Makes 1 lb.

2 cloves garlic
4 tablespoons unsalted
  butter
1 tablespoon Worcestershire
  sauce
½ teaspoon ground cumin
½ teaspoon cayenne pepper
1 teaspoon curry powder
½ teaspoon paprika
1 lb. raw nuts
coarse salt

1.   Chop the garlic finely. Melt the butter in a large skillet and add the Worcestershire sauce, cumin, cayenne, chopped garlic, curry powder, and paprika. Simmer over low heat for 1 minute.
2.   Add the nuts and stir until evenly coated. Spread on a baking sheet and bake at 325° for 15 minutes, stirring occasionally.
3.   Cool slightly, and toss the nuts with coarse salt. Store in airtight containers.

MARINATED OLIVES
Makes 1 lb.

8 cloves garlic
4 strips orange zest
4 strips lemon zest
¼ bunch parsley
¼ cup fresh lemon juice
¾ cup olive oil
1 bay leaf
2 dried chilies
½ teaspoon dried oregano
½ teaspoon coarsely ground
  pepper
½ teaspoon dried thyme
1 lb. Niçoise or Greek
  olives

1. Chop the garlic finely; strip the orange and lemon zest (see page 30). Remove and discard the parsley stems and chop the leaves. Combine the lemon juice with the oil in a small saucepan and bring to a boil. Remove from the heat and add the garlic, zest, parsley, bay leaf, chilies, oregano, pepper, and thyme. Cover and let stand for 20 minutes.
2. Place the olives in a bowl. Pour the oil mixture over and cover. Marinate at least 1 day before serving.

HORS D'OEUVRES ON SKEWERS

Skewered bits of meat, vegetables, or fruit are easy hors d'oeuvres to make and serve. The combinations are limited only by your imagination. Whatever the food served, be careful to place it near the end of the skewer so that it can be eaten easily. If you are using wooden skewers that will be baked or broiled, soak them for 30 minutes in water before putting them in the oven or broiler.

SKEWERED SHRIMP, SCALLOPS, AND AVOCADO
Makes about 16 skewers

32 shrimp (30 to a lb.)
½ lb. scallops
2 cloves garlic
½ cup water
½ cup white table wine
1 teaspoon salt
¼ cup lemon juice
½ cup walnut oil
1 large avocado
16 skewers
Rémoulade Sauce (see page
  87)

1. Peel and devein the shrimp. Clean the scallops and cut them into 16 pieces. Crush the garlic. Combine the water, wine, and salt, and bring to a boil. Drop in the shrimp and scallops, bring back to a boil, and drain immediately.
2. In a shallow dish, combine the crushed garlic, lemon juice, and walnut oil. Drop the warm shrimp and scallops in the marinade. Cover and marinate overnight refrigerated.
3. To serve, peel the avocado and cut into 16 pieces. Skewer a shrimp, scallop, avocado, and shrimp on a skewer. Arrange the skewered shellfish attractively on a platter and serve with Rémoulade Sauce.

This is my adaptation of an oriental dish. Hoisin sauce (a sweet plum-based sauce) is available in oriental food markets—the other "oriental" ingredients, soy sauce and fresh ginger are available in the supermarket. These skewered bits of meat are also delicious in combination, like pork with chicken, or lamb with sausage.

SKEWERED LAMB, BEEF, PORK, CHICKEN, OR SAUSAGE
Makes 24

1½ lbs. boneless meat
2 green bell peppers
2 red bell peppers
a 2-inch piece fresh ginger
  root
2 cloves garlic
3 tablespoons soy sauce
2 tablespoons hoisin sauce
¼ cup sherry wine vinegar
¼ cup sherry
½ cup olive oil
salt and pepper
24 skewers
olive oil
Dipping Sauce (see recipe
  below)
a baking sheet

1. Cut the meat into 48 small pieces. Remove the seeds from the peppers and cut them each into 24 pieces. Peel and chop 2 tablespoons ginger. Crush the garlic. Combine the soy sauce, hoisin sauce, sherry vinegar, sherry, olive oil, garlic, ½ teaspoon each salt and pepper, and the chopped ginger.
2. Marinate the meat and bell peppers in the marinade 24 hours. If you are using wooden skewers, soak them in water for 30 minutes before you use them.
3. Alternate 2 pieces of meat and 2 pieces of pepper on each skewer. Lightly oil a baking sheet and place the skewers on the sheet. Broil or grill 5 inches from the heat for 2 minutes each side. Serve with Dipping Sauce.

Dipping Sauce

1 cup sherry
4 tablespoons soy sauce
3 tablespoons sherry wine
  vinegar
2 tablespoons brown sugar
4 green onions

In a small saucepan, combine the sherry, soy sauce, vinegar, and sugar. Simmer gently for 5 minutes. Chop the green onions and add to the sauce.

CHEESE-BASED SNACKS

No chapter on hors d'oeuvres would be complete without at least one version of the popular cheese puff. Here are two of my favorites.

JALAPEÑO CHEESE PUFFS
Makes 16 pieces

1 medium-length baguette
8 cherry tomatoes
2 oz. aged gouda cheese
2 oz. jack cheese
¼ jalapeño pepper
4 tablespoons prepared
  mustard
olive oil
alfalfa sprouts
a baking sheet

1.   Slice off the ends of the baguette and make 16 slices, about ¼ inch thick. Slice the tomatoes in half. Grate the cheeses and combine.
2.   Preheat the oven to 350°. Remove the seeds and chop the jalapeño pepper finely—combine with the mustard. Spread the mustard on the slices of bread and sprinkle each slice with grated cheese. Place a half tomato on each.
3.   Place each slice on a lightly oiled baking sheet and bake 5 minutes or until the cheeses melt.
4.   Garnish each cheese puff with alfalfa sprouts.

BAKED CHEESE OVALS
Makes 36 pieces

¼ lb. sharp Cheddar
5 oz. flour (1 cup)
¼ lb. unsalted butter
18 large dates
36 pecan halves
olive oil
a baking sheet

1.   Grate the cheese. Combine the flour, butter, and grated cheese until it forms a dough. Cut each date in half lengthwise and remove the pit.
2.   Preheat the oven to 375°. Divide the dough into 36 pieces. Flatten the dough and wrap each piece around a half date. Place on a lightly oiled baking sheet and press a pecan half on each. Bake about 15 minutes, or until lightly golden.

Pinwheels are an attractive and very easy fingerfood. You can use any combination of deli meats or smoked salmon.

MANGO CHUTNEY PINWHEELS
Makes about 36 pieces

¼ lb. fresh goat cheese
3 tablespoons mango
  chutney
12 slices ham, turkey,
  smoked salmon, etc., ⅛
  inch thick

1.   Blend the cheese and chutney together until smooth.
2.   Lay out each piece of meat and spread the cheese mixture on top. Roll up tightly. Cover and refrigerate 1 hour.
3.   Cut each roll crosswise into 3 pieces each and arrange on platters with cut sides up.

MEATS

Raw meat preparations are extremely popular as hors d'oeuvres or light suppers. Meats used must have no visible fat and must be very fresh. The flavor of freshly chopped meat is what is so special about Steak Tartare, therefore it is crucial that it be prepared just before you serve it.

STEAK TARTARE
Makes about 20 servings

1 lb. lean beef
¼ bunch parsley
½ bunch chives
½ small onion
6 anchovy fillets
1 tablespoon Dijon mustard
1 egg yolk
½ teaspoon Tabasco
1 teaspoon salt
2 tablespoons capers
3 tablespoons brandy

1.   Coarsely chop the meat in a meat grinder or food processor. Remove and discard the parsley stems and chop the leaves finely; mince the chives, onion, and anchovy fillets.
2.   Combine all ingredients in a large bowl and blend thoroughly but gently. The egg yolk will bind the meat and seasonings. Serve immediately.
3.   To serve, arrange the tartare in a smooth mound on a large decorative tray or platter. You may garnish the platter with tiny Niçoise olives and sliced tomatoes. Arrange cocktail rye bread and black bread in alternating colors on one side of the platter along with a small crock of butter and utensils for spreading and serving.

Prepare this dish just before serving. Partially frozen meat is easier to slice, so put the meat in the freezer about 45 minutes before serving time.

THINLY SLICED RAW BEEF
Serves 8

1 green onion
2 tiny pickled gherkins
¼ bunch parsley
1 lb. beef top round
1 tablespoon capers
¾ cup Vinaigrette Sauce
   (see page 85)

1.   Clean and slice the green onion finely. Chop the gherkins finely. Remove and discard the parsley stems and chop the leaves finely. Remove all visible fat from the meat and chill the meat in the freezer 45 minutes (no more) before slicing.
2.   Remove the meat from the freezer and slice it across the grain into paper-thin slices and arrange it in an attractive overlapping pattern on a platter. Add the green onion, capers, gherkins, and parsley to the vinaigrette and spoon over the meat.

MENU PLANNING AND ENTERTAINING

I am sure you have encountered the child who, after studying the food on his or her plate says, "That doesn't look (or smell) good—I'm not going to eat it!" As infuriating as that response may be at first—listen to what the child says because he or she may be right. The presentation of each dish is one of the primary concerns in menu planning as is the course-by-course construction.

Interesting menus create contrasts in color, texture, shape, taste, and design. You eat with your eyes as well as your mouth; it matters how the colors, textures, and shapes, relate to each other and the plate. You would never for example, serve Cream of Potato Soup, Chicken Breast Fillets in a Cream Sauce, Puréed Potatoes and Turnips, and Rice Pudding on white plates—all at the same meal!

No food should appear more than once at the same meal, and no meal should be composed of all rich foods say, or all soft foods. You need to consider balance and proportion—a large baked potato and grilled T-bone steak would appear awkward on a flowered luncheon plate. Be aware of the character of the food (an elegant Roquefort in Puff Pastry would not be called for as a first course at a barbecue of hamburgers and sausage); the season (a hearty beef stew is inappropriate in the middle of summer); and type of meal (dainty crêpes filled with tiny shrimp have no place at a men's sports awards dinner).

Another aspect of menu planning is the ease or difficulty of preparation. Never serve two or more dishes on the same menu that require many hours of preparation (like Baked Lasagne and St. Honoré—you will be so long in the preparation that you will no longer enjoy the eating), or menus that have three or four dishes on them that all require the oven (and you only have one oven). Consider, too, the number of guests you will be serving. If you are having 30 people for dinner, and you are doing all the cooking and serving yourself, don't attempt to seat everyone, and then make and serve omelets (too difficult).

Like other aspects of cooking, menu planning is a skill that becomes easier the more it is practiced. The following menus composed of recipes from this book, will, by example, get you started with menu planning. Study each menu before cooking it, and visualize it in your mind's eye, served on plates, course by course. When eating, look at each course with a critical eye, noticing all the points mentioned above. There are dozens of possible menu combinations in this book—after trying the ones I've composed, start planning on your own. Within a very short time you will develop a "feel" for putting together attractive menus, and will be able to do it as easily as you are able to coordinate your clothing.

You may wish to add salad with a Vinaigrette Sauce (page 85) before or after any of the main courses presented here.

DINNER FOR 6 OR 8

Steak Tartare *(page 282)*

Chicken Breast Fillets with a Wine Cream Sauce *(page 132)*

Grilled Mixed Vegetables *(page 148)*

Fresh Orange Soufflé *(page 210)*

DINNER FOR 6 OR 8

Fettucini with a Basil Cream Sauce *(page 201)*

Poached Chicken Breasts With a Lemon Sauce *(page 103)*

Braised Leeks with Dill *(page 111)*

Frozen White Chocolate Mousse with a Dark Chocolate Sauce *(page 223)*

DINNER FOR 6 OR 8

Pasta with Clam Sauce *(page 199)*

Lamb Cacciatore *(page 115)*

Chocolate Mousse *(page 222)*

DINNER FOR 6 OR 8

Sausage in Brioche with Madeira Mushroom Sauce *(page 252)*

Chicken in Red Wine *(page 110)*

Steamed-Baked Potatoes *(page 104)*

Chocolate Almond Soufflé *(page 210)*

DINNER FOR 6 OR 8

Mixed Shellfish Salad *(page 163)*

Perfect Roast Beef *(page 126)*

Individual Spinach Soufflés *(page 209)*

Fruit Poached in Burgundy *(page 103)*

DINNER FOR 6 OR 8

Cheese Soufflé *(page 208)*

Shellfish Timbales with a Lime Sabayon *(page 156)*

Perfect Boiled Rice *(page 99)*

Apple Cream Turnover *(page 269)*

DINNER FOR 6 OR 8

Consommé *(page 53)*

Braised Meatloaf with a Wild Mushroom Sauce *(page 116)*

Mixed Vegetable Purée *(page 98)*

Little Pots of Chocolate Custard *(page 216)*

DINNER FOR 6 OR 8

Creamy Carrot-Orange Soup *(page 59)*

Steak with a Piquant Tomato Sauce *(page 135)*

Potato Gratin *(page 128)*

Hazelnut Meringue Cake *(page 230)*

DINNER FOR 6 OR 8

Cream of Potato Leek Soup *(page 57)*

Fish Baked in Parchment *(page 158)*

Orange Sponge Cake *(page 234)*

DINNER FOR 8 OR 10

Cold Cucumber-Yogurt Soup *(page 65)*

Vegetable Curry *(page 117)*

Lime Saffron Rice *(page 99)*

Fresh Fruit Tart *(page 259)*

DINNER FOR 8 OR 10

Risotto alla Milanese (page 101)

Osso Buco (page 113)

Sautéed Vegetables *(page 139)*

Pecan Fudge Cake *(page 238)*

DINNER FOR 8 OR 10

Gazpacho *(page 66)*

Chicken Baked in Bread *(page 249)*

Caramel Custard *(page 217)*

A WORD ON ENTERTAINING

Entertaining people at dinner in your home is a little like the art of creating a theatrical production. In a play, all the major elements are coordinated by the director, who makes sure that the lines spoken by the actors, the set, the lighting, the costumes, and the music are at their best and in harmony with one another—which is just the sort of coordinating the host or hostess entertaining at home must do. Once you have chosen a date and invited a group of guests, the menu must be selected, the shopping done, the wines chosen, the table set, and finally the meal prepared and served. Assuming that you are to be bartender, butler, cook, and waiter, there is the necessity to plan well. How can you make sure your "production" will be a success?

To begin with, if you want to have your guests seated and served at table, don't attempt entertaining more than eight people at a time. Six is ideal. After a menu is selected, make a shopping list, and complete your grocery shopping a day in advance, leaving only perishable foods like seafood to be purchased on the day of the party. The evening or morning before the dinner, set the table. Set out in the kitchen all the dishes, including the coffee cups, saucers, and serving dishes you will be using, ready to be warmed or placed on the table as needed. Check the liquor, mixes, wines and ice. When all of this has been accomplished, prepare any recipes that require thorough chilling.

Next, do all the advance preparation possible for the rest of the meal, like chopping vegetables, shelling nuts, grating lemon peel, etc. Cover these and store them in the refrigerator or on the countertop until needed. The rest of the preparation should be completed at least an hour before your guests arrive, so that you will be able to freshen up and relax. All that is left to be done is heating and serving.

To save yourself from dishwashing at midnight, arrange for a helper (it can be your own teenage child or a neighborhood girl or boy), to assist you that evening with the younger children, the serving, the final clearing of the table, and the dishwashing. Whenever you are unable to have that extra help, serve coffee in the living room and never start clearing the table or washing dishes while your guests are present. Have the dining room candles lit when guests arrive, and leave them burning after you leave the table. There is something lovely about a deserted table with candles burning low, wine glasses at varying stages of emptiness, napkins crumpled at each place—the warmth and closeness that people feel when sharing a good meal lingers on even when they have left the table. It feels good to be the catalyst that makes it all happen.

EQUIVALENTS
AND MEASURES

Measuring Ingredients

It is best for the beginning cook to measure ingredients exactly. With experience, the cook will realize that measurements down to the last ½ teaspoonful are not always necessary, and will develop a feeling for the necessary amount of herbs, onion, garlic, grated cheese, etc., without measuring to produce precisely the results wanted in a dish.

In fact, there are many recipes where the cook is asked to use his or her own judgment—to "season to taste." On the other hand, there are some ingredients in recipes that are critical, and should always be measured, like baking soda and baking powder, or flour in breads and pastries. For truly accurate measurement of dry ingredients—flour, sugar, nuts, etc.—use a scale. A cup of nut meats can vary if they are whole or chopped or broken—but ¼ lb. is always ¼ lb. on the scale.

The following charts will help with the most common equivalents, weights, and measures.

LIQUID MEASURES

1 tablespoon . . . . 3 teaspoons . . . . 15 milliliters

2 tablespoons. . . . . 1 oz. . . . . 30 milliliters

1 cup . . . . 8 oz. or ½ pint . . . . 240 milliliters

2 cups . . . . 16 oz. or 1 pint . . . . 480 milliliters

4 cups . . . . 32 oz. or 1 quart . . . . .0.95 liter

16 cups . . . . 4 quarts or 1 gallon . . . . .3.8 liters

DRY MEASURES

a pinch or dash . . . . ⅛ teaspoon or less
3 teaspoons. . . . . 1 tablespoon
4 tablespoons . . . . ¼ cup
5⅓ tablespoons . . . . ⅓ cup
16 oz. . . . . .1 lb.
1 lb. 1½ oz. (approx.) . . . . 500 grams
2.21 lbs. . . . . 1 kilogram

EQUIVALENT WEIGHTS OF
SPECIFIC FOODS

Note: Because of variables, these are approximations.

Almonds, in the shell, 2 lbs. ....1 lb. meats
Almonds, whole shelled, 1 cup .... 5 oz.
Beans, white, dry, 1 cup .... 7 oz.
Beans, white, dry, 1 cup ....3 cups cooked
Bread, 1 slice .... ¼ cup dry crumbs
Bread, 1 slice .... ¾ cup soft crumbs
Bread crumbs, dry, 1 cup .... 3 oz.
Butter, 8 tablespoons .... 4 oz. or ½ cup
Butter, melted, ¼ lb. .... ½ cup
Carrots, raw, chopped, 1 cup .... 4 oz.
Cheese, grated, 2 cups .... 8 oz.
Cheese, cream, 1 lb. .... 2 cups
Chicken, whole, 3½ lb. ....2 cups cooked meat
Cream, 1 cup .... 2 cups whipped
Cucumber, raw, peeled, seeded, chopped, 1 cup .... 5 oz.
Eggs, large, whole, 5 ....1 cup
Eggs, whites, large, 8 ....1 cup
Eggs, yolks, large, 12 to 15 ....1 cup
Flour, 1 cup .... 5 oz.
Lemon, 1 large .... ¼ cup juice
Raisins, 1 cup .... 5 oz.
Rice, long grain, raw, 1 cup .... 7 oz.
Rice, long grain, raw, 1 cup ....3 cups cooked
Strawberries, whole, 1 cup .... 5 oz.
Sugar, brown, 1 cup firmly packed .... 7 oz.
Sugar, confectioners', 1 cup .... 4 oz.
Sugar, granulated, 1 cup .... 7 oz.

APPROXIMATE WEIGHTS OF SPECIFIC FRUITS AND VEGETABLES

The following weight chart will give you something to go by when a recipe calls for a "medium" vegetable or fruit. Generally, for large, add 2 ounces, and for small, subtract 2 ounces. For dense vegetables like cabbage, cauliflower, or broccoli, add 6 ounces for large, subtract 6 ounces for small.

apple	6 oz.	cucumber	8 oz.
artichoke	8 oz.	eggplant	1 lb.
beet	7 oz.	leek	7 oz.
bell pepper	6 oz.	onion	7 oz.
bunch broccoli	1 lb.	potato	6 oz.
cabbage	2½ lbs.	tomato	6 oz.
cauliflower	2½ lbs.	turnip	8 oz.
carrot	3 oz.	zucchini	6 oz.

OVEN TEMPERATURES

Throughout this book, oven temperatures are given in degrees Fahrenheit (F), the standard measure used in the United States. Fahrenheit temperatures can be converted into degrees centigrade (C), the units used by most other countries, by using the formula $C = (F - 32) \times 0.556$.

	Fahrenheit	Centigrade
very slow oven	250° to 275°	121° to 135°
slow oven	300° to 325°	149° to 163°
moderate oven	350° to 375°	177° to 190°
hot oven	400° to 425°	204° to 218°
very hot oven	450° to 475°	232° to 246°

GLOSSARY

The following are terms used in this book that may not be familiar to you.

au gratin   A French phrase meaning a dish sprinkled with bread crumbs and/or grated cheese and baked or placed under a flame until brown.

albumin   Any of several simple, water soluble proteins that are coagulated by heat. If albumin is heated with a liquid, it forms a scum at the top which collects foreign substances. For instance, egg whites are simmered in a stock to clarify it in order to make a consommé.

bain-marie   *See* water bath.

beat   To stir or mix rapidly so as to blend or make lighter or fluffier.

bisque   A thick, creamy soup, classically made with shellfish, but sometimes made of puréed vegetables or meats.

blanch   To plunge briefly into boiling water, either to set the color and flavor of vegetables, or to loosen the skin of tomatoes or peaches, or to remove excess salt, as from bacon. Foods that have been blanched are usually cooked a second time until done. Also called parboiled or preboiled.

blend   To mingle and combine ingredients with a spoon, food processor, etc., so that the resulting mixture is uniform in texture, color, and flavor.

boil   To cook a liquid until bubbles break at the surface.

bouillon   The French word for broth.

chill   To cool but not freeze food.

combine   To mix ingredients together so that they cannot be separated.

cream   To mix butter that is soft but not melted with another ingredient, such as sugar, eggs, etc., to a creamy consistency. The best way to do this is to use the beater in your electric mixer or use the back of a wooden spoon in a bowl to press the ingredients into one another.

crust   *See* raft.

dash   A very small amount, often of a strong spice like cayenne.

deglaze   To loosen the pan drippings from a roasting pan or skillet by heating and stirring in wine, stock, or other liquid.

dust   To sprinkle with sugar, flour, etc.

egg wash   A mixture, as of egg yolk and water or milk, applied to pastry to glaze it.

fillet   To remove the bones from a piece of meat or fish. Also, the resulting piece of boneless meat or fish.

garnish   Anything that adorns or decorates a dish. It is usually edible, but its main purpose is visual appeal. A bouquet of watercress or parsley placed on a plate, or assorted carved vegetables or vegetable purées served with meat, are considered a garnish.

gourmet   A connoisseur of fine food and drink. The word is widely misused as an adjective.

liquor   Liquid such as broth or juice from shellfish as in clam liquor.

mask   To cover food completely, as with a sauce or an aspic.

parboil   *See* blanch.

preboil   *See* blanch.

purée   To put cooked or soft food, usually vegetables or fruits through a sieve, food mill, or blender, in order to obtain a thick, mushy pulp.

raft   The cooked, whisked egg white floating on top of a consommé. Also called a crust.

reduce   To boil liquid, such as a sauce, until the desired consistency and concentration of flavor are reached.

roux   There are two kinds of roux—white or blond roux and brown roux. A brown roux is equal amounts of butter and flour by the tablespoon, cooked to a good, brown color, and is used in brown sauces. A white or blond roux is also made with equal amounts of flour and butter, but is cooked for a shorter time—not browned—and is used for white sauces and veloutés.

sauté   A French term meaning to cook very rapidly in an open skillet. The equivalent American term is pan-fry.

savory   Piquant, pungent, or salty to the taste, not sweet.

short   A term used to describe pastry that is rich and flaky because it contains a large amount of butter or other shortening.

sweat   To cook covered over a low heat, without any added liquid. This method extracts juices and flavors from vegetables and is a technique used in making soups and sauces in order to intensify the flavor of the liquid.

velouté   A basic white sauce made of chicken, veal, or fish stock added to a white roux. It is similar to White Sauce.

wash   *See* egg wash.

water bath (bain-marie)   A container filled with about an inch of water. The container holding the food to be cooked is set in the bath and both are placed in the oven. The pan of simmering water will cook steadily at a low temperature. Since the water produces steam, the food will not get dry. Custards and soufflé puddings are always baked in water baths. The water in the bath should come about halfway up the sides of the dish set in the bath. If you need to add water during the cooking, it should be hot.

zest   The outer (colored) part of orange or lemon peel. It is usually grated and chopped, then used as a flavoring ingredient.

INDEX